Praise for
THE DOGGIE IN

"In this brilliant and unflinching piece of investigative journalism, Rory Kress pulls back the curtain on the industrialized and inhumane production of puppies for sale in this country and the utterly inadequate efforts by state and federal authorities to rein in even the worst abuses. We are killing an estimated one million dogs a year in shelters in this country—dogs that in the vast majority of cases would make wonderful companions—even as puppy mills turn out hundreds of thousands more, often in horrendous conditions, for profit. If ever there was a brief for why people should adopt and not shop for a dog, this is it."

—Peter Zheutlin, *New York Times* bestselling author
of *Rescue Road* and *Rescued*

"With passion and compassion, Rory Kress looks behind the cute puppies we see in pet stores and reveals the truth about the origins of commercially produced dog pups. Kress finds that the problem isn't just breeders acting outside the law, but laws and regulations that consider dogs much like any other agricultural product—a long way from how we know dogs need to be reared for successful, happy lives in human families. Seldom have I been as moved and as educated by a book about dogs."

—Clive D. L. Wynne, PhD, director of Canine Science
Collaboratory at Arizona State University

THE
DOGGIE IN
THE WINDOW

THE
DOGGIE IN
THE WINDOW

How One Dog Led Me from the Pet Store to
the Factory Farm to Uncover the Truth of
Where Puppies Really Come From

WITHDRAWN

RORY KRESS

Published by Sourcebooks, Inc.
P.O. Box 4410, Naperville, Illinois 60567-4410
(630) 961-3900
Fax: (630) 961-2168
sourcebooks.com

Library of Congress Cataloging-in-Publication data is on file with the publisher.

Printed and bound in the United States of America.
VP 10 9 8 7 6 5 4 3 2 1

For Race, who was with me all along.

My Favorite Mistake

I LOVE MY DOG IZZIE. BUT I HATE THAT SHE EXISTS.

Izzie is the gangly, self-possessed wheaten terrier who shares my home. Barely twenty-eight pounds soaking wet with a saliva-heavy tennis ball in her mouth, she's embarrassingly quick to lock eyes and spread her legs to solicit a belly rub from a stranger. She's imperious and strong-willed, marching all four paws to the beat of her own drum whether it's convenient for us or not. While her independence is unrivaled, she knows when to soften her moxie, when to comfort and keep company. On sleepless nights when I pace the halls of our home, she waits for me by my bedroom door before I even set a foot to the floor. When mired in stress at my laptop, I'll find her jet-black nose on my thigh before I can even think to call her to me.

Izzie is the first and only dog I've ever had. And like every dog owner, I've always assumed that Izzie is special and unique among the rest of the canine rabble. When I walk down the street, other dogs are just dogs. They're cute and lovable, but Izzie is set apart.

To me, she's more than a dog. And much the way most people feel about their human soul mates, I'm grateful that somehow I found her and she found me, certain that no other animal could ever take her place. And yet, by bringing Izzie into my home, I thoughtlessly supported an industry that ruthlessly harms animals just like her.

Izzie might be a puppy mill dog.

So where my world seems simple through Izzie's eyes—*Is it a bed? Can it be a bed? Is it food? Can it be food?*—her world is dizzyingly complicated through mine.

It all started out so innocently. I wanted a dog. My husband—then just my boyfriend—was bullied into wanting a dog. We asked around where we could find one. We were living in Brooklyn at the time, and a few family members recommended a pet shop on Long Island. I resisted. I thought I knew about puppy mills, and I was aware that pet shop dogs supposedly come from these horrifying places. But our relatives insisted that this shop was different and that they'd been buying long-lived, healthy dogs there for years.

"But aren't those puppy mill dogs?" I'd asked at the time, not even sure what puppy mills were exactly, but knowing that I must oppose them.

"No way. They're all from licensed breeders," we were assured.

I pulled up the shop's website. There, in big, bold letters: "**We do not support puppy mills, backyard, or hobby breeders.**" Then, below, in bigger letters still: "**Licensed breeders only**" with three logos: the American Kennel Club, the USDA, and the Animal and Plant Health Inspection Service arm of the USDA (APHIS). I was impressed. Until that moment, I hadn't even known that the USDA regulates dog breeding in this country.

The USDA's stamp of approval tells me what meat is safe to eat, which eggs are fresh, which milk I can drink. We all put a lot of faith in this government agency every single day without a second thought. So if these were dogs coming from USDA-licensed facilities, I reasoned, they could not be coming from puppy mills. It all seemed very official to me. But it's that very faith in the government that puppy dealers take advantage of, hiding behind the imprimatur of the USDA to give their work the appearance of legitimacy. And I was a perfect mark: I wanted to fall in love with a dog so badly, I just accepted that the agency in charge of so much dead meat governs the way living dogs are treated.

When I pictured puppy mills, like most people, I pictured something illegal. I imagined seedy, underground operations where dogs are tortured and bred to death in secret, canine sweatshops so far from the eye of the law that no one can know. That's what most of us have been trained to envision, so used to the horrific images on the late-night infomercials or the grainy, undercover videos aired on the evening news magazines. We see these facilities and assume they must be illegal. How couldn't they be?

But many of them aren't. Sure, those places we've seen on TV are puppy mills. And sure, as in any industry, there are bad actors, and some of them are illegal. But many of the commercial breeding operations that we've come to call puppy mills are, in fact, 100 percent legal. Thousands of them. Yes, even the horrifying ones we've seen on TV. Federal employees inspect them at least once a year. The owners are licensed by the USDA. The agriculture agency evaluates these facilities based on requirements set forth in a federal law signed in 1966 called the Animal Welfare Act. But even if these facilities pass government inspections with no violations every year, many are still unquestionably abusing their dogs.

Because, trouble is, if you're a dog, the lax standards of care laid out in the Animal Welfare Act don't do you much good.

More than two million puppies are sold every year from our nation's dog breeders. This number includes puppies born to breeders of all stripes: USDA-licensed and unlicensed, illegal puppy mills and meticulous show breeders alike, according to the Humane Society of the United States, the nation's largest nonprofit organization fighting animal cruelty. Just over one million of those puppies come from USDA-licensed facilities, born to the more than 165,000 dogs kept for breeding purposes on these properties—again, according to the Humane Society, which often keeps better records than our government on this issue. I wish I could give you official numbers, but the USDA has informed me that it does not keep a record of how many total dogs are produced nationwide at its more than two thousand licensed facilities because the Animal Welfare Act does not require it to do so.

Because Izzie was one of the million dogs who are born at USDA-licensed breeding facilities every year, I've traveled across the country investigating this federally regulated system. I wanted to understand how the government can do a better job of upholding and enforcing the Animal Welfare Act—the role the USDA has been charged with in overseeing our nation's breeders. Beyond that, I've interviewed veterinarians, rescuers, animal welfare advocates, dog breeders, and even a top official at the USDA who all agree that the Animal Welfare Act mandates a minimal standard of care at best. So if, in fact, the regulations do little more than promote basic survival in a breeding operation, even one small misstep could be the difference between life and death for a dog in one of these facilities.

But beyond Izzie, there's another reason I've focused my investigation on USDA-licensed breeders.

There will always be illegal operations in any industry. The commercial dog-breeding world is no exception. The government should do everything in its power to find and prosecute these operations, to be sure. However, the bigger lapse in my mind, as a dog owner and as a taxpayer who is bankrolling our country's agencies in their work, is how our government can be tasked with regulating an industry by holding it to subpar standards that, even when met, harm these dogs. What's more, how can the government agency tasked with upholding these minimal standards fail to do even that? In this way, the government is complicit in abusing the dogs that unwillingly produce the puppies we so cherish. And when it comes to those puppies, why are we, as a society and as consumers, so quick to lavish money and love on the animals in our homes after purchasing them from places where they are so callously used and even tortured?

So maybe Izzie, the dog who sleeps in my bed and eagerly snaps up green beans from my fingertips, has a happy ending to her story. Like Izzie, many dogs born in puppy mills for purchase in our nation's pet stores and on the internet surely go to happy homes where they're raised lovingly, appearing in family Christmas cards and dutifully serving as ring bearers in their owners' weddings. But what about these dogs' mothers whose lives have been commoditized so we could enjoy the luxury of raising their offspring? What if we took the time to imagine the life of the dog we purchased had it been kept behind as breeding stock instead of shipped off for sale?

The day we took Izzie home, we were satisfied customers of a broken system. Given how happy we are with her, we should have never questioned where our four-legged firstborn came from. For the most part, the people who have purchased from pet shops and now speak out about them are those who have ended up with a sick dog. We have not. That is neither our story nor my motivation in investigating this industry. I am not an animal rights activist but a journalist. Even then, animal issues have never been my beat. But over the years, as I went about my life, producing and reporting stories in my work for NBC's *Today Show* and other outlets, Izzie became unquestioningly an integral part of the fabric of my family.

As a journalist, I approach the world with an unremitting sense of curiosity. I see life through a binary lens: is this a story or not? For those first few years, Izzie fell into my journalistic blind spot. She was not a story as far as I was concerned. I'd toss her a treat and give her a kiss on the nose as I'd head off to work on stories that I thought people needed to hear. She was my pet, and I grew to love her more than I ever thought possible. But with time came a churning suspicion as I couldn't help but look at her and wonder: *Who the hell is this dog, and where did she really come from?*

It's an ugly thing to question the ones we love. Still, I only knew of one way to handle this nagging curiosity that would not leave me be. I would have much preferred to go about my life ignorantly and guiltlessly adoring my dog. But I couldn't. So I began researching, investigating, and searching for the truth about Izzie. But by entering into her world—the real world she came from and not the one we chose to construct for her in our home—I found a much more complicated story than the one about my own dog. Just as she does on our walks, Izzie pulled at the leash, leading me—ready or not—to find the truth about how all our dogs come into this world and how our government, time and time again, is willfully failing to ensure their health, sanity, safety, and well-being despite taking up the mantle of their protection.

So what happens when the Animal Welfare Act provides inadequate regulations for breeding dogs humanely and the USDA, a federal agency, is unable or even unwilling to enforce these regulations appropriately or transparently?

You get Izzie. And you get an American public wrongfully trusting a broken system to breed for us the animals we call family.

THE
DOGGIE IN
THE WINDOW

CHAPTER ONE

The Keep 'Em in Business Act

"SHE'S GORGEOUS," A DOE-EYED HIPSTER WITH TWO full sleeves of tattoos says to me as Izzie jumps up and plants her muddy paws on the woman's skin-tight jeans. We're at the Cipriani of the canine world: McCarren Dog Park in Williamsburg, Brooklyn. But here, the mutt is king, and any distinguishable breed is decidedly uncool. Izzie is just poorly groomed enough to pass. "Where'd you rescue her from?"

"Long Island?" I try awkwardly.

It's a question I hear often when walking Izzie: *Where'd you rescue her from?* The assumption runs deep. Even when people fail to word it precisely that way, they never ask where we bought her or what pet store she came from. The notion that I could be shamelessly parading around a pet store pup is unthinkable in many parts of the country, particularly in the urban enclaves where we've typically lived.

The other question I field most often with Izzie from passersby or other dog owners is this: *What is she?*

Well, she's a dog. She's a scavenger in the kitchen. She's a terror when she's moody. She's the light of my life. But yes—you guessed it—she's not a mutt. In short, she's a wheaten terrier.

Then there's the more subtly phrased *What's she a mix of?*

This question often comes from a more polite subset of the same people who ask where she was rescued from. They mean well, stroking Izzie's silky ears as she bows and flirts with them. Sometimes they'll add *She's just so unusual looking!* and hazard a few guesses of what breeds might be making up Izzie's special brew. The conversation quickly chills when I'm forced to break it to them that, to the best of my knowledge, she's not a mix of anything. Supposedly, she's all wheaten. I sense in these interactions that this answer creates discomfort with some—if she's not a mix, she's probably not a rescue, many will rightly assume. Statistically, they would be right: purebreds only make up about a quarter of dogs found in shelters, according to the Humane Society.

Over the years, their discomfort has become my discomfort and, to a greater extent, my anxiety. I see their faces when they hear my answers fall short of their expectations, and I know they are judging my compassion and love of animals as inadequate. I watch as Izzie shrinks in their eyes from a lovable, Dickensian orphan, rescued from an unspeakable fate, to just a puppy mill dog, the instrument of heartache for millions of canines nationwide.

Once it becomes clear that Izzie is neither a mix nor a rescue, a third question sometimes comes from the more intrepid and, admittedly confrontational, few: *Well, did you at least get her from a breeder?*

I try to dodge the question when things get this far. I make a joke, something like *Well, she's a wheaten terrier the way that a Coach bag from Canal Street is a real Coach bag.* The joke doesn't play quite as well outside of New York City, so sometimes I'll just say *She's a knockoff* and hope I'm off the hook.

My husband, Dan, handles these questions in his own way. Most of the time, he just says *Yep, she came from a breeder.* He's a lawyer, so he's comfortable with the semantics. As far as he sees it, he is telling the truth: *Obviously she came from a breeder. Someone had to breed her; she didn't just fall out of the sky.* Fair enough. But I know better: not all breeders are created equal. Or rather, not all breeders are creating dogs equally.

These questions I encounter while walking Izzie all zero in on a central anxiety that plagues most dog owners in this country: these pups may be our "fur babies" now—but whose babies are they really?

While Izzie may be one in a million to me, she's actually one of about ninety million—that's how many domestic dogs currently share our homes in this country. So where are all these dogs coming from? Only 23 percent of them are being adopted from shelters and rescues.[1] That leaves an overwhelming majority of us with an uncomfortable question to answer about the provenance of our pooches.

As a member of this quiet majority who has to come to terms with the truth of where our dogs came from, I can say that we all handle it quite differently.

Some of us believe what we want to believe. Take, for example, our friends who purchased a dog online. The puppy was shipped to them from out of state to be picked up in a crate at the nearest airport, sans escort. They would never admit to themselves or anyone else that this dog came from anything other than a reputable source—but without ever laying eyes on anything but pictures of their dog as a puppy posted online, how would they know?

Then there are the deniers who will rock their purebred, pet shop dogs to sleep in their arms every night while waging wars on social media against pet shops and puppy mills with the ubiquitous hashtag *Adopt Don't Shop*.

Or there are the foolhardy few, like me, who genuinely want to know the truth and are naïve enough to think they can try to understand it. Maybe that's why there's no hashtag to represent this curious but ashamed group; perhaps I'm the only one.

While surely there are responsible breeders among the thousands who hold a USDA license, the law does not require much of them to stay up and running. The price to obtain a license is relatively small and can range from $30 to $750, depending on how much money the breeder's operation brings in. Once bred, these dogs are sold in pet shops, online, and in newspaper ads. Like it or not, for many of us, these are the dogs we're curling up with every night in bed. With most designer puppies selling for anywhere between $1,000 to even $3,000 each, it's clear there's money being made on the backs of dogs just like Izzie without adequate oversight or protection that takes their unique needs into account.

So where did I rescue Izzie from?

Sure, she came from Long Island—but I did no rescuing. And when I was told that she came from a USDA-licensed breeder, like so many others, I heard what I wanted to.

I bought the story. I bought the dog.

While my story begins with Izzie, the story of our nation's laws regulating the breeding of dogs begins with Pepper.

In 1965, Pepper was a five-year-old Dalmatian living on the Lakavage family's eighty-acre farm just north of Allentown, Pennsylvania. In June, the children let her out back for her evening walk. When the usual time came to fetch her, she did not return. They called her name into the night. She didn't come running.

Pepper was gone.

In this era before Facebook and microchips, the Lakavages had to conduct the search for Pepper in person: papering nearby towns with MISSING posters and chasing down leads from their hometown in Pennsylvania to a farm in upstate New York to no avail. As the family scoured the region for "Peppy," she was locked away where they would never find her: in the bowels of a laboratory at Montefiore Hospital in the Bronx. There, she was used for the testing of an experimental heart surgery to install a pacemaker. She died on the table and was cremated, just nine days after she disappeared from her own backyard. By the time state police and humane societies got wind of the Lakavages' story and pieced together Pepper's trajectory—broker by broker—to the operating table, it was too late.[2]

Julia Lakavage, Pepper's owner, later summed up her grief to a local paper.

"Dogs are like family members," she said. "[They're] children that don't grow up. They're almost human."[3]

The story struck a nerve with dog owners across the country. At the time, there was no regulated network of breeders to supply the nation's laboratories with dogs or other animals to be used in experiments. Very few of the estimated one hundred thousand dogs used in laboratories every year at that time came from facilities breeding the animals explicitly for that purpose. Most simply came from the pound or were stolen from their owner's backyards or off the sidewalk.

"There was something called *pound seizure* going on. If dogs and cats ended up at the pound and they were not adopted, then instead of killing them—if they were healthy enough— laboratories would buy them," animal law expert Joyce Tischler tells me. She's the cofounder and general counsel for the Animal Legal Defense Fund (ALDF) and is known in her field as the mother of animal law. "[Pound seizure] was definitely in full swing in the 1950s and the 1960s, and there are still some places in the United States where pounds will sell their dogs and cats to laboratories to use in research."[4]

But as shocking as it is to hear that pounds are still engaging in this sale of dogs to laboratories today, it was upsetting to Americans even sixty years ago.

"It was a very controversial thing that the pounds were doing because they are supposed to be a safe place for animals. But also what was happening was that there were people making money from stealing people's dogs and cats off the street, from the backyard, and then selling them to research laboratories," Tischler says.

As the now-famous *Sports Illustrated* article from 1965 covering Pepper's story put it, the plucky Dalmatian's downfall was likely due to the very traits that made her such a beloved pet: she was trusting, friendly to strangers, and probably easy for a dognapper to coax into his truck without a fight, bite, or bark.[5]

But Pepper's plight won more than popular sympathy. It also attracted the attention of Capitol Hill; Senator Joseph Clark of Pennsylvania and Representative Joseph Resnick of New York took up Pepper's battle. Before the Dalmatian's fate was even known for certain, Congressman Resnick had already decided he would introduce a bill to the House that would prevent the theft of dogs and require records be kept on the breeding and housing of the animals destined for life—and more likely than not, death—in a lab.

"That was the initial impetus for the Animal Welfare Act: to deal with these dog thefts and cat thefts. When people's companion animals were ending up in research, it was really shaking dog and cat owners," Tischler says.

Representative Resnick's bill went on to become the Laboratory Animal Welfare Act of 1966, putting the federal government in charge of licensing and tracking the dealing of dogs and other animals destined for research facilities. Later shortened to be called the Animal Welfare Act, or the AWA, this piece of legislation appointed the USDA and later its Animal and Plant Health Inspection Service (APHIS) arm to enforce the regulations it set forth. Within a few years, this legislation would be expanded to encompass dogs bred to be pets.

Oddly, in 2002, the Animal Welfare Act, the only federal statute protecting lab animals, was amended to exempt rats, mice, and birds from its oversight. As a result, 95 percent of animals used in today's research are not protected by the law originally known as the Laboratory Animal Welfare Act. However, despite the fact that the USDA was tasked with enforcing it, the Animal Welfare Act has never been expanded to cover the care and handling of animals we most typically associate with agriculture: cows, chickens, pigs, and the like. And from the very beginning, the USDA has had a complicated relationship with the Animal Welfare Act because, by definition, the agency is historically cozy with the agricultural community.

"If you look at the cases today involving the USDA and the Animal Welfare Act, the USDA refers to regulated industry as its customers—its customers! So [the USDA] has a long history of having been coopted by the very industry that it's supposed to be regulating," Tischler says.

The agency did not deny this charge but told me it has many customers to answer to—including the breeding industry and the animals themselves.

So while the Animal Welfare Act is now primarily a document concerning the breeding and handling of dogs and other pets, it remains entirely insufficient even in this specialized area. Because when it comes to ensuring that dogs bred for life as our companions are brought into the world safely and respectfully, animal welfare experts tell me the legislation does not go nearly far enough.

Bioethicist Bernie Rollin, a professor of animal sciences and bioethics at Colorado State University, has a long history of attempting to reform the Animal Welfare Act. In 1982, he testified before Congress, calling for a sea change in how lab animals were treated, to take their pain into account, and require the use of anesthetic for the first time.

"I wrote the federal laws for laboratory animals that passed in 1985 to require pain control of animals that you hurt because it was not flat done. It was not done," Rollin tells me, still disgusted by this policy omission.[6]

As a result of his own involvement in amending the statute, Rollin is very familiar with where it is lacking.

"It's a bent reed to rely on if you want to make sure the animals are treated well," he says. "It's a biblical term: a bent reed won't hold anything up."

Among animal welfare advocates, the very name *Animal Welfare Act* is seen, at best, as a misnomer if not a cruel joke. Mary LaHay is the president of Iowa Friends of Companion Animals. The Hawkeye State has one of the nation's highest concentrations of puppy mills, and LaHay has dedicated her career to shutting them down. She recalls a conversation with one of the attorneys on the board of her organization as they were working through the regulations in the Animal Welfare Act.

"[The attorney] stopped and looked up and said, 'This isn't the Animal Welfare Act. This is the Keep 'Em in Business Act,'" LaHay says. "That's [the USDA's] purpose: their focus is to keep people making money... And if that means some dogs suffer in the process, so be it."[7]

So what, exactly, are these rules and regulations that the Animal Welfare Act lays out for dog-breeding operations around the country? And are they really as inadequate as these animal welfare advocates tell me?

I took the Animal Welfare Act's list of regulations for commercial dog breeding to Dr. Karen Overall to help me better understand.

Overall ran the prestigious behavior clinic at the University of Pennsylvania Veterinary School of Medicine for more than a decade and is currently a senior research scientist there. As a veterinarian, specialist in behavioral medicine, and a PhD, she has devoted her life's work to researching the neurobehavioral genetics of dogs and the ways in which canines develop normal or abnormal behaviors. She is a frequent consultant for lawmakers and various local, state, and international governments on canine-related legislation. In 2008, she was appointed to the Pennsylvania Governor's Canine Health Board and has been instrumental in the commercial breeding reform efforts in the

Keystone State. One by one, I ran each of the regulations in the Animal Welfare Act for commercial dog breeding by Overall's scientific mind.[8]

CAGE SIZE

Animal Welfare Act

Find the mathematical square of the sum of the length of the dog in inches (measured from the tip of its nose to the base of its tail) plus 6 inches; then divide the product by 144. The calculation is: (length of the dog in inches + 6) x (length of the dog in inches + 6) = required floor space in square inches. Required floor space in inches / 144 = required floor space in square feet.

Translation

For those of us who didn't excel in math, this is the Animal Welfare Act's formula for calculating the size of a dog's enclosure in a breeding facility. The space must be secure and free of debris with no rusting or jagged edges. If housing one dog alone, this equation roughly works out to a minimum space requirement that measures only about six inches longer than the dog itself and six inches taller than the dog's full height when standing.

Let's use my dog as an example: Izzie is twenty-six inches from the tip of her nose to the base of her docked tail. Using the Animal Welfare Act's equation, she's entitled to about seven square feet of cage space for the duration of her entire life. That amounts to a cage that's just a little over two and a half feet by two and a half feet—or thirty-two inches by thirty-two inches.

When I attempted to launch into the finer points of this regulation with Overall, she was quick to bring my mathematical dithering to a quick halt.

"Stop right there," she said. "Dogs by nature are not cage animals… No dog natively would choose a cage to be raised in or on. And no cage adequately meets a domestic canine's cognitive or physical needs. Period."[9]

I then asked Overall why the Animal Welfare Act would go to the trouble of painstakingly specifying calculations for how to determine cage size if it was simply impossible to humanely keep a dog in this fashion. Surely, I insisted, there must be some science behind those carefully dictated numbers.

"They have made it sound like science, but it is pseudoscience," Overall scoffed, pointing out that there is no scientific grounding in any of the current cage size requirements. For its part, the USDA has confirmed to me that the cage size regulations were based on common sense, given that there was not much science to go off at the time the Animal Welfare Act was written. However, unlike the authors of the Animal Welfare Act, my own, personal common sense best aligns with Overall's scientific opinion that no dog belongs in a cage.

"It's like the climate change deniers [who say] 'Well, the science isn't in…' Well, the science is in, the science has been in, and the science that's coming out is nailing nails in their coffin like crazy," said Overall. "You know, I could be talking to the local meeting of the Flat Earth Society."

EXERCISE

Animal Welfare Act

Dogs housed individually. Dogs over 12 weeks of age, except bitches with litters, housed, held, or maintained by any dealer, exhibitor, or research facility, including Federal research facilities, must be provided the opportunity for exercise regularly if they are kept individually in cages, pens, or runs that provide less than two times the required floor space for that dog... Dogs housed in groups. Dogs over 12 weeks of age housed, held, or maintained in groups by any dealer, exhibitor, or research facility, including Federal research facilities, do not require additional opportunity for exercise regularly if they are maintained in cages, pens, or runs that provide in total at least 100 percent of the required space for each dog if maintained separately.

Translation

If a dog lives alone in a cage that is twice the minimum size requirements, his breeder does not need to engage him in any additional exercise whatsoever.

For Izzie, this would mean that if a breeder kept her in a cage that was about 3.75 feet by 3.75 feet (or fourteen square feet), she would be allowed to spend the entire duration of her life enclosed. Under the Animal Welfare Act, she would never be entitled to set a single paw outside that crate.

Dogs kept in groups are assumed to be capable of providing adequate exercise for their cage mates. In fact, dogs kept in groups have no exercise requirements at all so long as their enclosure meets the minimum space requirements.

These are the Animal Welfare Act's requirements—or lack thereof, really—for exercising canines in a commercial breeding facility.

I read these regulations aloud to Overall, although she already knew them well. She responded by referring me to the Five Freedoms, a list of animal welfare protocols developed in the United Kingdom in the late 1970s. They include the freedom from hunger and thirst; the freedom from discomfort; the freedom from pain, injury, and disease; the freedom to express normal behaviors in an appropriate habitat; and the freedom from feeling fear and distress. Humane organizations and veterinary groups around the world, including the American Society for the Prevention of Cruelty to Animals (ASPCA) here in the United States, have since adopted these guidelines as standards for humane treatment of animals. The Five Freedoms are not, however, included or referenced in the Animal Welfare Act. As Overall and many other canine experts see it, these Five Freedoms must be taken into account as the most basic standard for care.

"When you look at the Five Freedoms, one of them is the freedom to exercise normal behaviors… There are basic exercises that every dog would want to go out and do," she explained. "They want to go out and sniff the urine and feces of other dogs. They want to stand and smell the breeze. They want to walk through a variety of habitats and explore them… I mean, come on. There are basic needs that every dog shares. Meet them. And if you don't meet them, you can't [be a breeder]."

And for a dog, none of those Five Freedoms can ever be met in a cage.

TEMPERATURE

Animal Welfare Act

When dogs or cats are present, the ambient temperature in the [indoor] facility must not fall below 50°F (10°C) for dogs and cats not acclimated to lower temperatures, for those breeds that cannot tolerate lower temperatures without stress or discomfort (such as short-haired breeds), and for sick, aged, young, or infirm dogs and cats, except as approved by the attending veterinarian. Dry bedding, solid resting boards, or other methods of conserving body heat must be provided when temperatures are below 50°F (10°C). The ambient temperature must not fall below 45°F (7.2°C) for more than 4 consecutive hours when dogs or cats are present, and must not rise above 85°F (29.5°C) for more than 4 consecutive hours when dogs or cats are present... When their acclimation status is unknown, dogs and cats must not be kept in outdoor facilities when the ambient temperature is less than 50°F (10°C).

Translation

Whether indoors or outdoors, the temperature must not dip below 45° for more than four hours. If temperatures spike above 85°, the breeder must provide fans or air conditioning. Exclusively outdoor facilities are generally prohibited without approval from a veterinarian. If approved, however, dogs must be able to access shelter from the elements and receive additional bedding when temperatures dip below 35°. It's up to the local veterinarian hired by the breeding operation to say which dogs are able to tolerate outdoor facilities depending on the region.

I asked Overall if these standards were appropriate for a dog destined to be a companion animal.

"No," she began. "For [a dog] to be able to work with those temperatures, [it would] need a primo diet and primo access to escape conditions and water and things like that."

Overall then offered the example of the Beagle Brigade, the team of dogs who are employed by the USDA's Animal and Plant Health Inspection Service (APHIS) to inspect luggage that comes into our nation's airports for banned agricultural goods. To get these beagles ready for duty, they are trained at the USDA National Detector Dog Training Center in Georgia, generally a hot and humid climate.

"Every one of those dogs has group and individual shade available for their outdoor runs," Overall said. "They have kiddie pools because they know that [beagles] can't self-regulate and they need to give them both sets of options. You would think that [commercial breeding] dogs should be treated at least as well as those [beagles]."

These beagles that Overall was referring to are, interestingly enough, employed by APHIS, the same division of the USDA tasked with regulating commercial dog breeders.

On the flip side, Overall noted that working dogs in cold temperatures are not only genetically selected for their ability to withstand those particular conditions, but also are provided a highly specialized diet to handle the day-to-day energy requirements that are necessary in extreme situations.

"When you get performance dogs that work on the cold end of things, I don't think people realize what goes on there. Not only are these dogs selected for a [particular] set of genes, but also you've trained and enhanced these dogs. And you're feeding them slabs of often fatty, raw meat or specialized diets that are high in fat," Overall said. "So they're on a specialized diet, and they are conditioned to those temperatures... Furthermore, there are huge immune effects of these extremes in temperature that are well known and established in laboratory animals of all kinds including dogs. But they have never made their way into a USDA regulation."

What's more, the Animal Welfare Act regulations do not account for any differences in dietary requirements in conjunction with temperatures in breeding facilities.

FOOD

Animal Welfare Act

Dogs and cats must be fed at least once each day, except as otherwise might be required to provide adequate veterinary care. The food must be uncontaminated, wholesome, palatable, and of sufficient quantity and nutritive value to maintain the normal condition and weight of the animal. The diet must be appropriate for the individual animal's age and condition. Food receptacles must be used for dogs and cats, must be readily accessible to all dogs and cats, and must be located so as to minimize contamination by excreta and pests, and be protected from rain and snow.

Translation

Breeders must only feed their dogs once a day. The food must be clean and appropriate for the dog in question. The Animal Welfare Act gives no specifics on what kind of food is best. In most cases, breeders will purchase whatever bulk kibble is cheapest.

WATER

Animal Welfare Act

If potable water is not continually available to the dogs and cats, it must be offered to the dogs and cats as often as necessary to ensure their health and well-being, but not less than twice daily for at least 1 hour each time, unless restricted by the attending veterinarian.

Translation

Dogs must be offered water twice a day for at least an hour each time. That is, if water is not continually provided throughout the day.

The statute here leaves a lot of room for interpretation—and optimization of the breeder's time and resources. In most cases, I've seen this instruction carried out by the breeders hooking PVC pipelines to the tops of the cages. These pipes then carry water to a type of metal nozzle that most people would recognize from its more common use as the nib of a rodent's or gerbil's water bottle. After all, continually refilling water bowls in a commercial dog-breeding facility where there are hundreds of dogs would be enormously time consuming for the workers.

When I read these food and water requirements to Overall, I noted that to my untrained medical eye, they seem to create a dangerous confluence of adverse conditions for a dog when taken in conjunction with the wide range of acceptable temperatures on the books.

"They are a perfect storm. What you're talking about are requirements that are minimally compatible with life," Overall said.

On the issue of providing water, Overall explained that while a dog might survive in the conditions mandated by the Animal Welfare Act, the animal's quality of life and long-term health would be severely compromised.

"What you're setting dogs up for with those schedules are profound fluctuations in electrolyte levels and dehydration levels," she said. "[Their] red blood cells will become more concentrated. We try to tamp out those extremes for health reasons."

She also noted that in her world of scientific research, where she has published hundreds of peer-reviewed papers and edits an academic journal in the field, any study that keeps a dog in conditions where water is similarly limited would not be eligible for publication in most scholarly journals—unless, of course, the study was specifically investigating the effects of water deprivation.

"Studies have to be done ethically with *ad libitum* access to water," she said.

I then described to Overall the water access workaround I'd seen quite frequently where, in many commercial dog-breeding facilities, PVC pipes line the top of cages with a thin metal tube dipping down into the dog's space for him to lick when he desires a drink of water. I asked Overall if these types of setups could be considered *ad libitum* access to water.

"That's not *ad libitum* access to water," she said unequivocally.

"Let's go back to the Five Freedoms and ask if that gives them the freedom to exhibit their normal behavior… Dogs are going to [drink from] a bowl of water because part of what they do with their tongue is thermal regulation, and they really like to coat it… [Dogs] basically fling [their tongues] back to get water."

The problem with licking-activated dispensers, as Overall summed it up, is that they do not give the dog the opportunity to drink and coat its tongue as its anatomy was designed to do. These water dispensers, however, are not banned by the Animal Welfare Act regulations or by USDA enforcement.

FLOORING

Animal Welfare Act

Primary enclosures equipped with mesh or wire floors shall be so constructed as to allow feces to pass through the spaces of the mesh or wire: *Provided, however,* that such floors shall be constructed so as to protect the animals' feet and legs from injury.

Translation

These enclosures are not your standard doghouse setups in a backyard. More often than not, dogs in breeding facilities live in kennels that are suspended above the ground and are often stacked, one on top of another. The floors of these crates are rarely, if ever, solid. For the most part, this is a practical consideration for a busy breeder so that most of the dogs' waste falls through the slats in the floor onto the ground below—or into the crate of the dog below. The solids that remain in the cages can then be hosed out easily without collecting puddles, as the Animal Welfare Act strictly mandates that surfaces remain free of standing moisture. The floors themselves must not sag or dip. If the floor is made of metal wire, these strands must be wider than one-eighth of an inch in diameter or be otherwise coated with plastic or fiberglass. By comparison, the width of this type of metal wire, known as nine gauge, is comparable to a lower-note string on a bass guitar.

"That's not very wide. When you actually go and look at these floors, it's appalling," Overall said. "These wire floors actually damage dogs' feet: they damage their pronation, they damage their ability to bear weight, they damage the articulation of the joint, and they certainly don't allow the dogs to have the full range of experiences they would choose to if they could have natural access."

While these standards are minimal at best, they are at least standards that can be enforced. More pressing, however, is what the Animal Welfare Act fails to regulate at all.

BREEDING FREQUENCY

The Animal Welfare Act imposes no limits on how often a female can be bred. Most commercial operations will at least attempt to breed a female on every heat—that's every six months or even more frequently in some smaller breeds. With no legal reason not to, it makes financial sense for a breeder to try and get the most of out of their breeding stock. But is it humane to the dogs?

"No responsible breeder would do that. No human would do it: you don't give your body time to recover," Overall said.

"Pregnancy is a toll, and it is not a benign procedure… You wouldn't breed yourself on every heat."

GENETIC SCREENING

The Animal Welfare Act has no provisions for preventing genetic abnormalities in commercially bred dogs—a point that several experts, including bioethicist Bernie Rollin, underscored. As such, a breeder might be routinely producing unhealthy, genetically compromised animals by pairing the same dogs for mating over and over again. Often, a breeder is not even aware that he is causing genetic abnormalities because the products of these infelicitous pairings are already shipped off through a broker to be sold elsewhere before the problem can present itself. In the pure breeds that most of these commercial operations are churning out, it is especially likely that dogs are being inbred to produce puppies that carry on negative genetic traits. Yet the Animal Welfare Act says nothing about preventing these problems.

Every purebred dog, by definition, is inbred to some degree. To breed them responsibly and have the best chance of producing healthy dogs takes great effort to source a genetically varied line and meticulous, long-term record keeping to see if, and more likely when, genetic disorders present. At USDA-licensed facilities, however, there is nothing to stop a breeder from taking two littermates and pairing them together again and again.

Izzie's breed, the wheaten terrier, is most often genetically predisposed to protein wasting disorders and Addison's disease. Knowing this, we run a pricey, detailed urine screening on her at every annual checkup. So far she's passed every test. However, it is a costly precaution that I began taking willingly during the reporting of this book, knowing now that she was likely inbred in one of these facilities where there is no legal reason not to.

HUMAN CONTACT AND SOCIALIZATION

Animal Welfare Act

[Breeders] should consider providing positive physical contact with humans that encourages exercise through play or other similar activities. If a dog is housed, held, or maintained at a facility without sensory contact with another dog, it must be provided with positive physical contact with humans at least daily.

Translation

This language is as good as an omission from the statute entirely.

The difference between "should consider providing" and "must provide" is stark. In the case of most commercial breeders, "sensory contact with another dog" may mean living in a stacked cage with hundreds of other dogs whose feces is hosed through the wire-mesh lid every day and where the round-the-clock barking never ceases. After all, not all sensory contact is positive sensory contact. No breeder would be penalized for failing to carry out this regulation with a daily trip to the local dog park or a nightly game of fetch. Ultimately, the Animal Welfare Act regulations fail to mandate any amount of human contact, interaction, or socialization beyond yearly visits from a veterinarian.

Considering that these animals are being mass-produced for

the specific purpose of living side by side with humans in their homes, it seems that nurturing a dog who is accustomed to and even enjoys a person's touch and presence should be a vital part of the breeder's process. As Overall sees it, this omission leads to problems both behaviorally and chemically in the dogs.

"Dogs probably coevolved with humans. Certainly they have the longest domestication history... We have had a unique relationship, and we know that we have had that relationship for at least thirty-five thousand years. We are part of their lives," she explained. "And now we know that how you interact with something affects which proteins are transcribed [from an animal's DNA]. If you have a parent who has never had these experiences and exposures [to humans], you may have a different set of transcribed proteins as an offspring. And certainly the offspring don't get adequate contact, which is what you want if you want a puppy to be as social as possible."

END OF LIFE AND "RETIREMENT"

Animal Welfare Act

Euthanasia means the humane destruction of an animal accomplished by a method that produces rapid unconsciousness and subsequent death without evidence of pain or distress, or a method that utilizes anesthesia produced by an agent that causes painless loss of consciousness and subsequent death.

Translation

A breeding facility can terminate a dog's life in any way its owners or operators choose at any time, so long as the method is quick and appears—to us human bystanders—to be painless. For specifics, the USDA refers breeders to the recommendations from the American Veterinary Medical Association's (AVMA) euthanasia panel. These recommendations do acknowledge that euthanasia at breeding facilities will differ from the process in a clinical setting but insist the procedures be done professionally and compassionately with veterinary oversight.

But gunshots, of course, are typically cheap and expedient at producing the mandated "rapid unconsciousness and subsequent death"—although the AVMA guidelines state that the group does not recommend death by gunshot for routine euthanasia of dogs. But just in case, the AVMA offers plenty of rules governing exactly what kinds of bullets are considered humane. The guidelines even include a helpful illustration of a dog with a red dot on its head, indicating exactly where a bullet should go—in case you couldn't figure that one out yourself.[10] And yes, your own pup's veterinarian is more than likely a dues-paying member of this very same AVMA.

Anatomic site for gunshot in dogs is located midway between the level of the eyes and base of the ears, slightly off midline with aim directed across the dog toward the spine. [11]

With Overall's expert take on the Animal Welfare Act in mind, I turned to the USDA to find out what kind of science went into developing the nuts and bolts of the statute. I was politely referred to Dr. Robert Gibbens, the western regional director for the USDA's Animal Plant and Health Inspection Service (APHIS), which runs the agency's Animal Care group. His office directly oversees the inspections of our country's breeding operations across the Midwest where the majority are concentrated. He's also a licensed veterinarian and a dog owner.

"The authors [of the Animal Welfare Act] were looking at common sense. Because I don't think back then there was a lot of science. There's still not a lot of science into how you measure welfare. You can certainly see signs of bad welfare. Like any animal, dogs exhibit a variety of signs if they aren't kept in conditions that are good for their health and well-being. But I think it's harder to measure good welfare. Is the dog healthy? Does the dog appear to be stressed? But you can't ask them," Gibbens says. "When those regulations and standards were written, we put a lot of what we saw as humans into those standards. And clearly we think as humans, we don't think as dogs… More science needs to be done."[12]

But then Gibbens affirms one of my chief concerns about the Animal Welfare Act: the USDA is operating on the hope that breeders will go above and beyond what the law mandates.

"We're not just encouraging [breeders] to meet our standards. We are encouraging them to exceed our standards," he says.

But without any incentive to do so—and without any repercussions for just meeting the bare minimum—why should they bother to do more? Especially when, to do so, it would cost money.

At some point, most breeders look at their litters and decide which pups to breed and which to sell. I think about Izzie: she's noticeably small for a wheaten terrier and has thin hair that, as a puppy, was patchy at best but has since filled out somewhat. Maybe she was the runt of the litter or her uneven hair growth disqualified her from becoming breeding stock. Whatever it was that sent her off on the long road to Long Island where I purchased her, her fate would have been very different had she been kept behind to breed in the USDA-licensed facility she came from. Now that I understand the Animal Welfare Act requirements, I can picture exactly what my Izzie's life would look like if her breeder had kept her as stock according to the rules, no better, no worse.

She could have lived her entire life in fourteen square feet of cage space. Because that small area is double the minimum required for her size, her breeder would not be required to provide her with any mental stimulation or exercise. The floor of this fourteen-square-foot cage could be constructed of a wire mesh material where the wires could be as thin as a bass guitar string and could be constructed outdoors so long as she had an area available to her for shelter from rain, direct sun, and snow. This wire mesh would allow the urine and the feces of the dog in a cage above her to fall through into her crate, as hers would fall to the dog below her feet. Her breeder would not be required to provide her with any temperature regulation so long as it stayed above 45° and below 85°. She could be provided with a self-feeder for her kibble and a water drip she can lick to access. If her breeder wasn't up for installing a twenty-four-hour water drip, he could simply give her a bowl of water twice a day for an hour each, temperatures notwithstanding. There would be no requirement that the breeder interact with her or otherwise socialize her with other humans or dogs as long as she was kept within earshot of the other dogs around her. She could be bred at every heat or once every six months until she could no longer produce a litter. Then she could be retired to remain in that cage until her life naturally ended or, if her breeder was one of the better ones, she might be adopted out to a rescue. But if neither of those options appealed, she could simply be euthanized. Or, more likely, shot.

This is the life of a breeding dog in a facility that is entirely up to code with the Animal Welfare Act. This is the treatment our government upholds.

At this time, seventeen states maintain their own additional regulations and require licensing on the state level to fill in some of the gaps left behind by the Animal Welfare Act standards and USDA enforcement. But only ten states actually subject their licensees to routine and unannounced inspections without complaint or cause beyond an initial inspection during the license application process.

Ultimately, this means that the conditions described by the Animal Welfare Act are completely legal—even if animal welfare experts like Overall and others agree that they are inhumane. Even in those states that have additional regulations, many do not go much further at all. A breeder's decision to go above and beyond this statute for the care of his dogs is just that: the breeder's decision.

CHAPTER TWO

Dogs Don't Vote

WE ALL KNOW ABOUT PUPPY MILLS. ASK ANYONE walking his French bulldog or her goldendoodle down the street how they feel about these industrial-strength breeders, and you'll surely get an impassioned tirade about how evil they are. But ask them where their dogs actually came from, and the majority will have to answer, just as I do, that their four-legged-friend came from a pet store, from the internet, or from a friend.

So what, exactly, is a puppy mill? What is a dog breeder? Where do they intersect, and where do they diverge? Many people use the two terms synonymously but, for the purposes of being as fair as possible, I will not.

Let's start with what the federal government considers to be a commercial dog breeder. The Animal Welfare Act defines a breeder as a person "whose business involving animals consists only of animals that are bred and raised on the premises in a closed or stable colony and those animals acquired for the sole purpose of maintaining or enhancing the breeding colony."

Translation: a breeder runs a business that produces new animals. The animals used for this operation are part of a business and are not the breeder's pets.

So who needs a USDA license to be a breeder?

Breeders are required to obtain a class A license to operate under USDA oversight only if they have more than four breeding females in their facility. Any breeder with four or fewer breeding females is considered a hobby breeder and is not subject to federal regulation.[1] Breeders who sell directly to consumers with all parties present at the time of purchase—buyer, seller, and dog—are also exempt from federal regulations and do not need to obtain a license, no matter how many breeding females they have. They are considered, in these cases, to be operating as retail pet stores, which are not regulated by the Animal Welfare Act. While it may seem egregious that a breeder with hundreds of dogs can claim exemption from federal oversight by selling in person, this regulation is actually now more stringent than it used to be. Until 2013, breeders were selling puppies online all over the country without any USDA oversight at all. But much more on that later.

In the USDA-regulated system, licensed brokers often transport the puppies from breeders to pet stores or even directly to consumers. These middlemen go breeder by breeder, buying up pups for a small fraction of what the consumer will pay. Then the brokers pack them up in vans or even eighteen-wheelers to drive them cross-country and wholesale them to pet shops where they can fetch an impressive price. These brokers are required to obtain a different class B license to stay in compliance with the USDA.

So now that we know what the government considers to be a commercial breeder, what does the government consider to be a puppy mill?

Well, the term *puppy mill* does not appear in any federal statute. It certainly doesn't appear in the Animal Welfare Act. But in the early 1980s, a federal court in Minnesota did define the term *puppy mill* for the purposes of its case, leading to the most commonly accepted definition used today.

AVENSON V. ZEGART (1984)

In March 1982, then-executive director for the Minnesota Humane Society Lesley Zegart was investigating commercial dog breeders across the state to determine who was running puppy mills. After receiving complaints about the Park Rapids breeding operation of Merle and Jean Avenson, Zegart teamed up with the county deputy sheriff to visit the property and ask the pair to voluntarily cooperate with a search of their facilities. Zegart and the officer knocked on the Avensons' door to find no one home.

Once he stepped out of the sheriff's car, Zegart spotted a barn housing several dogs who appeared to be displaying signs of the skin disease mange. While neither Zegart nor the sheriff's deputy physically entered the barn, their observations from the entryway were enough for them to issue a search warrant for the property. Four days later, the warrant was carried out. Some of the sickest dogs were seized from the Avensons' farm and had to be euthanized. As for the Avensons, they were arrested and charged with several counts of animal abuse. These charges, however, were later dropped by the county prosecutor.

The Avensons filed suit against Zegart seeking $1 million in damages. The breeders alleged that Zegart's first visit to the property with the sheriff's deputy violated their Fourth Amendment rights protecting them against any unreasonable search.

In 1984, the U.S. District Court for the District of Minnesota dismissed the Avensons' case. But the ruling was notable in that it provided the first and only definition in a legal context of what exactly constitutes a puppy mill. The decision defines a puppy mill as "a dog-breeding operation in which the health of the dogs is disregarded in order to maintain a low overhead and maximize profits."[2]

This is a definition that is now generally agreed upon by most attorneys and animal welfare groups.

In short, puppy mills are not illegal. Unethical? Sure. Cruel? No doubt. But if, in fact, the definition put forth in *Avenson v. Zegart* is the most widely accepted one for a puppy mill, then it's easy to see how almost any commercial breeder—even those with USDA licenses, following the regulations put forth in the Animal Welfare Act with no violations on their inspection records—could still be defined as a puppy mill. Profits first. Dogs a distant second.

So I asked the USDA directly: How can the regulations they enforce allow a licensed facility to be a puppy mill? After all, if I kept my dog at home in the exact same conditions as she would be kept in a violation-free, USDA-licensed breeding operation, the local police could seize her, fine me, or even send me to jail for animal cruelty.

"How do you reconcile that difference?" I ask Gibbens. "From what I'm allowed to do with a dog privately and what [a USDA-licensed breeder] is allowed to do with a dog?"

Gibbens surprises me with his response.

"I think we have to be careful to avoid reconciling that difference, or else we wouldn't be able to do the job we've been asked to do," he says frankly. "We've got to apply the standards that are in place… Whenever we can use those standards to help our animals, that's what we can do… I think it's important that our folks try to keep a very level-headed, neutral approach to what we are doing. And when we've got animals in trouble, it's pretty unusual we can't use our regulations or standards to help."[3]

It's worth noting that it is often local animal cruelty statutes that end up putting bad breeders out of business, not the Animal Welfare Act. For example, in 2016, the USDA terminated licenses for fewer than ten of its more than two thousand licensees, according to the Humane Society.[4] The USDA does have the authority to terminate a license at any time. Termination, however, opens the door for the breeder to reapply for a USDA license in a year or two, depending on judge's orders. Revocation of a license, while permanent, can take years of hearings and appeals through the court system. But these instances of termination and revocation are rare and are often reserved for repeat offenders who are truly the absolute worst of the worst. In most cases, the USDA simply inspects, cites, and then repeats the process over and over, giving even routinely bad breeders the chance to correct violations every time.

Still, as many animal welfare advocates and animal behavioral experts argue, it's the inadequate standards and regulations contained in the Animal Welfare Act that are actively to blame for putting animals in both physical and mental distress in the first place.

"The problem is that the standards as they exist are survival standards at best," John Goodwin, senior director for the Humane Society's Stop Puppy Mills campaign tells me. "A female breeding dog can spend her entire life in a cage that's only six inches larger than her body, and her paw may never touch a blade of grass.

She'll be bred until her body runs out, and even the most highly motivated inspector with the best of intentions is powerless to do anything about that because the rules are so abysmal."[5]

So if a dog in my home mandates one type of treatment under local animal cruelty laws and a dog in a breeding facility is considered an agricultural commodity requiring different treatment, is the USDA really the right agency to assign to the protection of animals destined to be pets?

To say that the USDA and its inspectors are in bed with American agriculture sounds like a nasty accusation, and it's one I hear often from the animal welfare side of the equation. However, the USDA would not be upholding its own mission if it did not work to support America's farmers, a group which, oddly enough, includes dog breeders. After all, it is the USDA's own self-described mission to help "rural America to thrive [and] to promote agriculture production."[6] Nowhere in the agency's mission does it say it is their job to protect the health and welfare of the animals themselves. As for APHIS, the department within the USDA that directly oversees the inspections of dog breeders, its topline mission statement is simply "To protect the health and value of American agriculture and natural resources." In its longer explanation of its mission statement, APHIS includes a mention that it is charged with "administering the Animal Welfare Act."[7]

I ask Goodwin at the Humane Society if he thinks the problem is, in part, that USDA inspectors side too frequently with the breeders as a result of the agency's core mission—or, as animal legal expert Joyce Tischler says, if the agency treats breeders as its customers.

"I think it's more nuanced because there's about one hundred inspectors nationwide, and that's not very many. And they're not just inspecting the two thousand or so puppy mills that are licensed by the USDA," Goodwin says, referring to the other facilities that the USDA is charged with inspecting outside of the dog-breeding world. "So you have a small number [of inspectors] to cover all these facilities. The rules that are given are very bare bones and minimal. Are [the USDA inspectors] on the side of the breeder? Not necessarily. It really depends. Probably about 30 percent of these USDA-licensed puppy mills can't go a year without a citation. So they are giving out citations. There certainly are some inspectors who will give a certain bad actor a less severe citation... and you're left wondering where the consistency is. There are some puppy mills that never get cited until a new inspector comes in. Then it starts getting citations. So there are definitely going to be bad apples, but that doesn't mean that all [the USDA inspectors] are bad apples. In fact, I think a lot of them are probably decent. But look at the rules that they have to work with. A lot of inspectors can and want to do the right thing, but we can't indict the individuals. Instead, we have to look at fixing the system."

Gibbens does not deny the Humane Society's assessment that manpower is a significant obstacle for his agency. He estimates that there are about 115 inspectors making the rounds on well over 2,000 licensed dog breeders nationwide. He says some 60 percent of these inspectors are veterinarians—a plus for an aspiring USDA Animal Care inspector but not a job requirement. Their job duties on a daily basis, however, are astonishingly varied.

"They might go to a circus in the morning and a dog breeder in the afternoon and an airport at night. So they have a wide variety in what they do. We've got around eight thousand regulated facilities right now. I think just over two thousand [of those] are licensed dog breeders. So 75 percent of what we do are not licensed dog breeders," Gibbens explains.

But does Gibbens think the Animal Welfare Act regulations that the USDA is enforcing are enough?

"You know, that's gotta be for society and for Congress to determine," Gibbens says. "Our role is to enforce the law as it is now. I'm sure if you asked our 115 inspectors what their opinion is on this, you'd get a pretty wide variance. As you know, we don't regulate the dogs at home, and we've been given specific, performance-based standards to apply to the dogs that are regulated under the Animal Welfare Act. So I know it sounds like I'm trying to avoid the question, but it's the approach that you have to use if you're an inspector in the field out there every day."

As I can personally attest from what I've witnessed in investigating these USDA-licensed commercial breeding operations, there is some room for interpretation with these rules. I ask Gibbens about it.

"The inspector calls it like they see it," Gibbens confirms. "And then, if the licensee disagrees, the licensee has the opportunity to file an appeal."

Gibbens tells me that fewer than 1 percent of his inspectors' findings are appealed by breeders annually. But there might be more to this impressively low number of appeals than meets the eye.

THE OFFICE OF THE INSPECTOR GENERAL REPORT

I'm certainly not the first person to point out the USDA's problematic and often failed enforcement of the Animal Welfare Act. As it turns out, even the USDA's own Office of the Inspector

General has put the agency on notice for being too lenient in its inspections of licensed dog breeders.

In 2010, the USDA's Animal Care group was subject to an internal audit from the Office of the Inspector General (OIG). The investigation yielded a sixty-nine-page report that was damning to say the very least. The audit found that Animal Care's enforcement of problematic dog breeders was "ineffective" and failed to adequately document violations so that appropriate action could be taken. Furthermore, even when the agency had been empowered by Congress to triple the maximum penalties it could slap on violators of the Animal Welfare Act, inspectors managed to actually "misuse guidelines" to calculate penalties that were 20 percent less than before. The report reads:

> Specifically, [Animal Care inspectors] inconsistently counted violations; applied "good faith" reductions without merit; allowed a "no history of violations" reduction when the violators had a prior history; and arbitrarily changed the gravity of some violations and the business size. [Animal Care] told us that it assessed lower penalties as an incentive to encourage violators to pay a stipulated amount rather than exercise their right to a hearing.[8]

But this report that brought into the light the deliberate failings of the USDA's inspections of dog breeders only came about after years of pressure from animal welfare groups.

Attorney Ed Green, senior counsel for the Washington, DC, office of law firm Crowell & Moring, worked with the Companion Animal Protection Society (CAPS) pro bono for years to help the animal welfare group make its case on Capitol Hill. He has been

a fixture in Washington for decades and served as an attorney for
the U.S. Department of the Interior drafting federal regulations.
When the audit report finally emerged, Green recalls being very
pleased with its hardline stance on the agency's failures. But as
time passed, it became clear the report was not having the desired
effect. Green recalls wading through a morass of excuses from the
USDA for why the agency could not tighten the inspection and
enforcement processes following the report.

"It all sounded nice, but it was all bullshit. They just truly
were stuck in the mud and did things the way they wanted to do
them," he says.[9]

I ask if this type of bureaucratic and uninspired mind-set is
typical of most government agencies. Green is adamant that the
USDA is unique in this regard.

"Most of the agencies with which I deal are much more
mission oriented than the folks at USDA. At least the [Animal
Care] group anyway. I can't speak for other parts of the USDA.
But I think USDA—parts of it are quite aggressive and enthusiastic in terms of what they do, but mostly it's sort of a humdrum
group that's been around for a century and a half now, and it
just does its business. Certainly the Animal Welfare Act imple-
mentation is, to say the least, modest in terms of what it does,"
he says. "These people are down in the bowels of the executive
branch, and they're down in the bowels of the U.S. Department
of Agriculture—nobody really gives a shit about them frankly.
Well, and the animals don't know—it's sad."

Because working directly with the USDA was proving to be
without much merit, Green took CAPS to Capitol Hill to try
and convince various committees and subcommittees in both the
House and the Senate to take action.

"We were always received sympathetically and, in some cases, even enthusiastically. But the bottom line was: dogs don't vote," he says.

When I spoke to Gibbens, I asked him what became of the hard-won 2010 OIG report. Did the audit actually change anything?

"After the audit that was released in 2010, the Secretary [of Agriculture] declared the 'Age of Enforcement,' which meant that we were supposed to cite every little thing we found," Gibbens tells me. "So we did that and wound up with hundreds of enforcement cases, more than the system could handle. So those were just closed out with warnings, and we focused on the more serious ones."

To me, closing out hundreds of cases does not seem to be in the spirit of an "Age of Enforcement." But as Gibbens explains, this new inundation of violations spurred by the OIG report inspired the agency to develop another tactic—one that has since been reviled by animal welfare groups.

"We needed another tool, simply besides citing every little thing," Gibbens continues.

So the agency began using what it calls "teachable moments."

A VIOLATION IS A VIOLATION IS A VIOLATION

There are two main categories of violations available to inspectors to describe the level of severity of their findings. The most serious type of infraction is called a direct violation: something that is immediately impacting the health of an animal. A nondirect violation is anything that is not having an immediate impact, like, for example, a backed-up drain outside of a dog's cage.[10] However, there is no master list that itemizes specifics of what inspectors must cite as a direct violation—there are a few overarching examples provided to inspectors, but they have to take it from there using their experience and common sense. Just as Gibbens says, the inspector calls it like he sees it, and it's up to the breeder to appeal the decision. But several animal welfare watchdog groups tell me this lack of specificity has led to inspectors finding ways not to document veterinary care violations as direct violations—even in cases of repeated noncompliances. Furthermore, I've pinpointed a theme in the inspection reports that I've obtained where the USDA inspector often gives only one citation for multiple sick animals when each one should be documented as its own separate noncompliance.

But if direct and nondirect violations are the two main categories that inspectors use to enforce the Animal Welfare Act, what is a teachable moment?

"A teachable moment is a minor noncompliance: it's not having any discernable impact on the animal or the dog...[and] it hasn't been a problem before. So we haven't seen it before, we haven't mentioned it before, it hasn't been cited as a noncompliance before, and it hasn't been a teachable moment before," Gibbens explains.

But according to Bob Baker, the executive director of the Missouri Alliance for Animal Welfare (MAAL), these teachable moments are intentionally being used to leave violations off the record and help keep USDA-licensed breeders in business—and they're part of a larger pattern of the USDA changing inspection report terminology to make it more difficult for states to regulate which breeders their retailers can purchase from.

Baker is widely considered to be one of the nation's top experts on commercial dog breeding and has been instrumental in leading the fight for better legislation and enforcement both in Missouri and nationwide. In fact, when I first started researching this topic, nearly every expert in animal law, behavior, ethics, and health that I spoke to would conclude our conversation by suggesting I speak with Baker. I've since found his perspective to be invaluable to my coverage as he is a very rare breed in the fight for improving animal welfare: he is able to zero in directly on the rational and legal arguments for what is wrong with the current system without falling into the trap too many animal activists do of overrelying on the emotional pull of their battle.

Baker also holds the distinction of being the person who first sounded the alarm about the USDA's teachable moment policy.

It was 2014, and Baker was attending a USDA breeder conference in Missouri. He recalled the room being hot with outrage over the fact that a growing coalition of municipalities and states were passing laws limiting the number of violations a breeder could have on his inspection reports and still sell to local pet shops.

"[The breeders] were just livid. They were claiming that [these laws were] very, very much affecting their business… So Gibbens said, 'Don't worry about that. We're going to get around this… If we see you have violations and they aren't real serious, we'll just mark them down as teachable moments,'" Baker recalls. "The dog breeders were all upset, and they said 'Will there be a record of these teachable moments?' And USDA said, 'No. The only record of it will be on a separate sheet of paper from your inspection report, and the inspector will write that down, but that will not be in his field notes or anything that can be obtained through a

FOIA [Freedom of Information Act] request. You will be the only one who will see it. [The inspector] will write it down on a sheet of paper, and he will give it to you.'"[11]

Gibbens confirms to me that he first announced the change in policy at that 2014 meeting fully aware that Baker and other animal welfare organizations were present.

But Baker points out one of the many reasons why this type of process is problematic: a repeated violation requires an escalation of enforcement action. But if a violation—even a minor one—is intentionally left off the record, how will an inspector know whether it is a new or a repeat violation?

Under pressure from animal advocates led by Baker, the agency released a stakeholder's report, coming out officially with the teachable-moment policy in January 2015. Today, the agency says that inspectors document teachable moments on a separate piece of paper from the official report but retain them on file. They are now available by FOIA request—but only if that request specifically calls for a breeder's teachable moments. Even a FOIA request calling for all a breeder's records will not include any teachable moments.

"The inspector has to believe that the issue can be corrected quickly and that the licensee intends to correct it quickly. There's some subjectivity to it," Gibbens tells me of the teachable-moment policy. "So at the end of the inspection, when they hand over the inspection report, there's also a list of any teachable moments. The licensee gets a copy, the inspector gets a copy, and a copy goes to the supervisor."

"Is there a punch list of deadlines on the teachable moments?" I ask.

"No," Gibbens tells me. "They're not treated as noncompliances.

If there was anything on there that was affecting an animal, it wouldn't be a teachable moment. It would be cited on the inspection report."

But as my own investigation has since found—and as I will demonstrate later in this book—that may not be entirely the case. In Missouri, one of the only examples of where state inspectors are empowered to create their own inspection reports, I have found multiple, serious animal welfare violations documented just hours before federal inspectors have visited the exact same facility and documented no violations at all—neither on the official record nor in a teachable moment.

It's easy to write all this off as mere semantics: a direct violation, a teachable moment, and so on. But words mean a lot when you fight for years to pass legislation based on these terms and then the USDA changes the rules of the game. This is exactly what those breeders were fighting for in that 2014 conference, when they were placated with the teachable moment policy. Now they can circumvent laws in a growing number of municipalities and states where pet shops are barred from purchasing dogs from breeders with one direct violation on the record. Other ordinances also limit the number of nondirect violations a breeder can have on its USDA reports and still sell to pet stores.

"If you have laws passed based on certain terms that are used at the time and then you have a new term that's introduced thereafter, it can obviously wreak havoc with a law that's been passed with much effort and of course can serve to undermine that law. And certainly it raises questions and concerns for us," says Cathy Liss, president of the Animal Welfare Institute.[12]

Bob Baker agrees that this type of labeling is "just another method of helping the breeders circumvent these laws."

"Inspectors, when documenting a teachable moment, write

that there were 'no noncompliant items identified.' It's a felony to falsify a federal document If they're writing up a noncompliant item as a teachable moment…there's an intent to be fraudulent to help the breeder get around the state laws," Baker says. "The USDA is undermining the consumer. You think your New Jersey pet store is only buying from good breeders, but you might be buying from one with teachable moments or a direct violation that's been knocked down to an indirect violation."

In one of my meetings with Gibbens, I try to drill down on exactly what constitutes a direct violation.

"If I'm an inspector," I say, "and I show up and—oh my goodness, there are dead puppies from a litter that didn't go right. Is that something you consider direct?"

I'd assumed the answer would be *Of course dead dogs are a direct violation*. I was wrong.

"It'll be based on what the inspector sees and finds out. It may still be occurring. So if it's still occurring, it would be a direct. If it was something that, it's done, and we're just seeing the results, and whatever caused it is not still there and likely to cause it with another litter, they'll probably not put it as a direct," Gibbens says, explaining that even with dead puppies found on site, the most damning designation of direct violation is not a certainty.

"It's outrageous," Liss says of the fact that a USDA inspector can find dead dogs on a breeder's property and still not slap the operation with the designated direct violation. "Well, they're dead, so it's not an animal at risk because the risk is over. It's dead."

Liss continues, citing her organization's concern with the USDA's overreliance on categories to define what's wrong and exactly how wrong it is. "I don't even like [to use] categories to the different types of citations that are made—direct or nondirect. A violation is a violation is a violation. And to me, you start creating all kinds of gray when you are separating some kinds from the others or deciding sometimes you don't have to note them," Liss says, pointing out that the USDA is now rolling out yet another new designation for violations on reports called *critical*.

"I think then you get caught up on which category they're in, instead of recognizing that none of it should be happening," Liss says.

But as I was chasing my tail, digging deeper into the USDA's ever-shifting nomenclature of violations, something even more outrageous happened.

MAKE AMERICA TRANSPARENT AGAIN

For much of the last decade, the USDA made its most recent inspection reports available through an online database on its website. While imperfect, this tool allowed consumers, animal welfare advocates, pet shops, and lawmakers to see how many violations a breeder had on the record—of course, with teachable moments omitted. As I conducted the bulk of my investigation into the industry, these reports were available online, allowing me to quickly reference the past three years or so. While I went on to discover that these online reports were often misleading in that they failed to actually document violations, they were at least an effort at transparency. In our initial conversation, the USDA's Gibbens gave himself and his department a pat on the back for being transparent by maintaining the database. So despite my reservations about the accuracy and thus the value of these reports, they were at least a starting point for a consumer wanting to make a more informed decision.

But on Friday, February 3, 2017, the online database of

inspection records for the USDA's Animal Care program disappeared. It was day fifteen of the newly minted Trump administration, which had yet to even confirm a Secretary of Agriculture. There was no press release, no tweet, no notice of any kind. After years of providing immediate access to these inspection reports to whoever was willing to search online, the tool was deactivated. Now, to access any records, one would have to submit a Freedom of Information Act (FOIA) request. And wait. And wait.

Most major news outlets missed the story at first, and for a few days, this change went relatively unreported. But animal welfare groups were watching.

By Monday, February 6, 2017, the Humane Society had fired its opening salvo against the Trump administration, sending the USDA an official notice that it would seek legal action if the files were not restored.[13]

The next day, the USDA responded to the mounting pressure, attempting to cast blame on the Obama administration for the decision. The agency released a statement on its website saying the move to pull these records began "in 2016, well before the change of administration" and came from an internal effort "to balance the need for transparency with rules protecting individual privacy."[14] In the days that followed, I spoke again with Gibbens, who declined to comment on the suppression of these records but did reiterate that the process began before the start of the Trump administration.

However, Matt Herrick, the former USDA communications director for the Obama administration denied that his team ever would have suppressed these inspection reports. He tweeted: "Decision by @usda 2 remove animal abuse reports not required. Totally subjective. Same option given 2 past admin. We refused. #transparency."[15]

So why does all this matter?

Currently, the state of California and dozens of municipalities both large and small ban pet stores from selling anything other than dogs obtained from a shelter or rescue. These include cities like Los Angeles, Philadelphia, Miami, Chicago, Las Vegas, and others. However, seven states plus New York City and several surrounding counties have laws on the books that regulate which breeders can supply pet stores in their jurisdictions. That's Arizona, Connecticut, New Jersey, Louisiana, Maryland, Ohio, and Virginia—plus New York City and Suffolk and Nassau Counties, which make up much of Long Island. These regulations, which impact tens of millions of American consumers, make it illegal for pet stores to purchase from unlicensed breeders or those with direct and nondirect violations on their recent inspection reports.

Unlike the outright ban on retail pet shops, the regulatory laws in these seven states and the largest city in the nation are now threatened even more than they were by the teachable moment policy. These laws are not enforceable without immediate access to USDA inspection reports that inform pet shops of who they cannot purchase from. Access to this database was a major consideration when these states passed laws restricting the types of breeders from whom pet shops could purchase. Now it's gone.

Put it this way: imagine if access to everyone's driving records was suddenly—and without warning—ended by an order from the federal government. A state trooper could pull a driver over, and he would have no way to view that person's record. Maybe that driver is a law-abiding citizen with no marks against him. Or maybe that driver is wanted in two states and has been arrested in the past for multiple DUIs. There would be no way to know, because all the records that would tell law enforcement how to proceed and do their job are now inaccessible without a FOIA request that could take years to be answered. Or never get answered at all. Now, the laws are effectively worthless.

Albeit unlikely, that example makes it easy to see how the Trump administration's suppression of USDA inspection reports neuters the hard-won legislation that aimed to put the bad actors out of business while keeping the responsible breeders in business. Any responsible, USDA-licensed breeders out there should be the first to cry foul as now they're indistinguishable from those who are not. For what it's worth, this move also marks a clear instance of the federal government swooping in to negate the rights of the states to decide how to regulate the retail pet sale industry—an interesting action for a Republican White House.

I spoke to the Trump administration's transition team leader for the USDA, Brian Klippenstein, several months ahead of his appointment. At the time, he was the executive director of farmer-advocacy group Protect the Harvest. In our conversation, Klippenstein made his views on pet sale legislation—both the laws banning purchase from licensees with violations on the record and those that banned pet shops from selling any animals not obtained from a rescue—very clear. Looking back on this conversation, the writing was on the wall for what his first steps would be in becoming the de facto leader of the USDA.

"There are over eighty jurisdictions in America where it's illegal to sell pets at retail. San Diego, Phoenix—big places. We have nothing against a rescue or a shelter—far from it. I'm delighted they're there," Klippenstein told me. "But it used to be that you could get a pet from any shelter or rescue [for little or no cost] but now, in some of these jurisdictions, you have to pay—and in some, you have to pay a lot. The interesting part of that to me, as a tactical point, is you have your competition outlawed so you have a local, legislative monopoly, and now they're in the retail pet sales business… It's a fascinating tool if you can get a legislative body to let you have monopolistic control."[16]

By withholding the USDA inspection reports from the internet, at least Klippenstein and his team can ensure that in the jurisdictions where pet suppliers are regulated and not all-out banned, the competition to rescues and shelters is alive but not well.

It's hard to say how the USDA will end up balancing breeder privacy with transparency. The agency would not give me any clues when I asked directly. It seems that if breeder privacy and transparency are both essential for a well-functioning pet industry, the USDA would have at least consulted stakeholders for a way to make this change responsibly, instead of simply yanking the entire database unannounced. I could foresee a situation where this move backfires and animal welfare advocates will respond by pursuing more of the all-out retail pet store bans that the industry so reviles. After all, if the federal government wants to prevent states from regulating the industry and enforcing their own laws, maybe the only way to crack down on bad actors is to encourage more states and cities to outright ban all pet stores from selling any puppies not obtained from rescues.

Whether the full database of inspection records will ever come back online has yet to be determined. Many of my sources tell me they are doubtful that it will ever be restored in full. My conversations with Gibbens at the USDA reveal a more nuanced perspective. Keep in mind, Gibbens is on the operational side of the agency and does not have much say into its policies.

"I know that the agency wants to be as transparent as it can be within the legal confines of the laws we have to comply with. Not to sound bureaucratic, but that's just the way it is," he says.

I ask if withholding these reports was a way of obfuscating the truth or if suppressing the reports was endangering the consumer who wants to know where his puppy is coming from before making a costly purchase.

"The agency is considering, in the face of this, to be as transparent as we can legally be... The industry—the pet distributor industry—used our inspection reports as well. And so now they're at a loss, because they can't look at those reports instantly and see if they want to buy from that breeder or not," Gibbens says.

In the meantime, animal welfare advocates seem drained of hope. One animal welfare lobbyist on Capitol Hill told me in our interview that perhaps it would be best for me to not report on anything dog-related at all during the Trump administration lest officials become aware and make things somehow even worse.

Maybe she's right and now isn't the right political climate to be publishing an investigation on this topic. Maybe by the time you read this, things will have changed. But I have to believe that even those who supported the Trump administration can agree that the welfare of breeding dogs must improve—assuming they can be made aware of the problems. Because our love for dogs is not a partisan issue. Look at it this way: in 2016, 54.4 million American households—or about 137.6 million people— owned at least one dog.[17] In 2016, around 130 million Americans voted in the presidential election. Sure, maybe not all the 137.6 million dog owners in America are eligible voters, and maybe dogs themselves can't vote, but all the same, it sure looks like a lot more of us voted for "dog" in 2016 than anyone else.

CHAPTER THREE

The Dog Farmers

WHAT ACTUALLY HAPPENS WHEN A COMPANION animal becomes an agricultural commodity?

To begin to answer this question, I speak with one of the most seasoned, undercover investigators of animal welfare cases out there. He asks me to call him Pete for this book instead of his real name. I agree. There are certain questions he won't answer so as to not reveal the tricks of his trade and preserve his cover for future investigations, which is okay by me.

Over the fifteen years he's been undercover, Pete has investigated more than seven hundred commercial dog breeders. He's worked undercover at several puppy mills as well as at every other type of farm and slaughterhouse under the sun. His hidden camera footage has been instrumental in shutting down some of the worst out there and in shedding light on the ugly but common practices at many of the rest. In fact, you've likely seen some of his footage on TV or in documentaries over the years, where his unprecedented access has been instrumental in raising public outcry. When it comes to comparing the day-to-day practices at commercial dog breeders to factory farms, there is no one better suited to illustrating the similarities.

As you might expect, during an investigation, Pete is extremely careful to always keep his cover—even when he is working at a facility day in, day out for weeks or months on end. But he nearly blew it on one of the biggest investigations of his career, when he accidentally revealed just one small shred of his compassionate mind-set for animals.

It was 2008. Pete had been hired by Kathy Jo Bauck to work at her notorious Pick of the Litter Kennel in Minnesota. With up to 1,351 dogs on the premises at the height of her operation, Bauck's was one of the bigger USDA-licensed facilities out there. And to keep such a massive operation humming, Pete says she ran her business exactly like the factory farms he'd worked at before.

"The practice from the word *go* in the morning was exactly like working at a factory farm," Pete says. "In fact, I made an undercover mistake: I was the only person who called it a kennel. It was pointed out to me by several workers on a lunch break. They said 'Kennel?... We've always just called it *the farm*. We've never called it a kennel.'"[1]

This mistake was a rare one for Pete to make in the field. The strict vegan and self-described animal lover, who says he doesn't even swat flies, knew he'd made an error. To call a breeding operation a kennel implies an expectation of humane treatment for the dogs. Many puppy mills even use the word *kennel* in their business names because the word is one that they know will sound familiar and comforting to pet owners. After all, many of us willingly pay good money to take our dogs to kennels to board when we go out of town or for doggie day care. But Pete should have known better—the workday at the Baucks' was nothing like a kennel; it was all industrial-strength farming practices at their worst.

"To [the other workers], it was a dog farm. And they'd worked on other farms," he says. "It was a dog farm. You start in the morning, and you get the chores done. You don't take care of the dogs; you get the chores done. You have to feed, you look for the dead, you're going to remove the dead puppies. You're going to remove the dead dogs, make notes about the sick ones that you may or may not treat. Then you're going to go about fixing things. It is exactly like you do when you're pulling dead at the broiler farm or at the egg farm or you're pulling dead piglets at the hog farm. Or at a calf ranch—it's identical… When I learned that's how they viewed it, I quickly went in with that mentality, and it was pretty easy to get by with the work. But the way they would treat the animals too was with a callousness that I think would be shocking to most people or confusing to most people. But I had seen it before on farms."

The unbridled callousness seen at Kathy Jo Bauck's operation is horrifying to hear recounted as Pete tells it to me. But it is another thing entirely to see it. The undercover video he shot there is harrowing: workers shoving puppies into wire cages or yanking them by a single paw to be moved; dogs with gaping open wounds across their jaws or ribs left to rot; a pug whose eye had come out of its socket and was never surgically removed to relieve his suffering; an emaciated, pregnant spaniel refused medical care; dogs simply lying dead in the cages where they'd toiled their entire lives.

But when the dogs did not just die on their own, Pete says he watched Bauck's husband, Allen, gather up the sickest for slaughter.

"Allen Bauck, the husband, one of the USDA licensees, was

done with other chores during the day, but now was the time he was going to collect the [sick]. I had seen this at a variety of farms, especially a hog farm I worked at," Pete says, comparing the Baucks' practice specifically to the way hog farmers would hang their dying sows once they'd long passed the point of needing a quick and humane death. "Why don't you take care of them properly from the word *go*? It just didn't happen. It was the same thing with these dogs. So it's time to start collecting the sick: there's too many, and [Allen had the] time. We start gathering them, and we put them in a truck. This one mastiff in particular is absolutely at death's door. Blood's coming out of his mouth… he's slowly dying. And Allen wants to take the time to wander off and go talk to someone who showed up at the farm and bullshit with the guy about fixing cars."

Pete watched and even recorded video to show just how long it took for Allen Bauck to return to the truck and take the three dogs he'd gathered to finally shoot them. He watched as the mastiff continued to suffer in agony for at least ten more excruciating minutes while Bauck chatted with his buddy about cars. Eventually, Bauck returned with his gun and finished the job.

But as Pete tells me, death by shooting isn't always the swift ending to a tortured life.

"There was one dog that [Allen Bauck] had mentioned that he had shot in the past. It was a chocolate Lab. And when he shot the chocolate Lab in the head with a .22 rifle, [the bullet] bounced off the dog's skull, and he said the dog just stood there panting and looking at him. It didn't even move. So he put the .22 in the Lab's ear and pulled the trigger in order to kill it," Pete says.

But Bauck's way of recounting the story of the Lab's death to Pete was somehow even more disturbing to him than the actual facts.

"It was the way of discussing it: casually, matter-of-factly, almost bragging with a gallows sense of humor and kind of like a piqued interest in the grotesque and the morbid that I have seen among people who club calves to death with hammers and throw chickens in trash cans alive and bury them beneath their own dead. It was almost the same thing. And you don't see that in [a USDA] inspection [report]."

This is a point Pete repeats several times throughout our conversation: that the USDA inspection reports are not indicative of what can be found in the commercial breeding operations on any given day.

Gibbens at the USDA oddly echoes Pete's sentiment that the inspection reports are only a snapshot—and not a fully representational one at that.

"We do ten thousand to eleven thousand inspections per year," Gibbens tells me, including the eight thousand facilities that his department regulates under the Animal Welfare Act beyond just the two thousand or so dog breeders. "Do the numbers, right? Most places, we see once a year. So we don't know what goes on 364 days a year at these facilities."

But this discrepancy between reality and what appears on the record can create a very ugly situation on the ground for those other 364 days a year.

"When I work at a facility, I always, 100 percent of the time, find many, many, many violations that inspectors never see and never write them up for," Pete says. "I am fully confident that every facility that I ever go to, that there are far many more things that are happening there than I can observe just by walking through it. And I get more statements from [the breeders] and see more than an inspector does when they go."

Having watched Pete's undercover videos and compared them to official inspection reports, I can attest to the fact that he has pinpointed and recorded images of violations that do not appear on the record even just a few weeks later. He's not surprised when I point this out to him.

"I have been involved in the process of gathering state and federal records for [dog breeders]. When I first started doing this work, what I would do was I would use those records to determine which kennels I would make a priority in visiting. I would also visit other kennels that had alleged violations if they were in the area. And what I consistently found is that, right or wrong, whether this makes sense or not, what I would find on previous inspection reports had absolutely no impact on what I would find at the time when I would visit a kennel. I would go to some of the worst actors on paper, and their place would be perfectly clean when I was there. Then I would go to places that had never received any violations, and I couldn't fucking believe that they were allowed to have a license, it was so horrible. You know: veterinary care violations, open wounds, those kinds of things."

I ask him how this is possible—how an official, government inspection report can be so utterly misrepresentative of the truth on the ground. Pete has seen exactly how.

"[The kennel workers] would be literally a minute ahead of an inspector. They would be cleaning things up and hiding things and putting them right back. Such as putting mats in cages for puppies and then taking them right up. Or trying to clean up moldy feed just right in front of the inspector while someone else tries to delay the inspector. Common sense would tell you people would be more careful than that, and they would have a better plan than that. But the reality was like something out of a bad TV show. And it worked. It worked every time," he says.

But those were just the violations that the breeders were able to slip past investigators. Far more insidious are the violations that investigators actually witnessed and chose to let slide. The USDA has repeatedly and publicly said that educating the breeders is a vital part of their mission—hence the teachable moment policy. And while the controversial teachable moment policy would allow for investigators to document these violations without slapping them onto the official inspection report, Pete says he witnessed even this permissive tactic being thrown aside.

"What many breeders would tell me is there would be a violation that they felt was nondirect…such as peeling paint, or there is mold in this area, or there is a structural problem, or you have rats, or something like that. Okay. And [the inspectors] would say, 'If you would just take care of that, I will just look the other way and I will just let that go,'" Pete says. "These are supposed to be teachable moments, where they get written up and then it goes off [the record] after a certain period of time. But what the vast majority of breeders are telling me is that it doesn't even get written up; it's just a verbal instruction of *please do this*. And they realize that if they do it, there won't be any problem with the inspector later on. And the inspector will just let the whole thing go."

"So much for transparency," I say.

Pete lets out a low, dark laugh.

It may seem like a small concession for an inspector to make. What's so bad about peeling paint or rust on a cage joint? When we think of puppy mills, it's the serious types of violations that Pete witnessed and documented at Kathy Jo Bauck's operation that seem to be the ones these inspectors should concern themselves with. Fair enough. But the trouble is that the teachable moments system is already in place to handle these smaller concerns in an informal way so that breeders can learn from their mistakes. At least in recent years, with the formalization of the teachable moments policy, these smaller violations would be available by FOIA request so that the public could evaluate just how minor these missteps were when they failed to appear in the primary inspection reports. But if nothing is being documented and it's all agreed upon in off-the-record conversations, how can anyone other than the breeder and the inspector be sure what's happening? And worse yet, if it's up to the inspector to leave something entirely off the record, who's to say that the violations would stop with peeling paint and not something more serious? Well, in short, there's no way to know.

Pete also points out another problem with the inspection system. At many of these breeders, the same inspector will go out to the same property year after year—you can see proof of it in the signature at the bottom of every report. As a result, the breeders and inspectors become collegial, and it gets harder for the government agent to remain unbiased.

"You have a system where you have federal inspectors. So that sounds great on its head, right?" Pete begins. "But you have inspectors who have to go out and see these people day in and day out. And human nature is to be nonconfrontational. So what do you do when you have to, every year, you have to see the same people, and you don't want to be the bad guy, and you don't want to be confrontational? You let things go. You start to side with them. And from what I've personally seen, the USDA gets mad at inspectors who rock the boat. [The USDA doesn't] want to pull licenses; they don't want to complain about cruelty. So I think that when you see that someone has a lot of violations, that doesn't necessarily reveal what their place would be like on the day that you go to visit them. And if you see that a place has no violations, in my personal experience, there is an equal chance that is because they are actually following the rules as it is that they are ignoring the rules. The inspector is just so corrupt that he or she does not care at all and never writes them up."

As familiar as he is with the USDA's inspection system across various types of agricultural operations, Pete remains somewhat perplexed as to why the agency is tasked with oversight for commercial dog breeders. He believes the USDA's involvement, in part, enables the factory-farming mentality that many of the breeders have in place. As he's seen, many of the commercial dog breeders are former cattle or hog farmers who have previously worked with the USDA inspection system in their prior livelihoods. As a result, Pete says it should come as no surprise that the bulk of puppy mills can be found in the Midwest, where most of the nation's agriculture industry is clustered.

"The vast majority of [my investigations have] been across the Midwest…which has also been a hotbed of animal agriculture. So it's no surprise that dogs are part of that ag," he says. "Puppy mills are animal agriculture. They are farmed dogs. I have been to so many places, so many puppy mills, where they used to have a hog farm and they converted the hog farm into a dog kennel because you could have a larger number of head in a smaller amount of space with a higher price per head for that type of livestock—that livestock being puppies. And then [the breeders] already understand the USDA because—for some fucking reason—the USDA is supposed to handle chickens, cows, pigs, and dogs and cats."

It seems to me that Pete has earned the right to question the USDA's capacity to inspect the welfare of companion animals over his long career in the field witnessing and documenting the holes in the system. There's no doubt that he's seen the worst of the worst, enough to make his outrage with the USDA understandable. But to gain that access to these breeders, Pete's hands are not entirely clean. In order to maintain his cover and gain unprecedented access to these farms and breeders, he's had to do work that he admits he's not proud of. Animal welfare advocates, the people I'd expect to be his kindred spirits, have not always been fans of his work and have, in fact, been some of his biggest critics.

"Some of them liked me, and some of them thought I was the worst person on earth. One person called me the next 'Son of Sam' on social media," he recalls of the backlash he faced on his first puppy mill case. "The case lasted five and a half months, and I had to do some really bad things to maintain my cover, but I was reporting the evidence to a U.S. attorney's office... I would go and take this evidence to law enforcement, and then law enforcement would use it to shut down this target and save over six hundred dogs and over one hundred cats. Ultimately, I got a civilian medal from the federal government."

Pete says that this memory of receiving an honor from the government gets him through the darkest moments of working undercover side by side with unscrupulous breeders and farmers, witnessing the horrors that he does.

"Fifteen years later, that really has stuck with me. There is a place for all people to do all kinds of things. I realized that I have an ability to compartmentalize my emotions and to place more of a value on withstanding suffering than just trying to be happy. If I can do that, I may not be saving animals personally. I may not be personally running around getting people to be vegan, making people adopt instead of buying puppies from puppy mills. But in my role, I can assist all those efforts. And the reason that has been easier for me is because I've seen the fruits of this labor from my first case," he says.

But I have to ask: How can an award from the federal government mean so much to him when he has seen firsthand the way that the federal regulations and inspectors fail these animals time and time again?

"I've always said I have kind of a punk rock mentality of, you know, 'Fuck the government for the terrible regulations,'" he admits. "But how do you measure success in fighting puppy mills? By how many lives you've saved? Or do you measure the success by how many puppy mills are shut down and how much adoptions are increased at shelters? Because those two things may be mutually exclusive."

But perhaps his biggest frustration lies in the Animal Welfare Act itself—the very legislation that the USDA is charged with enforcing. Without the right regulations, even the best enforcement is not enough. In particular, there is one omission in the Animal Welfare Act's regulations for dog breeding that troubles him above all. And this omission, in Pete's estimation, is subjecting dogs to even worse conditions than some factory-farmed animals.

"There is nothing listed in the Animal Welfare Act regarding the psychological well-being of dogs. And that is the most frustrating thing to me," Pete says. "My work in the last few years has been focused on factory-farm animals. I have worked at three egg farms, and I personally hate egg farms more than anything on earth. But I think about egg farms all the time when I go into a puppy mill, because we are pushing for a cage-free country right now [for eggs]. And it is completely related to the psychological well-being of hens. And yet there is nothing in the Animal Welfare Act regarding the psychological well-being of animals who unwillingly devote their entire lives to produce our pets. That's the biggest problem that I see in the system."

He's right, unfortunately. As we've seen, there is nothing in the Animal Welfare Act mandating the mental stimulation of breeding dogs. Pete raises an essential point: these dogs are animals we are breeding to be pets, not food. They are prized and bred because of their value as companion animals whose mental well-being enriches our lives by their sides. So why is this vital part of their makeup not being accounted for in how they're bred? I believe it's largely because the breeding stock are so rarely seen on the other end of the transaction. As long as the puppies seem well enough, who's to know the difference?

After speaking with Pete, I take Izzie on a walk to clear my head and process the ugliness revealed in our conversation. It's a brisk October day, and Izzie prances ahead on the leash. She seems happy and blissfully unaware in the afternoon sun. It strikes me that she's a perfect example for why the well-being of dogs in breeding facilities is ignored: she seems mostly fine to my eye. I wonder what damage could possibly be done if I was able to get her so early in her life—maybe twelve weeks old at the most. As we walk, a snippet of my conversation with animal neurobehavioral scientist Overall pops into my head. As we'd analyzed the regulations in the Animal Welfare Act, I'd mentioned, in passing, that the puppies shipped off for sale are too young to be fully scarred by their experience in the breeding operation.

"Maybe the breeding facility hasn't left enough of a mental impression on the puppies by the time they're shipped off," I'd said.

"Oh yes, it has," she'd said. "That is what the data are now showing us."

I stop in my tracks. Izzie looks back at me, confused by the sudden halt. I turn around and jog back to my desk, Izzie galloping in tow. She high-steps beside me eagerly, certain my change of speed and direction is a game. I reach out immediately to Overall, asking if she'd be willing to actually meet Izzie and demonstrate if she—happy as she seems to me—was somehow permanently scarred by her experience at the USDA-licensed breeding facility where she was born. To my surprise, Overall kindly agrees. I book a flight for Izzie and me to head to her lab in the Philadelphia suburbs within a few weeks. Until then, I stare at this dog, perched on my couch, and helplessly wonder: *What will Overall find? Has the damage really been done?*

CHAPTER FOUR

When a Dog Is Livestock

IN THE WEEKS AHEAD OF OUR TRIP TO DR. OVERALL'S
lab, I begin the challenging process of unpacking my assumptions about dogs. My only experience with dogs to date has been with Izzie, my pet. But that relationship does not reflect the entire spectrum of how dogs are owned in this country.

No one would ever question that Izzie, splayed across my bed, flat on her belly, laying waste to a tennis ball, is a pet. And yet in the context of a breeding operation, Izzie would not be considered a pet at all—she'd be livestock. As much as the notion of my Izzie being anything but a pet chills me, it's a question I have to ask in order to understand this industry: Is a dog livestock? After all, dog-breeding facilities are inspected by the United States Department of Agriculture. So, emotions aside, maybe there isn't much difference between a dog, a cow, or a pig? Or perhaps the more precise question would be *when* is a dog a pet and when is a dog livestock? As it turns out, that depends.

Before I launch into this point, I do want to say that

mistreatment of any animal—whether pet or livestock—is a terrible thing in my opinion. The thought of inflicting pain or stress on any animal upsets me, whether that animal is destined for the dinner table, the doghouse, or the foot of the bed. But I feel it is important to emphasize that you do not need to be a vegetarian or a vegan to appreciate the profound harm specifically being done to dogs when they are treated as farm animals or livestock. And while the conditions in our nation's factory farms for our food are abhorrent, there are many excellent books and documentaries on this topic already available. So in this book, I will focus exclusively on the farming of dogs for the purpose of becoming pets while remaining transparent in my belief that factory farming of any kind should be a national concern.

Most dictionaries define *livestock* as a farm animal that is viewed as an asset. It's easy to see how a breeder's dogs fit into that category. But it's not so easy to see how a dog kept as a pet could be viewed that way. After all, any assessor of my family's meager net worth would be more likely to classify Izzie as a loss leader rather than as an asset of any monetary value—even if, to me, she might be the most precious thing I own.

And there it is again: I do own her, don't I?

For as much as we come to love the dogs who take up residence with us, they lack the rights that many of us assume they have—which is to say, they actually have no rights at all. In every single state in this country, animals are property. In the context of most commercial breeding operations, dogs are considered livestock. In some states, a dog in a breeding facility is, in fact, legally designated as livestock. As an agricultural commodity, a breeder's dog is expected to put forth a healthy enough litter at least once every six months or on every heat until the animal can breed no more. Then, in most cases, the animal is euphemistically retired. For some breeders, as we know, the word *retired* is synonymous with *shot*.

More often than not, we treat our companion animals well because it brings us joy and because we love them. But when our relationship is not based on love and mutual enrichment and instead becomes about mass production and profit margins, things change. These animals are very much at our mercy to provide and care for them, to go above and beyond what the law demands. So why are dogs vulnerable to the will of their humans—whether breeder or pet owner—to treat them with kindness, indifference, or neglect? Precisely because we are their owners, not their family.

This legal understanding of animals as property cuts to the very complicated core of our relationship with them. And dogs, more than any other animal, have become commodities. We buy a golden retriever because it is loyal, dependable, and is expected to live a long, healthy life by our side. Our consumer behavior is in many ways similar to the way we buy an American-made pickup truck because it is strong, dependable, and expected to run for many years to come. We buy an English bulldog for its unique and unusual looks and because its high price tag denotes exclusivity—even if its lifespan will be curtailed and it will struggle to breathe from the day it's born. It's the same way we might buy a vintage sports car: it may not last long on the road, and it's certainly not practical, but we love the way it looks and what it says about us.

Breeds are brands; dogs are goods for sale. And just like any other commodity that we mass-produce in this country, dogs are being subjected to factory conditions. That is, however, until they're living in our homes and are sleeping in our beds. Then, as if by magic, they become family. The dog hasn't changed. The context has.

"All animals are property in every state. They don't have legal rights," animal law expert Tischler explains to me. "State anticruelty laws are protections, not rights. A legal right would be something the animal could have initiated on his or her behalf, and we can't do that. I can't sue on behalf of an animal, because they are property. That's the rule in every single state in the United States. When you're dealing with puppy mills, you have a commercial breeding operation, where all the animals are property."[1]

It is worth noting that the United States lags behind much of the rest of the Western world in our protections of animals. Most European countries began rejecting factory-farming practices decades ago and have upgraded the protections afforded to their animals. In 2009, the Treaty of Lisbon, which amended the constitution of the European Union, was updated to include a reference to animals as "sentient beings" who, going forward, would have their welfare considered in continental lawmaking.[2]

But even in the EU, animals do not have rights. India, however, includes actual rights for animals in its constitution, the top of the list being that it is "the fundamental duty of every citizen of India to have compassion for all living creatures."[3]

So back here in the United States, Izzie is my property, just like my TV, my dining room table, and my couch. But if my husband and I were to divorce, the TV, dining room table, and couch would be divvied up by equitable distribution. Both my husband and I may wish to keep our couch in the event of a divorce, but no court will consider that battle a custody dispute.

Izzie, on the other hand, might join the growing ranks of other dogs and cats around the nation who are increasingly involved in legal custody disputes. Then a court might treat her as something more than simply property.

But the law bears out contradictions. If Izzie had died in my arms as a result of irresponsible breeding, I could only sue for the price I paid for her. In some states, I might even be able to recoup some of her medical costs. But emotional damages would not be awarded; she would be treated in this instance, by the court, as property.

For most dog owners, the contradictions inherent in the legal status of our four-legged friends are a non-issue. By and large, most domestic dog owners are not breeding their pets. With any luck, most of us will not get entangled in a bitter divorce that sparks a custody battle over the dog. Hopefully, most of us will not watch our dogs die prematurely due to bad breeding. And for the most part, dog owners are not making money off of their pooches—reality TV talent competition winners and Instagram celebrity pups notwithstanding. But as consumers of the dog-breeding industry, it is clear we are buying into a business that manufactures the pets we love by turning their species into an agricultural commodity or livestock.

And as any farmer will tell you, with livestock comes dead stock.

Regardless of what I may think or what Joe Breeder might think about whether a dog is livestock, what does the law say? The answer depends on what state you're in. Sometimes statutes within the same state contradict each other. Over the years, state and even federal courts have occasionally waded into the morass—is a dog livestock or isn't it?

UNITED STATES V. PARK (2008)[4]

Perhaps the most famous instance of a court's struggle to define whether a dog is livestock got its start in Idaho. In the late 1980s, Ron and Mary Park purchased a parcel of land along the Clearwater River that was subject to a scenic easement. The easement allowed them to live on the land and engage in livestock farming, but it prohibited all other commercial activities. The term *livestock farming* within the easement was not defined. When the Parks purchased the land, there was already a chicken coop on the property, and later, the Forest Service gave them the go-ahead to add horse stalls.

All went without incident for about a decade until, in 1997, the Parks opened up Wild River Kennels on their property. They began advertising their new enterprise that offered dog training, boarding, breeding, and a German Shorthaired breed-specific rescue. Within a year, the Forest Service told the Parks that Wild River Kennels was in violation of the scenic easement on their land, as the new business was a commercial enterprise and did not qualify as livestock farming. The Parks, as you might expect, disagreed; as far as they were concerned, dogs are livestock.

This disagreement continued until 2005 when the federal government filed suit. The Parks argued that their dog-breeding and kennel business was, in fact, an instance of livestock farming—which would be permissible under the terms of the easement. The government shot back that under Idaho law, dogs are not livestock. The district court granted summary judgment siding with the government, agreeing that dogs are not livestock, but it did not dive into the process of defining what exactly constitutes livestock farming. The Parks were ordered to shut down the kennel, seemingly a victory for the dogs-are-not-livestock camp.

But the case escalated to the Ninth Circuit Court of Appeals, which set out to dig down into what exactly constitutes livestock. Ultimately, the court concluded that the term *livestock*—in this case—was ambiguous and could potentially include dogs. The Ninth Circuit reversed the prior ruling that the Parks shut down Wild River Kennels and sent the case back to the district court to sort out.

There, U.S. District Judge Edward Lodge filed a new ruling in 2009 that further clarified whether dogs are livestock—or, perhaps more accurately, *which* dogs constituted livestock.

"The court finds that the dogs being used on the easement property for breeding, hunting, and boarding are dogs being used for work and/or profit and can be considered livestock," Judge Lodge wrote. "A family dog that does not work on the farm, is not bred, or is not used to help produce food when a person hunts is just a family pet and is not livestock."[5]

The distinction in this ruling highlights a very strange but critical legal conundrum: if a farmer has two dogs on the same property, the one used for breeding may be considered livestock, while the other dog living in the house may be considered a pet or companion animal. As such, these two dogs have different legal protections.

"Same dog, different places, different protections, different classifications. The dog hasn't changed, the dog's threshold for pain hasn't changed, the dog's needs haven't changed," animal law expert Tischler tells me of this odd legal discrepancy.

While this may seem like yet another battle of semantics, it most certainly is not. Legal distinctions and definitions have significant implications governing how these two animals are treated—and the differences are stark. In some states, only the abuse of a companion animal can be tried as a felony. Livestock—not so much.

By way of example, let's go back to Kathy Jo Bauck, the breeder that Pete, my undercover investigator source, helped to bring down in court. She is the most famous example of how classifying dogs as livestock can have major legal implications.

When Bauck unwittingly hired Pete to work at her breeding facility back in 2008, he was operating undercover for the Companion Animal Protection Society (CAPS). His hidden camera bore witness to the nonstop parade of horrors at her facility, and his footage was shown in court at her trial. The images show seriously wounded dogs at her facility who were malnourished and, in some cases, actively undergoing seizures or being submerged in pesticides. With Pete's footage and testimony revealing the full extent of her crimes, a jury convicted Bauck of three counts of torture and one count of animal cruelty in a Minnesota courtroom in March 2009. However, she was acquitted of felony charges, and these acts could only be punished as misdemeanors. Why? Because the court considered her dogs livestock, not companion animals.

The judge proved to be even more lenient than the jury, sentencing Bauck on only one of these convictions. A $1,000 fine was slashed in half, and she was required to pay only $500. A ninety-day jail sentence became twenty days of work release plus eighty hours of community service and a year of probation. Shockingly, Bauck was allowed to keep her USDA license and required only to submit her kennel housing around nine hundred dogs and four hundred puppies to unannounced inspections from the Humane Society.[6]

But old habits die hard, and a year later in 2010, the USDA

declared Bauck "unfit" to retain her license and pulled it for two years, after which time she could reapply.[7]

Even though Baucks livestock defense got her off the hook on far more serious felony charges, she was initially allowed to keep her dogs because they were considered to be her own private property. But a year later, in September 2011, Bauck was permanently banned from ever obtaining a USDA license again.[8] The decision also fined and barred several of her family members from obtaining licenses, given their involvement in her prior operation. She and her husband, Allen, also agreed to disperse their operation, selling off hundreds of dogs. Any dogs they could not sell off were ordered to be donated to rescues or shelters. However, in spite of everything, the Baucks were still allowed to keep six of their dogs, three of which were allowed to be females who had not been spayed.

In effect, this decision barred the Baucks from ever breeding or selling another dog for commercial purposes again but not from ever owning a dog again or becoming small-scale hobby breeders.

The Baucks' case is, unfortunately, not unique. Every state carries different legal penalties for cruelty to animals—many of which change depending on whether that animal is considered livestock or a pet. Again, the dog doesn't change when it crosses state lines. But its protections do.

Hal Herzog is a professor of psychology at Western Carolina University and the author of *Some We Love, Some We Hate, Some We Eat*, a book that examines our inability to think rationally about animals. When I spoke with him, he highlighted the contradictions in how we treat animals with his observations on the treatment of lab mice.

Back in 1988, he observed that within the same medical

research facility at the University of Tennessee, there were three types of mice: the good, the bad, and the feeders. Each of the three had different protections under the law.

The good mice were the ones the lab was built for: the ones that were dedicated to unearthing the secrets of medical science through experiments. These mice were covered under the Surgeon General's U.S. Public Health Service animal care regulations, granting them prized moral status. These mice, it's worth reiterating, today would not be covered under the Animal Welfare Act and would not be inspected by the USDA because of the 2002 amendment to exempt rodents. But under the watchful eye of the U.S. Public Health Service, every experiment employing one of these mice had to be approved. By the same token, special regulations for humane treatment had to be followed in order to euthanize them.

The bad mice were the pests who scurried the hallways of the lab as illicit mooches. Unlike their protected counterparts, these mice were to be executed as swiftly as possible—often using sticky glue traps that are considered to be a particularly inhumane form of extermination. But the lab feared using poisons and toxins that, while swifter and more humane to the doomed mouse, could potentially disrupt the health of the good mice and their experiments in progress. The paradox is, these "bad mice" were almost universally "good mice" that had escaped. Once that good mouse leapt from lab table to the floor, its moral status irrevocably plummeted.

Finally, there were the feeder mice: those that had been raised and bred as food for reptiles being housed in the building. Their moral status fell into an even murkier area.

"It's the same thing with dogs," Herzog tells me. "In some

countries, dogs are livestock. In China and Korea, they have dog farms [for food]… But increasingly, we're thinking about dogs in the category as being one of us. They reflect big issues in terms of what it means to be a human being. All these sort of foibles and inconsistencies reflect human nature in a very deep way."[9]

Depending on the context, our society and our laws have precedent for treating the same animal in very different ways. And for many animals, these seemingly semantic differences can be the difference between life and death—or, at the very least, a humane life and death.

CHAPTER FIVE

Why Dogs Can Never Be Livestock

OUR HISTORY WITH DOGS PREDATES ANY LEGAL system. Our shared bond even predates the very notion of a legal code or the words we have to describe these animals. So when it comes to applying rules to our long human history with canines, our laws make up a relatively recent construct. And as such, these laws reflect an imperfect and one-sided comprehension of a complex and intricate bond that we're still learning more about every year.

The idea that a dog could be considered livestock by the law in some states seems to ignore an awful lot of what we know about these creatures. Cognitive scientist Alexandra Horowitz puts it best in her book *Inside of a Dog* where she writes that dogs can only be classified as animals "with an asterisk"—now too impacted by their long proximity to humans to ever be fully wild again.[1] Penn State professor of anthropology Pat Shipman has even argued that dogs are to thank for the survival of our species. She posits that humans' early domestication of dogs was the reason our long-ago ancestors bested the Neanderthals.[2] So today, tens of thousands of years since our human evolution became a shared evolution with dogs, it's far too late to legally lump them into the same category as the animals we keep at a distance and raise to be eaten.

"Dogs have been our companions for somewhere between fourteen thousand and forty thousand years. In that time, they have developed an incredible bond with us. They hijack the oxytocin loop that is normally reserved for our children. They also prefer the company of humans to other dogs," Dr. Brian Hare, founder of the Duke Canine Cognition Center at Duke University tells me.[3]

Hare points me to an article he wrote for *Science* with his Duke colleague Dr. Evan MacLean. In it, they delve into a particularly fascinating area of research: the ways in which our common, domestic dog can outperform primates—our closest relatives—in relating to humans.

"Even as puppies, dogs spontaneously respond to cooperative human gestures, such as pointing cues, to find hidden food or toy rewards. By contrast, great apes must have extensive experience with people to show similar skills," they wrote.[4]

Hare and MacLean went on to elucidate the ways in which puppies mirror young humans in their reading of social cues— even making mistakes similar to those that newborns make in interpreting eye contact. Wolves, however, require considerable human interaction and contact to learn to interpret our gestures. But unlike domestic dog puppies, wolves do not innately recognize humans as potential friends to be cajoled for assistance with problems they cannot solve alone. Hare and MacLean concluded that this divergence must suggest that today's domestic dog did not inherit these abilities from wolves—they learned it from us and evolved separately from wolves over the course of millennia living by our side. Now, they're born with an ability to relate to humans.

"For an animal to be so bonded to us, then to be isolated and abused by the very species who is supposed to take care of them, this is cruelty at its worst," Hare tells me.

This is a notion that animal cognition experts I've interviewed raise time and again: humans are betraying our prehistoric bond with dogs when we fail to treat them not just humanely but with the closeness that our shared evolution demands. Dr. Marc Bekoff, professor emeritus of ecology and evolutionary biology at the University of Colorado–Boulder, goes so far as to say that when we disrespect this bond, we are actively betraying these animals, who are bred to have a certain expectation for how humans will treat them.

"The dog comes to us from thousands of years of domestication and expectation. That's not froufrou. I really believe that your average dog comes into this world with some sort of expectation about how he or she will interact with humans. From birth. It's almost innate. They have these expectations, so when we abuse them, it's a real double cross… We betray their belief that we'll do the best we can for them," Dr. Bekoff explains. "For dogs, it's genetically in them to expect certain treatment from humans. From the domestication process."[5]

With all this information, it's easy to argue that dogs are special and unlike other animals. I'm not sure I even needed these experts to help me make this argument. Leaving aside the matter of whether dogs are inherently different in their needs from cows, goats, and chickens, it's quite clear to most of us when we lock eyes with a dog that our relationship with this animal is truly unique. Moreover, it's way too late now to undo the past forty thousand years of domestication.

Either way, this relationship now mandates a certain level of treatment from us. But with the twentieth century imposition of factory-farming conditions on the breeding of dogs, a long history together is now being subverted in a distinctly new way. And just as humans have made this change for the worse, it's up to humans to right the wrong.

"The change has to be on the human side," Bekoff says emphatically. "The dogs aren't changing."

So if dogs aren't going to change back into wild canines, we need to better understand the evolutionary modifications that have brought them to trust and rely on humans as they do today. Let's start with the fact that dogs demonstrate a preference for human companionship over that of their own species.

PREFERENCE FOR HUMANS OVER CANINES

In a 1996 study published in the *Journal of Comparative Psychology*, researchers from Wright State University and Ohio State University tested adult dogs who had been living with a littermate since they were eight weeks old.[6] For the two years leading up to the experiment, these pairs had never been separated at all, even for a moment.

In the first stage of the experiment, researchers separated the pairs for several hours while keeping one of the dogs in its familiar kennel. The remaining dogs, even when alone, did not display outward signs of anxious behavior as they stayed in their home base kennel. Blood tests showed no elevation of cortisol, the stress hormone, in their systems.

However, when the same dog was isolated without its

littermate in a new kennel that it had never seen before, things changed dramatically. The isolated dog's cortisol spiked by more than 50 percent, and the dog displayed outwardly anxious behavior. Even when the pairs were reunited, if moved to an unfamiliar kennel together, the nervous behavior persisted, and the littermates did not display signs of finding comfort in the presence of their lifelong partners.

But it was the next part of the study that changed the way many animal cognitive scientists would forever interpret the human-canine bond. These same dogs, when isolated and placed in strange surroundings with the human who they had come to recognize as their caretaker, would cling close and soothe easily when stroked. Blood tests confirmed this apparent effect, showing that cortisol levels in the dogs' system only elevated slightly when remaining with their human.

This study appeared to show that dogs can experience a bond with humans that is more profound than their bonds with their own species—even their own littermates and lifelong companions. And, it's worth noting, the dogs in this experiment were not companion animals. Rather, they were laboratory dogs who had a caretaker they recognized as their owner. But these were not dogs who lived in their caretaker's home, shared their caretaker's bed, and enjoyed the same kind of personal relationship most of us share with our pet dogs. They were kennel-bound with their littermate in a research facility for life, but the soothing effect of their recognized human caretaker in contrast to the lack of comfort provided by their brother or sister was apparent all the same.

Next, I should address the skeptics among us who might argue that a dog's affection is simple and easily won: humans have food, and dogs love treats. No mystery there, no need for a scientist to dissect forty thousand years of domestication to explain it. Izzie has often been the target of this argument when friends and family have caught me sharing a bowl of blueberries or a plate of sashimi with her. It's true—she shudders with excitement to see me flip my chopsticks around to dangle a slab of fatty salmon into her impatient jaws. But a 2016 study from the department of psychology at Emory University challenged this misconception that treats alone buy unconditional canine love and devotion.

PREFERENCE FOR HUMAN PRAISE OVER TREATS

Gregory Berns, neuroscientist and author of *How Dogs Love Us*, put dogs in an fMRI scanner while awake and untethered to a leash. He then showed these dogs several household objects and offered them a hot dog, verbal praise, or nothing at all. Berns found that on the scans of thirteen out of fifteen of his test subjects, the dogs' brains lit up just as much for human praise as for the treat—if not even more so. In fact, Berns pointed out that the dogs who responded most strongly to praise were more disappointed when it was withheld than when they went sans hot dog.[7] While not all the dogs in the admittedly small study responded with a preference for praise over treats, the researchers concluded that the two rewards are very equally weighted in the mind of a dog and that many pups even prefer a resounding *Good boy!* to a juicy piece of meat.

Okay. You get it. We all get it. We love dogs. Dogs love us. Our interspecies bond is special—even if you're not, yourself, a "dog person." But at least maybe it's now clear to see how a dog should never be classified as livestock given its unique domestication history. It may now be easy to recognize that these studies show how dogs who spend their lives toiling away in USDA-licensed commercial breeding operations are especially harmed by their treatment.

Lifelong confinement, overbreeding, exposure to extreme temperatures, a lack of positive socialization or human contact—it all adds up to years of misery. Even worse, this lifelong subjugation seen in breeding dogs is on an order of magnitude that is uncommon in the rest of the factory-farming industry. When comparing the life of a breeding dog to that of the animals who are farmed for food, John Goodwin of the Humane Society tells me that the dog's plight is worse even if only for its protracted length.

As I am digging into the research, trying to get a handle on the science of our relationship with dogs, Overall sends me a note. She has some relevant studies she wants me to read before Izzie's testing. But before I recount what the research suggests, I should pause here to address my own mea culpa.

Yes, as I've said, Izzie is a happy and healthy dog whose well-being seems to belie the likely facts of her birth in a USDA-licensed breeder. However, she does have a very serious noise phobia. Overall had told me that noise phobias in dogs are the easiest types of anxiety to spot and that owners are most likely to report these over other, less obvious but still very real psychological traumas. Obvious indeed: anyone who has spent any amount of time with us knows that if Izzie comes to visit, you'd best silence every beep and chirp that any phone, computer, or security system in the home can make.

The default *ping-ping* of an iPhone receiving a text message is a major source of terror for her. One text message and she will freeze in her tracks and turn the entire neighborhood upside down with surround-sound barking and moaning. It's so predictably bad that when my husband or I hear this alert outside the home, when Izzie is not around, we both tense up, preparing for the barkfest.

While this phobia has mostly seemed like a curse, there was one instance when it came in handy. Once, when she was just a puppy and we were playing with her on a beach at the Jersey shore, she gave in to the lure of the endless, sandy expanse in front of her. Before we could react, she was galloping off at top speed. Dan and I raced behind her, trying to catch up. Faster and faster, her wheat-colored hair blending in with the sand, she gained more and more ground on us and became increasingly difficult to spot in the distance. Finally, winded and in utter desperation, barely even able to spot her on the horizon, I opened my phone and triggered it to make that *ping-ping* sound she so hates. Far off in the distance, I could hear her barking. Her outburst gave Dan—admittedly a much faster runner than I am—time to gain ground on her and scoop up the barking sand monster that was our dog. But other than that moment, her noise phobia has not exactly brought much in the way of convenience.

When we first had our home security system installed, we quickly learned that the single *beep* of the alarm being set was enough to set Izzie ablaze for hours, crying and pacing with worry—our very own Raymond Babbitt. Now, when Dan is on his work trips and Izzie and I are alone, I cannot set the alarm unless I've locked us both in the bathroom with the fans, shower, and faucets all running. Even then, she's smart enough to know I'm hiding something and will still let out a few, mournful whimpers.

And while her noise anxiety can be tremendously disruptive to our lives, we can only imagine how the repeated stress is hurting her. Dan recently cut our doorbell and invested in a fully digital system that would be silent and send notifications straight to our phones. As he slaved over the frustrating circuits and systems throughout an entire weekend, he repeatedly reminded himself that the doorbell had to go, because it was taking years off her life.

So as I pore through the research sent by Overall, I quickly see how things I'd always dismissed as Izzie's "quirks" might be signs of something much more insidious.

PSYCHOLOGICAL IMPACT OF LIFE IN A BREEDING FACILITY

A growing number of academic studies are now demonstrating the long-term impact of living in a commercial breeding facility. A 2011 study led by Franklin D. McMillan, published in the journal of *Applied Animal Behaviour Science*, examined a group of nearly twelve hundred dogs that had worked as breeding stock in commercial dog kennels. On average, the dogs in the study had already been retired from their former working lives and had been living in their adopted homes as pets for two years. When comparing these dogs to those that had never served as breeding stock in commercial operations, the former breeding dogs displayed higher levels of fear, demonstrated more compulsive behaviors, and were more sensitive to touch. Somewhat surprisingly, however, these dogs were found to be less aggressive than their nonbreeding counterparts.

"At first glance, this would seem to be an unconditionally positive finding," McMillan wrote of the retired breeding dogs' lack of aggression. "But when we look at the totality of changes in the puppy mill dogs, it becomes apparent that this finding, albeit desirable in and of itself, is likely due to the paralyzing and intensely elevated levels of fear that these dogs experience. In other words, unlike the typical animal who will use aggression to ward off something threatening, these dogs are often petrified with fear and incapable of striking out."[8]

The variety of anxiety-related behaviors combined with a lack of aggressiveness demonstrated that the breeding dogs had spent most of their lives in a state of constant fight-or-flight stress. By chronically activating this response for years, these dogs had developed an ingrained proclivity toward flight. McMillan determined that the most important distinguishing mark that differentiated the breeding dogs from the nonbreeding group was fear. McMillan compared this mental state to the post-traumatic stress disorder (PTSD) seen in humans.[9]

These long-term psychological scars make sense when the environment of the breeding dogs is fully understood and considered. But what about the puppies, like Izzie, who are whisked away from these commercial breeders at an early age? Surely they're spared the trauma and are able to lead normal, healthy, social lives. After all, why would consumers shell out thousands of dollars for pet store puppies that are irretrievably broken?

As it turns out, that's exactly what we're doing. The McMillan study suggests that dogs may be damaged by commercial breeding operations before they are even born. Mother dogs exposed to chronic stress both before and during pregnancy tend to breed hypersensitive, psychologically abnormal, and dysfunctional puppies.

In view of the fact that the prenatal life of breeding dogs occurs in [puppy mills], the conditions and events during this period may play a role in the psychological development of the fetus... Offspring of pregnant animals exposed to various stressors have been documented with neurohormonal dysfunction and...abnormal response to, increased sensitivity to, and impaired ability to cope with stress; exaggerated distress responses to aversive events; impaired learning; abnormal social behavior; increased emotionality and fear-related behavior and fearful behaviors that increase with increasing age...and behavioral deficits and molecular changes in the offspring similar to those in schizophrenic humans.[10]

When I read this paragraph—"abnormal response" to stress, "impaired ability to cope," "exaggerated distress response"—all I see is Izzie. This description of the psychological damage done to my dog before she was even born and purchased by me as a puppy rings all too true.

I read it again and again, and McMillan's words bear repeating: dogs born in commercial breeding operations are at an increased risk of physiological and psychological problems similar to schizophrenic humans. And all this due to damage done to the mother dog before the puppy is even born.

Once born into a commercial breeding operation, the life-altering trauma continues as the puppy remains "hypersensitive to distressing psychological or physical stimuli" up to around eight weeks of age.[11] This is the minimum allowable age to transport a puppy from its place of breeding to where it will be sold, according to the USDA.[12] In this extremely sensitive period, McMillan noted that even one negative experience could have a lifelong impact on the dog. Given that the vast majority of commercially bred dogs are separated from their mothers and littermates and moved across hundreds or thousands of miles in a truck or van by a broker before being deposited in pet shops of varying conditions, a puppy will undoubtedly encounter an array of major stressors and likely negative experiences along the road to its future owner's home.

Even the USDA's Gibbens tells me that he is concerned about the physical and psychological effects of transporting puppies for sale in the federally licensed supply chain. He broached the topic on his own when I asked him about a specific case in which a buyer had filed a complaint with his department after purchasing a sick puppy.

"The transportation history is interesting to look into, because the puppy may have gone to a distributor for a couple of days and been housed there," Gibbens says. "Then it may have been transported—in some cases—across the country and put in a pet store over there. It may sit in that pet store for who knows how long: a few days, a couple of weeks. That's tremendous stress on an eight- to twelve-week-old puppy—which is what most of them are. They've probably been through a couple of rounds of vaccinations, their immune system is coming into play, and they are exposed to a lot of other puppies with a lot of other germs and a lot of stress—transport is stressful for these animals."[13]

Tremendously stressful—but entirely legal.

As Gibbens mentioned, most of the puppies transported from breeder to point of sale are between eight and twelve weeks old. The question of the age at which a dog is removed from its mother to be transported and sold is not an insignificant one. In a 2011 Italian study led by Ludovica Pierantoni, researchers found that dogs separated from their mothers between thirty and forty days of life had very different behavioral and psychological outcomes from those separated later, around two months of life. As it turns out, puppies pass through a highly sensitive socialization period from the age of two and a half weeks to around fourteen weeks.

"If puppies stay with their dam and siblings during the socialization period, they have the opportunity to learn from them about behaviors that are attendant with social development during this time," Pierantoni wrote.[14]

Puppies rely on their family unit to learn how to process new experiences and stimuli. Without that stable support system, a puppy who is placed in a new environment will display signs of severe anxiety and stress.

Worse yet, Pierantoni found that the pet store environment itself may augment the negative impact of removing a young puppy from its dam and littermates too soon. If this is indeed the case, the current system of commercial breeding with the pet store as the destination is setting these puppies up for a lifetime of emotional and behavioral problems.

"Early separation from the dam and littermates, especially when combined with housing in a pet shop, might affect the capacity of a puppy to adapt to new environmental conditions and social relationships later in life," Pierantoni wrote.[15]

Overall believes that this Pierantoni study is particularly significant in its implications for the way that commercially bred dogs are brought to market.

"This is important from the puppy mill standpoint because the puppies leave early. So [the researchers] were looking at family separation, and they found out that the puppies who were separated by six weeks of age had more reactions to noise, more fears, and more reactivity when they looked at these dogs eighteen

months later," Overall says, discussing the study's comparison of
the difference between dogs who experienced this separation at
six weeks versus those who did so at eight weeks of age. "The
only difference here is these dogs got separated from their families
two weeks before the recommended time to separate them, and
they have all these problems that the other dogs didn't at eighteen
months of age. Statistically, significantly different… So that is the
first set of solid data that says, you know, what if you are taking
them away too early?"[16]

Overall points out that while the minimum legal age to sell a
puppy is eight weeks, many commercial dog breeders try to ship
their pups sooner. After all, as any business owner knows, you
have to clear out the old inventory to make way for the new.

Overall herself adopted a dog that was shipped off for sale as
early as five weeks. That early separation from the litter left him
with cognitive damage so severe that the rescue called Overall
personally to come take him, knowing that it would take an animal
behavioral expert like her to raise him and not euthanize him.

McMillan revisited this question of the early life experiences
of dogs from puppy mills in a 2013 study for the *Journal of the
American Veterinary Medical Association*. Here, he too pointed
to the eight-week mark as a time of significant sensitivity in a
puppy's life. But he took the argument even further by explaining that the stress of being transported—a common theme in the
lives of most commercially bred puppies—can add significantly
to the animal's stress.[17]

Taken together, these studies point to a perfect storm for
commercially bred dogs in the USDA-regulated system. First
there's the epigenetic influence of stress passed down from the
mother dog to her puppies before they are even born. Then there's

the damage done by separation from the family unit at a hyper-sensitive age. Next, add in the early life trauma of being transported cross-country on a crowded truck or van with hundreds of other dogs—a stress so significant that even the USDA's own Gibbens points it out as a serious concern. Then deposit these puppies in a pet shop where conditions are not federally regulated and hope for the best. By the time you or I show up to purchase our puppy, the lifelong damage has already been done. And that's before you even start to concern yourself with the well-being of the mother this dog left behind, soon to be pregnant with her next litter as we happily walk away with our seemingly unscathed eight-week-old puppy, hundreds of miles and a world away from where she came.

But to me, all this research still just amounts to a pile of paper. Izzie is my case study, born in a USDA-licensed breeding facility and then transported across the country to the Long Island pet shop where she languished for several weeks until she met me at around three months of age. Noise phobias aside, she'd always seemed fine enough. Until reading these studies, I naïvely thought that all dogs bark at irrationally minor infractions. This research suggests a very different truth. And now we're on our way to Overall to see exactly what that means.

CHAPTER SIX

The Capacity to Feel Joy

IZZIE AND I ARE CIRCLING PHILADELPHIA FOR THE second time as our plane tries to land. My feet straddle her torso as she lies pressed to the floor under the seat in front of me. The turbulence is oppressive, even for someone like me who never gets motion sickness. Izzie smacks her gums and lets out an anxious yawn, pressing her dripping wet snout onto my thigh. I know she wants me to scoop her lanky bones into my lap—that much she's made abundantly clear. But with the small army of flight attendants on high alert amid the wind shear, I know now's not the time to try any funny business. I press my forehead to hers and whisper softly to her.

"We're almost there."

We've traveled across the country from our home in Denver to visit Overall's lab in the Philadelphia suburbs, where she has agreed to perform her cognitive test on Izzie so that I can better understand her work. And also so that I can better understand Izzie.

This particular test is funded by the Department of Defense, the Army Research Office (ARO), and the Defense Advanced Research Projects Agency (DARPA). They're trying to learn more about the attributes that make for a good military working dog. For her research, Overall has enlisted pet dogs to see how they stack up when compared to elite, professional canines. She also received some funding from the American Kennel Club for her work running this test on aging dogs to see how—and if—mental decline impacts their abilities.

"We need more and better dogs, because for the rest of your and my and everybody else in this building's natural life, dogs are going to save you," Overall explains of the military's interest in her work when Izzie and I arrive. "[Dogs] can go places we can't go."[1]

She leads me and Izzie through the veterinary hospital, where she has set up her testing facility. We coax Izzie onto a scale and see that she has dropped a few ounces from her last checkup and is now around twenty-seven pounds. She looks nervous. To her, this has all the hallmarks of a trip to the vet: anxious dogs in the lobby, a weigh-in. So far, this day is not looking good.

Overall leads us into her lab. It's a converted storage area with a poured concrete floor that's gridded up into one-foot sections with red electrician's tape. There are two cameras mounted on tripods trained on the gridded area, poised to record and document our every move. Overall introduces me to her research assistant, Jess, and the three of us sit in chairs to give Izzie time to freely roam the space and get comfortable in her surroundings. Jess scatters a colorful mess of toys on the floor for her to nose through—the canine equivalent of a stack of magazines in a doctor's waiting room, I assume. Slowly, Izzie warms up to the experience, understanding that this is not how her vet visits typically go.

"[The military spends] huge amounts of money on dogs," Overall says. "We need for them to be good enough to train in the first two years of their life, and we need for them to last at least ten or twelve years working. We would like them to be biddable, we would like them to be flexible in their jobs, and we would like them to be healthy. We would like them to be smart. The smarter dogs can be more flexible and do more things and will be easier to train and will save us money. When you're flunking 75 percent of your dogs, that's a big chunk of change that is leaving."

"So then why bring in pet dogs?" I ask. "Why put a dog like Izzie in your data set?"

"Well, the question becomes, are our [working] dogs the best dogs, or do they overlap with the pet-dog population?"

Prior to conducting the in-person part of the test, she has all participating owners and professional handlers complete a lengthy questionnaire. After the test, all the dogs in the data set provide a small blood sample. She wants to know if a dog's breeding, early puppyhood, and upbringing have any bearing on its cognitive performance. Unsurprisingly, all these factors play a role.

The impact of early puppyhood living conditions on cognitive development is the intersection between the military's interest in Overall's work and my own. For me, Overall's findings are applicable to the conditions in American licensed breeding facilities. For the military, her findings could illustrate the problems with the current supply chain of working dogs, many of which come from breeders overseas.

"They come out of puppy mills in the Balkans, and the U.S. military buys them for five or ten thousand dollars—which is what we pay per dog on training—and then they're shipped to contractors who are really privateering," she explains. "Honestly, I feel very strongly. I think most—not all but most—of the canine contractors are privateering. They have taken advantage of the instability of the world to just churn out dogs. And they have no real interest in the dog and maybe even less in the military."

But even though Overall's work for the military is interesting, I'm really here to learn more about that massive oversight Overall pointed out in our first interview several months prior. I had assumed that the damage done by puppy mills was largely borne out on the dogs who toil their lives away there while the actual products—the puppies—are taken away early enough to live normal, healthy lives. Overall had said I was wrong. Dead wrong. I've read the studies that confirm her reasoning, but now, she's going to actually demonstrate this effect on my own dog who was born in a USDA-licensed commercial breeding facility and shipped off for sale while still a puppy. Overall believes that her cognitive test designed for the military could also prove how even my dog, as lovingly raised as I think she has been, may be permanently broken.

I ask Overall to walk me through what to expect from the test. She explains that most dogs very much enjoy the test and that it is tremendously fun and exciting for them to be mentally stimulated. It helps that so much of the day will involve treats and toys. With the exception of the brief blood draw at the end, to Izzie, much of the experience should feel like a series of new and unfamiliar games.

Izzie gingerly paces the room, nose to the ground, as Overall and I speak. Periodically, Jess tosses lamb lung treats onto the floor for Izzie to peck at. She happily accepts these scattered offerings. Once Izzie settles down on a dog bed with some toys, Jess clasps a bulky rubber tracking collar onto her and begins gathering baseline measurements. The tracker was made by a now-defunct brand called Voyce that engineered special firmware just for Overall's study.

"It takes data every second and averages it every minute," Overall explains as Izzie relaxes into wearing it. "So we can have a minute-by-minute analysis of three-dimensional movement for these dogs. It also does heart and respiratory rate."

"So it's like a Fitbit," I offer.

"Yes. But they hate when you say that," she says with a sigh.

Overall ushers Izzie and me out of the room so she and her assistant can prepare. We sit in the hall, and Izzie laps from a water bowl while we wait. Just a few minutes later, we're invited back in to begin the test.

The door opens, and I'm instructed to make Izzie sit on a big, red X taped on the floor. I crouch next to my dog, holding her still, my hand threaded through her Voyce collar.

In front of us, the two camcorders are rolling on the red, gridded space where Overall and Jess have arranged about a dozen bankers boxes. Some boxes are overturned; others are stacked. Some boxes have lids loosely laid on top. In most of them, I can see toys sticking out from corners or out from under a lid: a plush monkey arm here or a bushy squirrel tail there. Other boxes have toys hidden but within easy access if Izzie so much as taps the box and checks to pull it loose.

Izzie is excited. I can feel her heart beating against my palm as I hold her on the red X. Jess starts a timer and signals me to release my grip so Izzie can explore the space and they can observe her behavior. I let go, and Izzie scampers toward the boxes.

Izzie flits around the space with interest, her nails clacking on the concrete floors. She seems confused and unsure as to what she should be doing but not distressed. She can certainly see that some of these boxes have toys available for the taking, but she doesn't go to snatch them from where they lie. And just like that, the first sign of her impairment becomes apparent—but not to me. It takes Overall to point it out. Without her expert eye, I would never have recognized Izzie's behavior for what it is.

"This is a very classic response for a dog with her background," Overall says.

I don't understand what she's talking about. I watch as Overall tries to encourage Izzie to take a toy for herself, even leading her straight to one box, pulling a ball from it, and rolling it to her. She happily accepts it, sits on her haunches, and gnaws at the ball she's been given, ignoring the pile of boxes packed with toys and taking no initiative to explore any further. Izzie is clearly not willing to interact with this unfamiliar environment on her own and disturb the boxes.

"What is the classic response? To not be curious? Or to not be interested?" I ask. I'm not sure what she's seeing in Izzie. This looks pretty normal to me if only a little bit shy. After all, I've never given her an exercise like this to complete—this is entirely unfamiliar to her.

"It's not that she's not curious," she says. "But the idea that she would go and disrupt things and find stuff…the idea that she has control over this environment and that she can go take this apart?" Overall shakes her head.

She explains that many dogs who have had a more advantaged puppyhood and upbringing come into this part of the test and knock the entire setup apart, eagerly seeking all the toys hidden inside it.

"This is very classic. [Izzie's behavior says] 'I never learned to have that amount of control and explore things and take advantage. I never had that experience. I didn't do this.' And it's an early, early development thing," Overall says. "She never really learned to get out there and explore and get into trouble and recover from it... It's not that she's not interested in stuff we have... I think it's about risk. I think she doesn't know how to take risks successfully."

"So she's afraid if she turns over a box, something might come out and grab her?" I ask.

"I don't know what she's afraid of. [But] the idea that she would take control of the environment and find out what it does? That's not in her repertoire."

I bring up the Pierantoni study and mention how it found the reason for risk-averse behavior in dogs separated from their family unit too early is that they never learn how to take chances as puppies within the safety of their known litter. Overall elaborates on this.

"They're separated from something they know. In a good situation, the puppies will have begun to separate themselves when they're ready to start taking risks on their own."

This test complete, Izzie and I are ushered out of the room so that Overall can execute her scene change. Then we reenter and are instructed to sit on the red X again.

For this next test, Jess is standing behind three bankers boxes turned on their sides with the openings facing away from Izzie and me. She tells me that while Izzie and I were out in the hallway, she hid a toy in one of these boxes.

"Izzie," she says to get her attention. Then Jess points her finger at the box containing the toy. She signals me to release

Izzie, who is already lunging forward to escape my grasp. I let go. Without any hesitation, she makes a beeline for the box with the toy and happily grasps it in her teeth. This is not a task I have trained Izzie to perform, but she completes it with ease.

While simple in design, this test demonstrates something very powerful about my relationship with Izzie and the human relationship with dogs as a whole. In showing her ability to read Jess's hand gesture and find the toy, Izzie has demonstrated that she is capable of interpreting social cues across species lines. Many of us take this type of communication with our dogs for granted given how commonplace it is. We see dogs respond to these types of cues every day. However, it's a task that even our closest relatives, primates, are not capable of without extensive training. Significantly, I'm witnessing as Izzie successfully performs a task that even wolves fail, showing that interpreting human social cues is not innately canine—but it is innate to the domestic dog, just as Dr. Brian Hare had told me.

But Izzie is no prodigy. If anything, as this test will show, her smarts are somewhat below average—not that there's anything wrong with that. But she doesn't need to be a genius to execute this impressive feat. This type of social cue interpretation is something that most domestic dogs are born with and can do without any trouble, even as primates and wolves cannot.

"These are exactly the same tests that they've done with the chimps and the wolves, and none of them do as well as domestic dogs do," Overall explains.

"So a regular, old, run-of-the-mill dog, nothing special, not a working dog, like Izzie here—she'll outperform a chimp?" I ask.

Overall says yes. "There's something about thirty thousand years of living together where we're used to working together, and it may have changed some affiliative neurochemistry," she says as Izzie drops the toy to score an affectionate head scratch from Jess.

"So while the causality is not certain—" I begin.

"Correct," Overall says.

"The effect is very obvious."

"The effect is very obvious," she concurs.

We repeat this test several times with the toy hidden in a different box each time. Each repetition brings the same result: Izzie has no problem reading the social cues of a human to find the toy without needing to search for it.

But then the test changes. Overall sends Izzie and me back out into the hallway. When we return, the three bankers boxes remain in their original places with their openings facing away from Izzie and me. Overall's research assistant, Jess, remains in her initial position behind the boxes. As before, I crouch down with Izzie at the red X where we are supposed to wait until I'm signaled to release her. But this time, there is a small blue flag sticking out of one of the boxes. To me, it's immediately apparent that the flag indicates where the toy is hidden. But what does Izzie think?

Without a gesture, Jess tells me to release Izzie.

Izzie wanders over to the boxes, checking all three of them. She sniffs the flag, demonstrating that she can see it, but it doesn't appear to mean anything to her. After she wanders about, sniffing each box aimlessly, Jess points Izzie to where the toy is, and once again, she goes to it, having now understood a signal from a person. It's immediately clear that, to Izzie, the flag provided no signal that she could recognize, interpret, or understand.

"She's saying, 'Well, that didn't go how I thought it would,'" Overall says. "She was waiting for the signal, and she hasn't put it together. And that's the difference between a social referent and a nonsocial referent. [The blue flag] is not a social referent."

"Do most dogs pick up on that?" I ask, wondering if anyone else's pet dog managed to understand what the blue flag indicated.

"Most dogs in this study do. But the military dogs and working dogs without exception do not."

"The military dogs did *not* pick up on that?" I ask, sure that I misheard her answer.

"The vast majority of them did not because they work with humans... By and large, they were terrible [at this task]."

"And the pet dogs outperformed the military dogs?" I ask again.

"Yep. Of course, not her," Overall says of Izzie. I'm somewhat heartened to hear that she's at least in good company.

"So what does this tell you about her?" I ask.

"She just doesn't do this," Overall says, ever the scientist, unwilling to assign blame or to give a single, definitive answer as to the cause for Izzie's behavior. "But is it stimulation or is it the way they were born? Well, dogs who've had all the advantages can do this test... You certainly can teach her. I think as adults they can learn these things... It's not like what you're born with is what you're stuck with. But [early development] certainly is going to affect the response surface that you have available to display. Which is the way I tend to look at it."

Overall makes a fair point that is becoming clear: I could certainly be doing more to enrich my dog's mental development. While her birth in a commercial breeding facility may impose a ceiling on her abilities, my work as an owner is an important component of her continued development. In short, you can and should teach an old dog new tricks. As much as it might seem like Izzie enjoys our walks and couch-potato jam sessions, I admittedly do not do much to enhance her cognitive skills with mental stimulation games like these tests. Given that I've worked largely from home over the past year or so, I always assumed that we spend so much more time together than the average owner and dog, and I'm therefore giving her adequate stimulation. But time together is not the same as time spent actively engaging her mind.

Overall acknowledges that this is a point that is challenging for people to accept.

"This is not going to go down well in consumer education, that it's not just starting with the right dog, but you have to engage them," she says.

As much as we'd like to blame the conditions of a dog's birth for its behavior, the willingness of an owner to engage in mental stimulation activities has a major impact on the dog's psychological well-being. We exit the lab once again and wait for the next test.

Again, the door opens. But this time, there are no boxes to explore. Now, I am instructed to sit on a chair in the middle of the empty testing area. Izzie is given a few rubber toys stuffed with treats. She chooses the one bulging with hot dog slices—an excellent choice. Overall plays an audio file. It starts off with the sound of a thunderstorm. Izzie stops eating for a moment and freezes. The audio transitions to a vibration sound, and she resumes eating. Then the track advances to play the sounds of a mortar attack. Again, she freezes and looks around. In my mind, this is a huge success. After all, everyone who has ever met Izzie has endured one of her noise-induced panic attacks—they're practically a calling card. The fact that she's simply freezing and looking around the room without a yap? I'm impressed with her performance.

After the track finishes playing, I proudly tell Overall that I think Izzie did very well on this test. She doesn't hesitate to inform me that Izzie actually did abysmally: the fact that she stopped eating a high-value treat when she heard a sound that frightened her demonstrated that she was undergoing an uncontrollable parasympathetic response. What I had thought was a typical dog barking at certain noises is, in fact, a dog who likely suffers from anxiety or at least a serious phobia that is creating psychological stress for her.

Overall's test continues for several hours. Izzie must extract a tennis ball from a puzzle box. She succeeds. She must circumnavigate a Plexiglas panel to access a food treat she can smell but not immediately extract. She succeeds again with some effort. But at the conclusion of the day's testing, Overall reveals that Izzie's middling performance on any individual part of the exam accounts for only one small component of her final assessment. Instead, there's a larger pattern to Izzie's behavior that Overall has been tracking throughout the test with concern.

"She's at a disadvantage from experiencing joy," Overall says matter-of-factly.

Stunned and horrified, I look at Izzie, who is now blissfully nose-deep in a rubber toy stuffed full of Philadelphia cream cheese.

"She had a good time, but we have dogs who have true joy," she continues.

"So less than her performance on the individual steps of this test, it's how happy the test allows her to become that tells you something?" I ask.

"I think so," she says. "This dog has the capacity [to experience] joy… I think that she thought, 'This wasn't as bad as I thought it would be, and this was pretty good.' But you see some of these dogs, and at each step, they are just getting more joyful and more joyful and they're thinking *This is great!* She didn't. She was happy she did it, but she wasn't thrilled, and I think that's what [puppy mill breeding] takes away from these dogs is real joy."

I want to throw my arms around Izzie's neck, pick her up, and shower her in kisses and treats. I want to show Overall that this dog feels joy. I've seen her bounding up the Colorado Rockies, lording over cliffs, and terrorizing squirrels. I've watched her zoom up and down our block in the snow with a manic thrill in her eyes. I've curled up in bed with her and watched countless movies as she's slept with her head on my belly, peacefully and shamelessly snoring. How can Overall tell me that none of these experiences bring her joy?

"The world is a complex place," Overall says. "All I can do is try my best to sculpt out the complexity and leave it there for [people] to consider. Even if they end up saying, 'Well, he's just not a very outgoing dog because awful things happened to him.' But now, they have a greater depth of understanding of what that meant."

"Do you think that life in a commercial breeding operation diminishes the ability to have that joy?" I ask.

"I think it sucks the joy right out of you. I think it sucks the joy out of being a mom, and it sucks the joy out of being a puppy."

"Is some of that genetic?"

"A lot of it could be genetic, and those are the dogs we do see that are anxious or depressed."

Overall goes on to describe her own dog, Linus, who she was called in to rescue at just five weeks. She says that when she took him home, he was cognitively a "vegetable." Through years of her expert enrichment efforts, she was able to make him somewhat

functional; however, he lacks the flexibility to willingly partici-
pate in a wide variety of environments. He even flunked this test,
unable to cope with the anxiety of going through it. His distress
was so apparent, she vowed never to repeat the test on Linus.

"He can have great joy. And he's happy 99 percent of the time.
When people come to visit, he's the dog they love... But if they
met him outside of our property, they would never see that joy. So
how do we capture that in a test?" she asks with a shrug. "What
we can tell you is that the dogs who have joy in all parts of these
tests are very plastic, flexible dogs. So maybe that's what we want
in a working dog."

"Well, don't we also want that in our companion animals?" I ask.

"Do we? Because then they need for you to do things with
them."

She describes a set of working dogs trained in Sweden. The
puppies who turned out to be the most effective working dogs
were the ones that proved to be the most destructive in their
owners' homes. These were the dogs who, unlike Izzie, would
have tackled the bankers boxes in Overall's first test, tearing them
apart to find all the hidden toys.

"They'll start early training, and these dogs will blossom,"
she says. "They are supersmart. But they need [training], and if
they don't get that, they are figuring out how the Venetian blinds
work—which I think is charming. Most people wouldn't."

"But wouldn't you argue that you want a pet like that?" I ask.
"I mean, we love these animals. We spend billions of dollars on
them over the course of the year—"

"Dollars isn't time," she says.

"Don't we want them to feel joy?"

"That's the time part," she says. "But most anxiety problems are not caused by understimulation. They're caused by things that go wrong in the dog's head that then may be worsened by the environment. It's a biological process going on. That's not what we are talking about when we talk about joy in the richness of life."

I explain to Overall that many people end up purchasing a puppy from a pet store or online instead of adopting an adult dog because they feel that a puppy is a blank slate. They worry that a rescue dog comes with emotional and psychological baggage acquired over the years of its life. Puppies, however, seem free of that concern. They're young and, therefore, are worth the investment of a purchase, because they will be easier to train and mold to a family's lifestyle even if they do come from an ugly birthplace. I ask if her research confirms this assumption or upends it. She points to Izzie.

"Well, you're seeing it with every single thing she does: Where's that *umph*?"

I ask what that means—what would Izzie look like if she had been bred responsibly?

"You would see a dog that is more willing to try stuff," she says. "Learning to fail successfully is the single biggest skill we could give any social animal."

"And that can be disrupted in the first eight weeks of life even?"

"Absolutely," she says. "They freeze. They stop doing stuff. They get no feedback, and when you get no reinforcement, you stop offering behavior. And she offers very few behaviors in cognitive situations."

"So the notion that if you get a puppy from a [pet shop], it's not damaged—"

"That is probably completely wrong," she says. "Are there

really clean slates? The best clean slate is a good breeder who does early enrichment and allows a dog to develop its potential to the extent possible, you know, and build in flexibility. And if you're not going to do that, then that's a problem."

After our interview with Overall, Izzie and I drive back into Philadelphia to meet up with my husband, Dan. The moment we walk in the door, he's pelting us with questions, dying to know how our girl Izzie did on the test. I take out my recorder that I used for the interview and play back the part of the tape where Overall told me that Izzie's breeding and puppyhood have diminished her capacity to feel joy. Dan is horrified.

"Joy? This dog feels joy. Look at her," he says. Izzie rolls onto her back, her eyes darting back and forth from him to me suggestively, hinting that a belly rub should be on its way. "She doesn't know what she's talking about."

"Maybe *we* don't know what we're talking about," I say, certain that if anyone knows what they're talking about in this situation, it's Overall. "It's not that simple. It's not that black and white. She can experience joy in the situations where she is comfortable and in the environments she's come to know. She has the capacity to feel joy. But she lacks the flexibility to feel it in every situation. It just closes up the world to her a bit. But that doesn't mean she's a lost cause. We can still keep enriching her. And we should."

Dan bundles up Izzie's dangling limbs into his embrace.

"You feel joy, don't you?" he asks her, rocking her back and forth like an ungainly baby. She answers by taking a swipe at his nose with her tongue.

I understand his reaction, and I know that his denial and outrage might be similar to what most other dog owners would feel had they not seen the test with their own eyes and read the research that's out there as I have. It's hard to accept that something you love unconditionally might be broken. It's painful to have someone pull back the curtain and objectively demonstrate that you've been oblivious to the ways in which a member of your family is hurting. And it's even worse to know that our ability to overlook that pain puts money directly into the pockets of the people who perpetuate these conditions.

"I think she feels joy right now," I say, trying to reassure him. And as we hold her close, I'm almost sure she does.

CHAPTER SEVEN

From Man's Best Friend to Fur Baby

"IF THIS DOESN'T WORK OUT, CAN WE GET A SECOND dog?"

It's not the first time I've asked Dan this question. He puts the car in park outside of the fertility clinic. The bitter-cold wind lashes the windows as the snow swirls around us.

"Sometimes I think you're rooting for the dog," he says.

"Win-win?" I try.

He turns off the car.

Inside the building, we separate. Dan is taken down to the clinic's man cave to provide a new sample. I'm whisked away to a room that looks like it was designed by a space-age Torquemada, where a radiologist double-checks that I've pregamed with plenty of ibuprofen for this test.

"Just put your feet in my supercomfy stirrups," she says, gesturing to her table with large, black leather holders for my feet and legs. "Everyone loves 'em because they're so much comfier than the plastic ones."

"They look a little lethal injection-y," I say. She takes offense. "I just mean that they really look ready for action."

I hop up and try to breathe calmly as she inserts a catheter into my cervix and shoots dye through my uterus and fallopian tubes. They darken like a storm on the monitor. She says that's a good thing, that they look like they're flowing well. After the test, I scurry to the bathroom, holding a towel between my legs as the dye and some watery blood rush out of me.

My husband is in the plush waiting room, commiserating with a pink-haired woman about our respective insurance policies. He jumps up when he sees me and leads me back out into the gray morning. Tonight, it'll be Christmas.

"So?"

"One small bit of luck: at least the tubes are clear."

He hugs me. It's the first time we've left the doctor with good news. The past few visits have all been doom and gloom: *Consider an egg donor; find another clinic because you're not even eligible for IVF here; it's rare to see such diminished ovarian reserve at such a young age.* This time, I can tell he's relieved.

"What about you? How was the masturbatorium?"

"They had everything you could possibly want in there."

"Like?"

"A big recliner—"

"Weren't you grossed out to sit in it?"

"Absolutely. But they had it lined up just right to see the TV—"

"There was a TV?"

"Of course there was a TV."

"A little 8:00 a.m. porn?"

He laughs shyly. Dan's old-fashioned, and my probing is making him blush.

"You didn't just use your phone?"

"No service."

"So they just had porn playing on a loop?"

"No. They had a DVD collection."

"How'd they have that organized? The Gooey Decimal System?"

It all sounds so easy—fun, even—compared to the invasive tests I go through every time we visit the clinic. After all, repeating the tests is a formality; we know Dan's numbers are fine. I, on the other hand, am an exercise and health-food junkie just a couple of months past my thirtieth birthday and have the fertility prospects of an elderly, chain-smoking coal miner. This is the second clinic we've tried—the first one rejected me unless we would agree to use donor eggs, so sure we could never conceive with my own. This one accepted us and our cash but not our insurance. Good enough.

My mother had me when she was nearly forty. I always thought I'd tackle my career first and start considering children in my late thirties. I just hadn't had the itch yet. So as a precaution, we decided to do some baseline fertility tests to make sure we had time adequately on our side. After all, it hadn't yet seemed as though our lives had reached enough of a stasis for us to create new life. In our first five years together, we'd moved cities four times and changed apartments and homes seven times. Our careers had been on uncertain trajectories, and we were still finding our footing. It only seemed fair that we'd have a couple of years to enjoy the happy calm of young coupledom without any major disruptions. But of course, those just-in-case tests turned up a much grimmer answer than we knew to expect. So here I was, working my hardest to have a baby I wasn't even sure I was ready for yet—but didn't want to miss out on forever.

But then there's Izzie. She's been the one constant in our lives. Often, I introduce Dan as "the father of my dog" to get an easy laugh—but there is some truth to it. When we've come home, time and again, heartbroken by the news from a fertility specialist, she's always been there. She doesn't know; she doesn't care. When I hole up in bed to mope, she hustles upstairs like a nurse racing to a Code Blue, her paws beating an urgent song against the hardwood steps. She noses open the bedroom door and presses her back to my empty belly and waits for me to pull her close as a teddy bear. She doesn't recoil when I cry into her feathery neck, though I know she hates even a drop of rain to land on her hair.

But Izzie couldn't be the sole bearer of our secrets forever. At one point, I decided honesty was the best policy. My parents knew what was going on, but I wanted Dan's parents to be informed as well. When I told them that I might not be able to give their son the children he was otherwise perfectly capable of having, Izzie just lay on the floor on her back, waiting patiently for someone to address her available tummy. She didn't care whose fault it was, if there even is such a thing. I focused on her as I told our dreary tale. Sometimes love means not caring at all. That's how it always feels with Izzie.

Sure, these days I ask Dan a lot if we can get a second dog if having a human child doesn't work out for us—as if another dog could just be like Izzie squared and could replace the hole in our lives that we assume would be left. But there's another question I ask him too: Would we be happy if Izzie is the only baby we ever have? It's a silly question, meant to surf above the undercurrent of tension in our lives. Dan always says he'd be happy no matter what. That's the easy answer the supportive husband is supposed to give to his fertility-challenged wife. But I'm not Izzie's mother. Dan's not her father. We love her. We care for her. We've spent our fair share of nights holding her shaking body and cleaning her bloody vomit and diarrhea when she's fallen ill from a shared water bowl at the dog park. Nevertheless, she's not our baby and never will be. She's a dog.

But the more I try to become a mother myself, the more I have to come to terms with the fact that I'm not Izzie's mother. So who is—or was—Izzie's mother, and what happened to her?

     ———

Dog used to be man's best friend. Woman's too. The dog was a loyal companion, a trustworthy pal. While Izzie was the first dog for both my husband and me, my parents grew up with dogs in the 1950s and 1960s. They were happy, tail-wagging creatures that enjoyed their dominion mostly outdoors: in a suburban yard, in a doghouse. The dogs don't appear in family photos. In fact, there's no evidence of their existence at all other than a name remembered now, more than half a century later. Neither of my parents speak with overwhelming feeling about these animals. *He was a dog*, my mom has said with a shrug of Sparky, her family's cocker spaniel. *He was great.*

Dogs, then, were kept at a distance. The doghouse, so common a concept that it became a part of popular speech—*Dad's gonna be sleeping in the doghouse tonight!*—is now a largely antiquated concept. Along with urbanization, our dogs have been forced to come inside to live with us. Today, they sleep in our beds, not in the doghouse.

Dr. Leslie Irvine is a professor of sociology at University of Colorado–Boulder. She has written extensively about the human-animal bond—and, in particular, the ways in which we relate to dogs. She too has noticed a growing trend of dog owners infantilizing their pets.

"I don't think we have a vocabulary to describe the relationship other than to say: *Oh, my baby, my little girl, [she's] like a child to me.* It's not enough to say that we're friends or even *my best friend.* Because we don't let our best friends sleep with us—although I guess sometimes we do," Irvine says with a laugh. "The family is the closest place we can put that relationship."[1]

Dr. Alan Beck, director of the Center of the Human-Animal Bond at Purdue University, cites studies that reflect this increasingly close relationship with our dogs.

"You ask people 'What's the role of the animal in your family or your life?' The response is, 'It's a member of the family.' They don't mean it biologically, but it's the best metaphor we have for giving something more importance than just the simple description allows. It's like having a good family friend and calling her your aunt. It's capturing that our relationship with dogs has been evolving—and the dog itself has been evolving, so it really is now different than a food animal," Beck explains, noting however that by sheer numbers, there are still more people on the planet who would eat a dog than those who would keep it as a pet or consider it a member of the family.[2]

Beck says that studies done today to measure human attachment to animals would never have registered even a decade ago.

"When we measure how attached people are to animals, some of the tools we use would not have made any sense ten or fifteen years ago. Like: 'Do you carry pictures of your animal on your phone or in your wallet?' or 'Does your animal sleep in your bed or bedroom?'" Beck says. "Part of it is generational, and part of it is that more and more people are coming to urban environments, and that's where you see the indoor cat, the indoor dog—the dog may even be in the bedroom. Whereas you don't see that in the rural farmer's dog. It's a very real phenomenon, no doubt about it."

As a result, there's an inherent culture clash between the rural parts of the country, where dogs can often be detached from family life, and the urban areas, where the dog lives in close quarters and is considered to be a member of the family. That difference of opinions is what, in part, causes puppy brokers and transporters to thrive: transferring the dogs that are churned out by breeders in rural areas of the nation's heartland to be sold at a five- to tenfold profit in cities thousands of miles away.

Once these puppies find a home, however, we can see the way that we increasingly treat them as members of the family is reflected even in their names. While certainly not every dog in the 1950s was named Rover or Fido—my mother's dog, for example, was the aforementioned Sparky, and my father's was Taffy—for the most part, dog names seem to have had a decidedly whimsical, nonhuman quality. Even Lassie is a name you're unlikely to hear in any kindergarten classroom.

In the past, the national trends in dog names weren't widely documented and surveyed as they are today—perhaps proof in itself that this was not as consequential of a question to most. However, anthropologist Dr. Stanley Brandes of the University of California–Berkeley, turned to the pet cemeteries of America to document naming trends in dogs of generations past. While certainly not every pet dog is interred with a headstone, Brandes's technique demonstrated at least some trend toward increasingly human names.

Before World War II, Brandes noted dog names like Jaba, Teko, Dicksie, Punch, Snap, and Rags. Between the 1950s and the 1980s, nonhuman names continued to prevail, Champ, Happy, Clover, and Freckles to name a few. But at the same time, more and more human names begin to appear: Rivka, Daniel, Rico. But from the 1990s and 2000s on, the names become not only predominantly human but also very gender-specific: Oliver, Max, Timothy, Chelsea, and Maggie. Brandes pointed out that whereas in the past, it would be impossible to know if Jaba, for example, was a male or a female dog, today, human names often tell the tale. In cases where the name is non-gender-specific— Izzie would be an example—Brandes wrote that many owners add a feminization in either the spelling or the writing of it. For example, Nickie might become "Nickie Girl" but certainly not "Nicky," which could be misconstrued as a male dog.

Perhaps even more indicative of the role that our dogs have come to play in our households: only recently have they been afforded the luxury of the family's surname on their headstones, a trend that Brandes wrote only seems to have arisen in the last twenty years. Same goes for dogs that, from 1990 onward, are given headstones bearing religious iconography to match their parent families.[3] I've even seen this odd trend at Izzie's own groomer, who is now selling Star of David dog tags with a Jewish prayer engraved in Hebrew to add to our pup's collar. Then again, I live in Denver, where this same store also sells cannabidiol drops to help our dogs bliss out right alongside their owners who pop into the marijuana dispensary down the block. Dogs: they're just like us.

Sometimes Dan and I joke that we shouldn't have given Izzie

the name we did—it would have been our go-to choice for a child. But human-animal naming is a one-way street. A dog can take a human's name. But it's simply insulting for a human to be named after a dog.

Right?

According to the American Kennel Club, the top ten female dog names in 2015 included Chloe, Sadie, Lucy, and Bella.[4] These four also appear in the top one hundred female names for human babies born in 2016, according to the Social Security Administration's most recent ranking.[5] Of the top ten male names for puppies registered with the American Kennel Club, two also make the top one hundred list for human babies born in 2016: Cooper and Jack. With so much overlap, it's getting harder and harder to say who is being named after whom. More importantly, it's clear we now see dogs as deserving of human names we once reserved only for our offspring.

I can say—reluctantly, I might add—that as a child, family friends named their dog after me. I don't know whatever happened to the other Rory, although I do know that the other Rory was a male dog, which, neutered or not, added insult to injury. But perhaps if it weren't my own name, I might have agreed. Rory is a pretty great name for a dog.

CHAPTER EIGHT

From Hogs to Dogs

IF URBANIZATION IS HAVING SUCH A STRONG IMPACT on our relationship with our dogs, it is important to understand how rural America also has an effect on these animals. After all, the reality of the American puppy mill is inextricable from the history of our nation's agricultural industry—a fact that is underscored by the USDA's assigned oversight of commercial dog breeders. While these facilities may now churn out high-priced, designer puppies to be purchased for thousands of dollars in big-city pet shops, they are the product of shifts in the farming industry more than half a century ago.

So how did we get here?

Before World War II, family farms were commonplace. At the start of the twentieth century, nearly half of the country's workforce was employed in agriculture, and the majority of the nation's population lived in rural areas. But with industrialization and new technology, the work of the farmer changed. No longer was the family farm a reliable source of income as tractors began replacing horses and mules and small operations simply could not keep up and compete with the new order.

According to the USDA, the number of farms in this country has fallen by 63 percent since 1900 while the size of the average farm has ballooned by 67 percent over the same time period.[1] In short, these figures mean that, by and large, the family farm that once relied on around five products to sustain its income is now a thing of the past. In its place are today's larger commercial farms, devoted to a single commodity that is churned out by industrial production techniques and technology.

After World War II, these improvements in technology spurred a mass migration to urban areas, leaving the nation's family farms in a particularly challenged state. In an effort to help farmers find another source of income, some animal welfare advocates allege that the USDA actively encouraged down-on-their-luck farmers to raise and sell puppies. While I searched high and low to substantiate this claim, I was unable to find a direct link between the USDA and this initial impetus to breed puppies. However, it is clear that farmers, one way or another, realized that puppies were a veritable cash crop that could be grown right in the rabbit hutches and chicken coops that were otherwise sitting empty.

"When the industry got started, most of the breeders were farmers' wives who, in the past, used to raise chickens for egg money. When the egg business was taken over by these large corporations, they didn't have a way to supplement their income, so [dog breeding] fell right into their hands," Bob Baker of the Missouri Alliance for Animal Legislation (MAAL) tells me.[2]

When Baker first started his fight to improve animal welfare in the heartland more than thirty years ago, he took a job selling kennel equipment to gain access to dog-breeding facilities that otherwise would have never given him entree. His first red flag that these dog-breeding facilities were more like factory farms came when one dog broker he was visiting told him to rethink his footwear for this job.

"He said, 'You better get yourself some tall boots for when you go into these places...[because] you'll probably find more dogs in chicken coops nowadays than chickens.' He wasn't too far wrong, and it was certainly true."

Because of the deep agrarian roots underlying the history of commercial dog breeding, the majority of these facilities are concentrated across the farm belt of the United States: Missouri, Iowa, Kansas, and Arkansas. Other states like Ohio and Pennsylvania that are somewhat geographically separated from this area but have larger farming communities are also home to a high concentration of commercial dog breeders.

Baker notes that as family farms died out and their industries were taken over by big, agricultural conglomerates, the trend toward raising dogs as a crop became increasingly evident— particularly in Missouri.

"That was a main problem in Missouri because...in the 1980s, the pork industry was taken over by these large conglomerates like Smithfield Foods and Cargill and places like that. We lost a lot of pork farmers," Baker explains.

Baker recalls one particular lawmaker's protest during the battle to pass Missouri's 2010 anti-puppy-mill legislation.

"His biggest argument was that he had a lot of veterinarians who were unemployed because of all the hog farms going out of business. They were making up that business by working for the dog breeders," he says. "That was as recently as 2010 to 2011 that you were still seeing that effect."

Most haunting is the way the trend is so easily summed up in the Show-Me State. "Here in Missouri," Baker says, "we went from hogs to dogs."

This sharp decline in the fortunes of Missouri family farmers was the cause of the state's particular explosion in dog breeding. As of 2016, Missouri was home to nearly 678 USDA-licensed pet breeders, more than any other state in the country. At a distant second place is Iowa with 208.[3] Given this unrivaled concentration of dog breeders in the Show-Me State, Missouri has had to create additional legal protections for commercially bred dogs with its own legislation and state inspectors to enforce it.

Former Assistant Attorney General of Missouri Jessica Blome was instrumental in crafting the state's anti-puppy-mill legislation known as the Canine Cruelty Prevention Act. Passed in 2011, the law heightened state regulations and allowed her office to prosecute commercial breeding operations that, while still licensed by the USDA, were very much violating the dogs' welfare. Her work led to the rescue of more than six thousand animals and forced hundreds of substandard breeding operations—both licensed and unlicensed by the USDA—to shut down.[4]

"The way we treat farm animals is absolutely abhorrent," Blome tells me. "People are entering into the pet-breeding business with that same mind-set that these dogs are just there so that we can manage their reproductive systems in order to turn a profit. So you're going to see that the dogs are treated the exact same way that they might treat a pig in a confinement operation or a dairy cow that lives its entire winter in a barn."[5]

The USDA's failing to protect dogs in commercial breeding facilities was, in large part, the impetus to close the gap with state regulations. Before Missouri's Canine Cruelty Prevention Act was signed into law, Blome recalls witnessing the USDA's unwilling-ness or inability to enforce even its most lax regulations.

"USDA licensure means absolutely nothing because there's no enforcement," Blome says.

But the story behind the fight to pass the Canine Cruelty Prevention Act tells a far more nuanced tale of the way that the dog-breeding industry intersects with Big Agriculture. Initially known as Proposition B, an earlier version of the legislation was floated to a Missouri ballot initiative in 2010. It narrowly passed with a little more than 51 percent of the vote.[6]

This initial ballot initiative called for raising the bar for the care of breeding dogs while also capping the number allowed per facility at fifty. With many facilities in the state breeding anywhere from 100 to 750 dogs at a time, it's clear that this numeric cap would have forced an enormous change for the industry. But it wasn't just the dog breeders who gnashed their teeth at the number. That fifty-dog cap sent the far more powerful agriculture industry into a tizzy, and as a result, lawmakers began to bow to pressure to repeal Proposition B even after voters had passed it.

Animal welfare advocates were furious to see the will of the voters undercut as legislators worked to create what they dubbed "the Missouri Solution"—a compromise that would weaken Proposition B.

"Lawmakers should never have substituted their judgment for the people of Missouri and gutted core provisions of Prop B," President and CEO of the Humane Society Wayne Pacelle said at the time. "The so-called compromise was not about protecting animals. It was about placating agri-business."[7]

Blome agrees.

"Make no mistake—make no mistake," Blome says adamantly.

"Puppies are considered an agricultural commodity by the agricultural community. Any move to improve the regulations and improve the circumstances of puppies is absolutely viewed as a direct attack on all agriculture."

As Blome's office and its partners worked to hash out this compromise, the national farm lobby marched into the fray.

"I've never been more breathtakingly astonished than I was… when the compromise was happening, to see national pork, national beef, and national poultry interests flood Missouri with money and messaging in order to stop regulations that were meant to improve the lives of dogs in puppy mills," Blome recalls.

Brian Klippenstein remembers the fight against Proposition B as well—but from the other side. Before his ascent to the transition team leader for Trump's USDA, Klippenstein was the executive director of Protect the Harvest, a farmer and animal owner's rights advocacy group started by Forrest Lucas, founder of Lucas Oil. In that role, Klippenstein was instrumental in battling Proposition B on behalf of big agriculture.

"What they cleverly did was try to eliminate dog breeding— but they don't say that: they say you can't own more than fifty dogs," Klippenstein says of the fight over the fifty-dog cap. "Anybody in the business of breeding—anybody responsible, and not all of them are—will tell you that you can't make a living with fifty. It drives you into some other field."[8]

Klippenstein explains that, fearing for their livelihoods, licensed pet breeders approached their better-funded allies in agriculture to help fight the legislation.

"There is a kindred spirit among those who work with the land, the people who work with animals—most of whom would say they're God's creatures. To some degree, as the Allied Forces and NATO say, we should consider an attack on one of us an attack on all of us. Not necessarily an attack on a bad actor, but just when they go after one group, the other groups should care for several reasons. One is they should know they're going to be next," Klippenstein explains of the reasons behind the farm lobby's battle against the Proposition B legislation. "[Forrest Lucas] came in with enough money to do some radio and TV ads to tell the competing side of the story…and that fifty number disappeared."

Surprisingly, Blome herself was ultimately instrumental in removing the cap of fifty dogs from the legislation to forge the compromise on Proposition B that became the Canine Cruelty Prevention Act.

"The ones who wanted puppy mills abolished wanted to keep that fifty-dog limit. That's where I came in and said, 'Look, give us enforcement authority,'" Blome says. "You can have the best regulations. You can have the best standards for care in the world. But [it doesn't matter] if they're not being enforced… They gave the attorney general's office that authority so that we could actually make a difference. So the puppy mill opponents agreed, and we traded away the fifty-dog limit for enforcement authority at the attorney general's office."

Klippenstein's argument against the fifty-dog limit provides a window into what exactly is at stake for the agricultural community and the farm lobby in the fight over dog breeding.

"If there's a number that separates responsible ownership from irresponsible ownership for dogs, then it would only be logical that there would be [a number] for swine, bovine, and equine," Klippenstein explains. "There are irresponsible people out there but…it's not because they're small or big. It's because of what they're committed to doing. Often the bigger ones have highly trained people, more modern practices, more oversight, and more regulatory scrutiny. If it's bad, it's bad."

Compromise in hand and fifty-dog cap stricken from the legislation, the regulations formerly known as Proposition B were revised and signed into law as the Canine Cruelty Prevention Act. For the care of breeding dogs, these new restrictions made some real changes: requiring constant access to outdoor exercise areas, increasing cage sizes, and mandating that veterinarians have hands-on visits to these facilities at least once a year. The law also added funding to hire three small-animal veterinarians who could respond to violations or illnesses reported on-site. Before the law was passed, the USDA exclusively employed large-animal veterinarians for this purpose—workers trained only in the care of pigs, cattle, and other traditional farm animals.

"[The large-animal veterinarians] just didn't know exactly what would rise to the level of abuse or neglect in a companion animal, because what they see on a daily basis is comparable to the way we treat pigs and cows and chickens," Blome explains of these vets who had not been trained to work on the delicate anatomies of dogs and cats.

As you may recall, the USDA inspectors who are tasked with evaluating these facilities are not required to be veterinarians— the agency's Dr. Gibbens told me that only about 60 percent of them are.[9]

But Blome believes that the most important change that came with the new regulations was the way dogs began receiving access to water in Missouri.

"Missouri now requires constant access to potable drinking water, whereas the federal regulations require watering twice a day, and that's it. Or as often as needed, it says. So, if it's 115 degrees…and the water dr.es up, they still don't get any water until that evening. I mean that's crazy. That's crazy that that's the rule in every state but Missouri," Blome says.

With new enforcement authority and tightened regulations, Blome and her team went into action. In 2010—before the Canine Cruelty Prevention Act—1,414 USDA-licensed breeders were up and running in Missouri.[10] By 2016, that number had dropped to 678.

But there's still a tremendous amount of work to be done in Missouri. The state still topped the Humane Society's "Horrible Hundred" list in 2017 with the highest number of bad breeders in the country for the fifth year in a row.[11] This even as commercial breeding operations continue to go out of business on their own because they are unable to conform to the new regulations. But with its work still very much unfinished, the Canine Cruelty Prevention Act is on tenuous ground in Missouri: every year, the battle rises anew, and animal rights advocates are forced to defend the legislation. And the battle is not likely to get any easier. As of this writing, the director of the Missouri Department of Agriculture is fifth-generation hog farmer Chris Chinn. Chinn has openly admitted to using controversial gestation stalls for sows on her farm. In 2010, she spoke to *National Hog Farmer* magazine about her fears that reform to pet breeding in Missouri would negatively impact the livelihood of the state's farmers.[12]

But farmers' allies within the agriculture department aren't the only threat to the legislation. There are also independent groups that have sprung up in outraged response to Proposition B and the Canine Cruelty Prevention Act. Mindy Patterson, together with her husband, founded perhaps the most prominent of these organizations, called the Cavalry Group, back in 2010. Her group's stated mission is to protect and defend animal enterprise. Patterson is a vocal proponent of private animal-ownership rights and sees dog breeding as falling under that umbrella. Her group works as a liaison between attorneys and commercial breeders she feels are in need of a good defense. Often, she speaks on behalf of the industry when stories about bad breeders arise in the press.

"Prop B had much more to it than met the eye. The definition of 'pet' within the legislation was 'any domesticated animal living near or around the house.' So it set a precedent. If it was about dogs, then why didn't it say 'canine?' It said 'pet,'" she explains.[13]

She's right: the ballot measure known as Proposition B did originally define *pet* as "any domesticated animal normally maintained in or near the household of the owner," although the legislation did only refer to "pets" contextually as the products of breeding dogs. Still, Patterson and other farmers' advocates successfully argued that this type of regulation on the books would lead to a slippery slope wherein any farm animal could come to be defined as a pet. The revised Canine Cruelty Prevention Act that was ultimately signed into law ended up revising the definition of a *pet* as "any species of the domestic dog, *Canis lupus familiaris*, or resultant hybrids, normally maintained in or near the household of the owner."

"So you know, [Prop B] could have easily been amended or expanded to regulate cattle, pork, pigs, chickens. I mean, that's the thing: [the Humane Society] doesn't do anything without setting a precedent to come back for more," Patterson says. "If the government can tell you how many animals you can own, then you're a breath away from government telling you how many cars you can sell a year. We have got to get away from government telling us what we can and cannot do in every little aspect."

In spite of her vehement opposition to Missouri's Canine Cruelty Prevention Act, Patterson says she believes that reform to the dog-breeding industry should come at the state level— just not the way it was done in the Canine Cruelty Prevention Act. Fair enough. But Patterson's argument against government overregulation quickly becomes contradictory and leaves me somewhat perplexed.

"You know, we have regulated the textile industry out of our country...just by tightening the regulations so that people give up, and they take their companies to other places. Personally, I am very worried about what is happening—and dog breeders are one thing, okay? But they are doing the same things to our food producers, and they are going to regulate farmers and ranchers out of existence, out of America, and we are going to be importing all our food like we do oil and energy. And I don't want to buy food from China. I don't want to buy food from other countries that have looser regulations," Patterson says.

I point out to her that her argument is contradictory. She wants less regulation here in the United States. But at the same time, she doesn't feel comfortable purchasing goods from countries with laxer regulations than the United States. She responds by clarifying that the regulations in place on breeders now are based on emotion, not science, and they are tailored to putting people out of business.

To wit, Patterson takes issue with the USDA slapping breeders with violations for problems that are not immediately impacting the health of the animals—rusty cages or peeling paint in the kennels, for example. She says these measures are impinging on the breeders' right to do business unmolested. So I ask if she would defend a breeder who has violations on his record from the USDA that directly impact the health of the dogs on his property. It's worth noting that she has done just this, speaking to the press in defense of breeders who have wound up on the Humane Society's Horrible Hundred and have been blasted in the media. I ask her why she would be willing to protect these bad actors, and I list a few examples of what I've seen on the USDA reports of Horrible Hundred facilities: bloody stool, rotten teeth, dead puppies left in cages with their mothers.

"We do not defend those who do not abide by the law. And if they are not upstanding in their industry, then how can you possibly defend someone legally or otherwise that's not exemplary in their industry?" she insists.

But those are exactly the types of breeders she has defended in the media. For what it's worth, she's blasted the Horrible Hundred list as "nothing more than a fundraiser" for the Humane Society.[14]

The Humane Society is a frequent target of Patterson's ire in our discussion. She says that the media panders to the Humane Society and other like-minded groups and bemoans the fact that animal welfare advocates have the stronger emotional argument but that no one reports the other side—hers and the breeders' side—of the story. So I ask her, in the interest of fairness and getting her side of the story out in the media, if she can hook me up with one of the breeders in her membership who she considers to be exemplary. I tell her that I will be more than happy to report in my book that breeding can be done on a large scale without harming the dogs if that's actually the case. I explain that, to date, I've only seen hobby breeders who are able to bring dogs into the world humanely—and they are not able to do so as a primary source of income. I do want to show both sides of the story, and in order to do so, I would need to go see for myself the facility she selects and review their USDA inspection reports. In short, I won't be able to simply take her word for it. She can pick a breeder anywhere in the country—I will be happy to travel anywhere at any time. Patterson says she has many breeders in her membership that immediately come to mind and would be more than happy to demonstrate to me that dogs can be humanely and commercially bred in a large-scale facility. She just has to check with them and get back to me. I circle back with her in the weeks that follow our initial conversation, asking if she's found a breeder who is doing right by their animals that I can visit and interview. She responds that she is working on it. But a breeder she believes is doing great work that I can visit for myself never materializes.

Maybe Patterson is right, and there is a great commercial breeder out there somewhere. But for Izzie and me, the damage may have already been done. She was born in Missouri in 2010, before the Canine Cruelty Prevention Act was signed. But to truly comprehend the value of state regulations, I have to go deep into the heartland. I need to make the comparison for myself, to see how Missouri's additional laws impact its breeding dogs while its neighbors adhere to the Animal Welfare Act alone.

CHAPTER NINE

On the Rescue Run

MELISSA* IS SITTING IN THE OPEN BACK HATCH OF HER dusty SUV, whispering to an apricot-colored corgi in a cage. She's a dog breeder in her late thirties and has her black hair pulled back into a tight ponytail. She wears a Bluetooth earpiece and faded jeans. Her car bears bumper stickers from Protect the Harvest and slogans like *My other auto is an AK-47*. Melissa has met us at her mother's house outside Lebanon, Missouri, where both she and her younger sister have come to give up a few longstanding members of their breeding stock to a rescue—the more humane form of retirement. They followed in their mother's footsteps, continuing the family breeding business. The younger sister opens up her car to reveal two rambunctious Boston terriers and several Pomeranians in a separate cage. The rescue team approaches her car first, careful to avoid the emotional outpouring coming from her sister Melissa with the corgi.

---

*   All breeder and all dog names in this chapter have been changed. In the case of the dogs, I've tried to stay true to the spirit or tone of the original names.

"Will you guys keep in touch and let me know where they end up?" the younger sister, Jamie, asks. "Maybe even send me a picture of them with the families they go to?"

"Of course," one of the rescuers says as she takes a pair of Pomeranians in her arms and makes her way to one of the two Sprinter vans filled with nearly one hundred rescued dogs.

Jamie approaches the van cautiously and looks at the cages of dogs stacked and tethered together all the way to the ceiling.

"People are really going to adopt all these dogs?" she asks incredulously. "Like, they'll all get homes?"

"Some might take a while longer than others, but yes. Eventually, they all will," Theresa Strader, the head of the National Mill Dog Rescue, informs her plainly. Since 2007, her Colorado-based organization has rescued, rehabilitated, and found homes for more than ten thousand dogs from breeding facilities. She's agreed to let me tag along on one of her monthly rescue trips across the heartland.

"Melissa is really struggling," Jamie whispers to us, nodding toward her sister, now openly weeping over her ten-year-old corgi's cage. "I don't know if she's going to give him up."

With the corgi as the last remaining dog on the list to rescue at this stop, Theresa approaches Melissa with a tenderness she typically reserves only for four-legged animals.

"I don't think I can let him go," Melissa says, brushing her tears into her slicked-back hairline. "He's my lapdog."

"I know," Theresa says as gently as she can. But she knows that this corgi has never been and never will be a lapdog as long as it stays here. "It's time he got to retire and enjoy his life as a dog."

Melissa slowly opens the cage. Instead of handing him over to

Theresa's waiting arms, she pulls the animal awkwardly into her own cumbersome embrace.

"He's Corn-Husk. That's his name," she says, attempting to rock him in her arms. He blankly allows the gesture, his bat ears brushing against her cheek.

"That's a perfect name for him," Theresa says, trying not to telegraph her impatience, as the team has several more stops to hit and about fifty more dogs to rescue before midnight. "He's going to be so happy in his new home. I can promise you that."

Melissa sucks back her tears and asks to have her picture taken with Corn-Husk. She smiles for the flip-phone camera and then bursts into tears as she finally hands him over—a clumsy exchange as the chubby corgi goes stiff amid the commotion.

"This one's never missed a meal," Theresa says, grunting to lift him. "That's okay, Corn-Husk. Neither have I."

Melissa hiccups out a laugh through her tears.

Theresa's team scans the corgi's microchip, gives him a paper collar with a number, and stows him in a large crate in one of the vans. Within twenty-four hours, they'll give him a new name, erasing Corn-Husk from the record so that a new family can make him theirs.

We hit the road, heading for the next stop on Theresa's rescue itinerary.

"You see that corgi?" Theresa asks me.

"Of course," I say. "I didn't think she was going to give him up. She seemed to really love him."

"For as much as you can love a dog that lives in a cage, they do," Theresa says. "Did you see his feet, though?"

"No," I admit. I was just so struck by the breeder's grief that I didn't notice anything else. Typical—I'm always looking at the human; Theresa is always looking at the dog. "He seemed healthier than most of the other dogs you've gotten today."

"He had splayed feet and interdigital cysts," Theresa says of the painful red sores and welts that are almost universally found on the dogs she rescues. "That means he's likely lived his entire life on either pea gravel or in a wire mesh cage."

So much for being Melissa's lapdog.

After months of research into the Animal Welfare Act and the USDA, this is my first time being up close and in direct contact with commercial breeders and their facilities. On the ground, it's a very different scene than anything I was able to learn from inspection reports and in interviews with either side of the dog-breeding debate. Moments like this, where a breeder weeps to give one of her dogs up to a rescue, were not at all what I had expected to find.

"People see these breeders crying to give up the dog, and they think it's bullshit," Theresa says. "It's not. They really feel it. But they live out here where the life of a dog is not very revered."

It's true. Melissa might have let Corn-Husk live out his days and escape the gunshot that so often accompanies the retirement of a breeding dog. But the scars he bears demonstrate that he did not live the kind of existence most of us would bestow on our pets.

Theresa's organization is unique for its inside access to commercial breeding operations. Over the past decade, she has built relationships with breeders across the heartland so that when a breeding dog stops churning out litters that are healthy enough to sell, they call Theresa to come pick it up and find it a home where it can become a pet. In return, the breeder agrees not to shoot it or otherwise euthanize it. It's for this reason that I have changed all the names of the breeders and dogs in this chapter: I don't want to interfere with Theresa's hard-won relationships and her ability to continue rescuing dogs in the future.

Most of the breeders on this rescue run seem relieved to have the option of releasing these dogs to Theresa, happy to not have to kill them when their economic value diminishes or fades. It's a self-selecting group: the very worst puppy millers out there would likely not give Theresa or any other rescue the time of day. But even among this group, plenty of these breeders are bad enough.

After watching one breeder callously yank a half dozen cowering shih tzus from their cages by their paws and matted scruff, Theresa loses her cool in front of the rescue team.

"He hands us over dogs from '05, '04?" Theresa says, referring to the dogs' birth years, eleven or twelve years ago. The fact that the breeder has opted to spare the dog from certain death is not enough. "I mean, give the dogs a break. If you retire them at five or six, they at least have some life left in them."

But her anger is short-lived as a bigger issue soon arises. One of the rescuers radios Theresa to let her know that a dog is missing from the list. All three vans in the convoy pull over on the dirt road where we're traveling. A breeder at the last stop had told Theresa she'd be bringing a husky but forgot to pack it into the open bed of her pickup with the rest of her dogs and bring it to our meet-up.

"They're going to go back and kill it," Theresa says, preparing to divert the mission and return to the breeder's farm with her. To do so would mean driving all three vans carrying about one hundred dogs a full hour off the itinerary, delaying the five stops and meet-ups arranged with breeders for the rest of the day. Theresa performs the mental calculus, taking into account the poor condition of the rest of the dogs from this facility—so covered in mats that the breeder had pulled her Maltese dogs from their cages by the painful clumps in their fur as if they were handles.

Theresa jumps from the van and hustles to catch the breeder on the road. She makes her promise not to kill the dog and to hold it until Theresa swings through the area on her next monthly run. Theresa reluctantly moves the caravan ahead on the day's mission, still grumbling about that husky, not so sure that the breeder will keep her promise.

Not all breeders are created equally. As we log hour after hour on these rural roads, I see firsthand how a breeder in Missouri, where the Canine Cruelty Prevention Act raises the bar for dogs' treatment somewhat, differs from one in Oklahoma, Kansas, or Arkansas.

Theresa does not paint breeders with broad strokes. She operates in an unusual gray area where few, if any other advocates for dogs are willing to. Where most would find it abhorrent to even speak to a breeder who runs what can only be called a puppy mill, Theresa is willing to build relationships that, to the observer like myself, appear to even border on friendship. Many of the breeders we meet along the way hug her and her team, happy to see them again. With the breeders, Theresa is a brighter, friendlier, warmer version of her otherwise cynical, New York–native self. When one ragged Havanese with bloodied paws is transferred into her care and the breeder tells her its name is Jolene, Theresa breaks out into the Dolly Parton tune of the same name and gets everyone merrily singing along, even the breeder. The dog doesn't blink—she doesn't know her name; no one's ever called her anything before. Once we're safely back in the van and out of the earshot of the breeder, Theresa unleashes her fury on the state of that breeder's dogs. It clearly isn't easy to walk the line she treads every day.

While some animal rights activists decry the breeding of dogs altogether—be it in a puppy mill or a sparkling clean and ostensibly humane facility—Theresa sees a more nuanced palette. Of one commercial breeder she works with in Missouri that we do not get to visit on this trip, she says, "If every facility was like hers, we wouldn't have a problem. There wouldn't be any puppy mills." But then again, Theresa does not consider herself an activist.

"I'm a person who believes in all living things' right to humane treatment. I'm not a humaniac," she says, creating a portmanteau of the words *humane* and *maniac*. "I'm not even an animal rights activist. Animal rights and animal welfare are very different. I do want animals in my home and in my life. Animal rights people think we never should have done that… There's nothing radical about the way I act. I go in and very diplomatically work with these people to bring dogs home. Some people say it's like I'm in bed with the breeders, like I'm protecting them… We've rescued over ten thousand mill dogs in less than nine years. How many times do you think we could bully [breeders], push them around, stab them in the back, whatever—and continue to bring these dogs home? At the end of the day for us, it's about bringing these dogs home, out of that life. Nothing else."[1]

For their part, the breeders are wary and know well their reputation as purveyors of so-called puppy mills. Theresa points out to me on our travels the hallmarks of the breeding facilities that could easily qualify for the ignominious distinction of puppy mill: dogs that never see the light of day, wire-mesh cages, relentlessly repeated breeding and botched C-sections sewn up with fishing line until black or green ooze pours from the females' genitals.

In one windowless building we visit in Arkansas, the stench is so powerful that I have to leave and reenter multiple times just to scan the room fully. Inside are sixty-four elevated cages filled with snow-white Havanese, French bulldogs, Yorkies, and their puppies. Theresa confirms that many of these operations favor the smaller breeds: you can pack more in per square foot and, as a result, make more money. Here, the dogs yap, nap, and nurse their clementine-sized puppies on wire mesh with gaps about a square-inch wide. They drink like gerbils from a metal nib attached to PVC piping that carries water to every cage but can never drink as their oral anatomy was intended, lapping from a bowl. As a result, dogs in these types of conditions suffer from their mouths rotting dead in their skulls, even as they live on. But still they breed. After all, a rotten mouth isn't genetic, and it isn't going to pollute their litters.

Below the wire mesh of their cages are white, slanted pieces of plastic that channel into a makeshift gutter, carrying away their urine and excrement. Lining the walls of the facility are cages on the ground for the larger dogs, mostly English bulldogs. They have the modest luxury of metal dog doors that they can bang in and out of to a small, fenced, outdoor area on concrete.

At this facility, it's clear how much worse conditions can get without state provisions and inspections. This breeder is only beholden to the USDA and the Animal Welfare Act. This facility would never pass in Missouri, as most of the dogs lack any access or even view of the outdoors. But it's good enough to pass federal inspections—and that's all it needs to do. Don't get me wrong. I certainly am not saying that conditions are humane or optimal in Missouri breeding operations. It's simply that the breeders there are at least expected to meet somewhat higher standards than they are in other states like here in Arkansas. Which, alas, doesn't say much.

But heightened state regulations are only part of the story. It's surprising to me to see just how little standardization there is for care from state to state and even facility to facility. What I'm finding, as we drag on through the heartland, is that every breeder comes to work with dogs for a different reason. Often these reasons determine the kind and quality of care the dogs receive and not the federal or state regulations.

Back in Missouri, Maude, a pleasantly stout, elderly breeder gives up fistfuls of Pomeranian puppies, some with heart murmurs. It's rare that Theresa's group gets puppies unless they're born with a health issue that makes them impossible to sell or breed: a missing limb, a heart problem, fused joints. As I pace her facility, I note that some of Maude's animals at least have some ability to see the light of day and walk around together in a fenced, concrete enclosure, relatively free from their cages.

The heart murmurs on Maude's puppies are relatively mild. They may even go away with age or some medical treatment, and she could easily get away with selling them on the internet to an unwitting buyer, as cute and fluffy as they are. She could probably even breed them if she wanted to. The Animal Welfare Act certainly doesn't stop her from doing so.

"Can't take no chances," Maude says, shaking her long, gray ponytail. She isn't interested in gaming the system. She cites a childhood tenderness for this particular breed and has now devoted her life to proliferating their puppies. "I been breeding Poms for twenty years. I always wanted one as a little girl and never could afford one."

Later, when I pull up her USDA inspection reports, I find she has no violations on the record.

Other breeders transition from livestock to dogs. In many of these cases, there is no fondness for the dogs other than for their profitability.

Take Bert, for example, a longtime dairy cow farmer in Missouri. He wears aviator glasses and a trucker hat with the logo of a local farm supplier.

"I tried to get out of the milking and into dogs," he tells me, still the owner of a farm with a few dozen Black Angus cows. "The dogs are a lot more work," Bert says with an air of annoyance before striding off to pull a weary and bedraggled twelve-year-old West Highland white terrier from its crate by the scruff of its aged neck. Unfortunately, no state or federal regulations can stop that kind of treatment.

Another breeder, Jeff, gently hands over two Yorkies, one Havanese, and a Maltese to Theresa's team in Arkansas. The rescue group has stopped at one larger breeding facility here, and four other breeders have driven in from miles around to drop their dogs off too. Some come because they don't want Theresa on their property—either because they don't want her to see the condition it's in or because they don't want to be ostracized by their fellow breeders should they spot the rescue vans paying a visit. It's a relatively small community, and people talk. Other breeders come to Theresa's scheduled meet-up just to speed the process along and shoot the shit with their fellow breeders. But Jeff stands apart from the others, looking reluctantly at his dogs being loaded into Theresa's van. He strokes his graying goatee.

"My wife didn't want me to bring this one, so make sure she

finds a good home," Jeff tells Theresa, pointing to one of the dogs. "We fell in love with her."

Jeff bred horses for a decade before turning to dogs about seven years ago.

"The horse market went to nothing," he says. He then tells me in a whisper so that the other breeders can't hear him, "Our kennel is very different. We play with our dogs every day. My wife sits in their kennels for hours just playing with them. Because we love animals, and that way, they're not stuck in a cage all the time."

For what it's worth, Jeff's facility also has no violations on record with the USDA.

But as Theresa says often, "No one thinks they're running a puppy mill. It's always the other breeder down the road."

Arkansas breeder Jane meets us at the same kennel. Just as Theresa says, she's quick to point out that the worst of the dogs she's relinquishing did not come from her facility.

"These Yorkies come from a woman down the road from me," she says, becoming enraged, pointing to the dilapidated and malnourished dogs, puppies no more but still small enough to fit in the palm of the hand. "She was going to put them down. I said, 'Give them to me to take to this rescue.' She said, 'Rescue? Oh no!' It's because rescues make us look bad. But not all rescues are alike, just like not all breeders are alike."

As Jane preaches to the other gathered breeders and rescuers, I notice that the owner of the property where we've met is quietly cashing in a ginger-colored miniature poodle to another breeder who'd just finished retiring her dogs to Theresa. She hands him a wad of fresh twenty-dollar bills in exchange. He licks a thumb and counts out the money as a white bulldog named Panzer looks on, sitting on his distended, black testicles—the size of ripe grapefruits—oozing into a towel.

I ask Theresa if this bothers her, to see breeders meet up to retire dogs to her and then purchase new stock from each other at the rendezvous she'd arranged.

"It's about the lives of the dogs we save," Theresa says. "I don't think they're replacing the dogs they're retiring."

It's hard for me to be so sure.

Virtually every breeder of the nearly twenty that we meet on this trip says the same thing to Theresa as they hand off their dogs: *Find my dogs a good home.* But the contradictions run deep.

A breeder named Tom meets us in the parking lot of a Cracker Barrel in Wichita, Kansas, rather than have us come onto his property. I can guess at what it might be like though when he opens the door to his truck and the stink that pours out is nearly unbearable: rotting mouths, vomit, and shit. He hands over a half dozen Havanese and a single black pug to Theresa. Several of the Havanese are covered in mucus-heavy vomit stringing down their chests.

Tom is shy. He doesn't make much eye contact, mostly looking down at his stained overalls. He wears a camouflage baseball cap with a ragged gray ponytail stuck up inside it. As the dogs are transferred, he quietly says, "I may be a breeder, but I still take care of them." None of the rescuers seem to hear him as they work, or at least they don't respond.

He notices Theresa smoking as she works and shakes his head.

"I won't tell you what to do, but I never do smoke around my dogs," he admonishes in a low voice.

Theresa chooses to let the comment go.

Tom asks for USDA disposition forms he can fill out on the

dogs he's relinquishing. This is the paperwork that allows the agency to monitor where the dogs go when they are nowhere to be found at his kennel at the next inspection—dead or alive, sold or rescued. In spite of the more than ten thousand dogs Theresa has rescued, she says that the USDA has only come to her facility once in ten years to make sure that these disposition forms actually tell the truth, showing that the dogs did in fact end up with her as the paperwork states and not in a shallow grave just a few yards from where they were born or bred.

"Do you put biters down?" Tom asks. "I've got one, but if he's gonna go out and bite a bunch of people, I'll just put him down."

Theresa quickly insists that no, she will not put down a biter. Instead, she promises that she'll work with the dog to train it, rehabilitate it, and change its behavior so that it can find a suitable home. Tom agrees to bring it to her next time she's in town about a month from now.

Theresa pulls one of the male Havanese out and prepares to crate him in her van.

"Can he go with a female?" she asks, looking to pair him up for the journey with a crate mate that he won't attack.

"Depends on how good she cooks," Tom says, smiling, warming up to Theresa and her crew.

After the dogs are loaded and packed away, Tom and Theresa light up together. They lean against the hood of a Sprinter van as they smoke, and Tom tells us about the tornado that hit his mobile home last year.

"It happened on Good Friday. Wasn't nothing 'good' about that," he says.

The storm came with no warning in the dead of night and knocked over his home. He nearly lost an ear.

"You wouldn't hate all these people," Theresa had warned me before we left for this rescue mission. "Many of them got into this because it's what their families did. This is all they know. They don't live much different from the dogs. They really don't. A traditional shit hole is a traditional shit hole. We all know what that's like. I wonder how willing people are to sacrifice what they want with what is right. If people saw what I have seen over these last nine years, I'm quite certain that they'd never want to support animals living in that way despite how badly they wanted whatever type of dog. I say this to people a lot: you're not going to turn somebody who wants a [certain breed of] puppy for their kids to grow up with…into somebody who is just going to go to the shelter and get any dog, an older dog or a pitty mix or whatever—you're not. It's just an unfortunate truth about people that they want what they want. And many people are willing to put anything aside in their mind to get what they want, even suffering."

Theresa sees the hopelessness of a consumer base that is willing to ignore the truth about their dogs. She may be right—but I see that problem as the effect, not the cause. At fault here may be neither the consumer nor even the worst breeders out there. Instead, it's a fundamental disconnect between the things we love and the way they're made. As long as convenient access to a commodity is a must, an industry will arise to meet the demand—and few people will question it, especially when they can't see it with their own eyes. But in spite of the billions spent every year on our dogs, these animals are not simply commodities that can be mass-produced and sold without enormous consequences.

CHAPTER TEN

All About Izzie

THERESA IS RIGHT: THERE'S A PART OF ME THAT doesn't want to know any more about Izzie than the life she's had with us. Her story is my story, and being so close to learning the truth feels like it could unravel the innocence that underlies our relationship. I'm not alone in this unwillingness to know the truth. Time and again in interviewing owners of puppy mill dogs, I find the same willful naïveté.

There's no question that I feel connected beyond description to my dog. *To my dog.* Even referring to her that way feels inadequate. She's not my dog: she's Izzie. She has a mind, she has a heart, and she has her own set of priorities. She has moods. Sometimes, she's my shadow, trying to follow me even to the shower, her wet nose pressed against the steamed-up glass. Other times, she seems to resent me for whatever unknown transgressions I may have wrought against her, and she slinks away from me to isolate herself in an unoccupied bedroom or under a table. I respect her complexities and appreciate her unwillingness to offer constant, unquestioning love and affection—it makes her more real, more human, more like me. I wonder if it's easy to forget and overlook a dog's individual needs when you're a breeder with hundreds to tend to, none of which share your living space. As a pet owner, it seems so obvious.

When I look at this animal, I'm not seeing a dog. I'm no longer seeing millennia of symbiotic interspecies friendship. I'm not seeing the centuries of breeding that created the frizzy-haired, black-nosed, terrified-of-cell-phones creature that can distinguish between the sound of the cheese drawer opening and that of the freezer door opening. I'm seeing a piece of my heart.

But it didn't start out that way.

When we first brought Izzie home, Dan and I expected to feel the magic of human-canine bonding from the get-go: puppy love at its finest. We thought that we'd just throw a leash on her, and she'd know what to do. She'd naturally fetch a ball and learn quickly to do her business outside. She'd snuggle us to sleep each night, and her every action would be an outward expression of her undying loyalty to us. That's what we assumed. Neither of us had ever had a dog in our lives. What could go wrong?

We drove out to the American Dog Club on Long Island, the store our relatives had recommended, the one proudly declaring that it only purchased dogs from USDA-licensed facilities on its website. I'd called ahead and had been informed that there was one female wheaten terrier still available for sale—but I had to hurry before someone else got her.

Dan and I walked up to a wall of cages and searched for this last wheaten. We scanned through the Maltipoos, Yorkies, and goldendoodles, all yapping at eye level, begging for our attention.

But there, in a cage on the bottom row by our feet, sat a puppy much larger than the rest, her hair a mismatched tangle.

I spotted her first and crouched down to get a better look. Dan leaned over and peered into her cage.

"Is that it?" he asked, first words I still needle him about, even to this day.

"I think so," I said, clicking my tongue and cooing through the bars at her. She gave no sign that she even knew we existed. No eye contact, no glance. Nothing.

We summoned the staff to let her out so we could hold her. They placed her in my arms. She was compliant but stiff. I remember looking around at the other shoppers as they solicited kisses and cuddles from the puppies they took into their arms. I felt a grip of doubt in my chest. But I had decided that a wheaten terrier was the breed we needed because I am, sadly, allergic to dogs, and wheatens are known to be hypoallergenic. With no littermates to comparison shop, it was this dog or nothing.

A saleswoman ushered us into a small stall, similar to a changing room in a clothing store. This is where the store lets prospective buyers interact with the puppies outside of their cages. I sat with this unfamiliar creature in my lap and tried unsuccessfully to engage her interest or her gaze. I set her paws to the floor so she could walk unfettered and stretch her legs after a day in her cage. She moaned and moaned and, after some skittish pacing, peed on the floor. Brilliant dog psychologist that I was, I assumed that she had moaned because she was actually housebroken and wanted to be taken outside to pee, expressing her frustration at having to soil the floor. I took this as a good omen. The saleswoman rushed in to clean up the mess.

After about an hour of watching her pace our little stall and wavering back and forth on what we knew was a life-altering decision, Dan and I decided to rip off the bandage and purchase her. For $1,000, they turned her over to us with just a zip of our credit card, no questions asked. They handed us a sheet of paper with the name and USDA license number of her breeder, along with a referral to a vet who would finish her vaccinations for free, and sent us on our way.

I clutched her close to my chest as we drove her home on that rainy winter evening, along with more equipment than seemed logical for a ten-pound puff of patchy hair. We'd done our research and had overzealously prepared a Great Dane–sized crate for her in our living room and resolutely planned to do our due diligence with the housebreaking process. We'd read that dogs love their crates and some return to them voluntarily to sleep for their entire lives. So we put her in her new home with some toys and a pretty, pink sleeping mat. Dan headed to bed, and I bundled up to catch my ride to my overnight shift at the *Today Show*.

It wasn't long before the text messages started. I was elbow-deep in scripts, assembling my news blocks in the bowels of Studio 1A at Rockefeller Plaza, trying to choose which stories our millions of viewers would wake up to that morning.

she sounds like a shofar

It was 2:00 a.m. I'd barely been gone an hour.

its so loud and sad

can i just let her out?

Already, we were failing as dog parents.

I texted back.

the books say not to let her out of the crate

she needs to learn to be self sufficient

or she's going to have separation anxiety forever

An hour passed. Nothing. I settled into my predawn routine, bouncing around the abandoned newsroom, preparing before my team's writers came in. I felt self-righteous: Dan had followed my instructions, the still-unnamed dog had self-soothed, and all was well. Puppyhood accomplished. This was going to be easy. Then came the 3:00 a.m. texts.

she hasn't stopped shofaring yet

i'm going in

Before I could even reply and warn him not to—again—the next text rolled in.

she's covered in her own shit

this is a nightmare

I blamed Dan. Maybe he didn't give her enough of a chance to do her business outside before bed. Maybe he fed her something he shouldn't have after I left. Surely once she was under my supervision after my night shift ended, these types of problems would be unthinkable.

I got home from the studio just before noon. Dan was off at work, having walked her before he left a couple of hours before. But sure enough, there she was, alone in her crate, cowering away from a small puddle of piss in the corner. I scooped her out and took her down to the street. She just looked down at the grass-free Brooklyn sidewalk and tried to yank her head out of her collar, pawing at it resolutely.

"Well?" I said.

She circled my legs, wrapping me up in her leash.

"Go," I said. "Make."

Nothing. The commands were meaningless. I thought dogs instinctively knew these things.

"Come on. Just go pee-pee."

She yanked forward on the leash, lunging to pick up a cigarette butt her in mouth. I jumped down to free it from her needle teeth. She chomped, leaving tiny bite marks in my hand. Frustrated, exhausted, and betrayed, I took her back inside. It was almost 1:00 p.m., my bedtime. I set her back in her crate and began powering down in the bedroom. With the curtains drawn and my eye mask on, I began the long, slow process of trying to sleep by day.

scratch scratch scratch scratch scratch

I sat up in bed.

scratch scratch scratch scratch scratch

I tiptoed to the bedroom door. She was clawing wildly at the base of her crate, trying to escape. Her bed was balled up in the corner—what had once been pink velvet now turned brown.

scratch scratch scratch scratch scratch

Once again, I freed her from the crate and hastened her to the bathtub to wash the parts of her feet that had plodded straight through her own shit. Her bed—barely twenty-four hours in our possession—went straight into the trash. The crate was a mess. I scrubbed at it as she ran, crazy-eyed and dripping wet, around our small apartment. Finally, the clock nearing 3:00 p.m., I gave her another fruitless walk in my pajamas and put her back in her crate with some old towels for a bed.

I slunk back to the bedroom and closed the door. Curtains closed, eye mask on, I began trying to sleep again.

scratch scratch scratch scratch scratch

I tried to sleep through it.

scratch scratch scratch scratch scratch

I couldn't. And it wasn't stopping.

scratch scratch scratch scratch scratch

I sprang back out into the living room, fearing another feces explosion. But there she was, just scratching away for the hell of it. I threw a blanket over the crate. I'd seen people do it with birdcages before. Maybe she'd think it was nighttime and go to sleep. It didn't work. This was no bird we were dealing with. This was a puppy on a mission to destroy me.

By the time Dan got home from work that night, I was crying on the living room floor as the puppy darted wildly around the apartment, pausing occasionally to shred a stack of magazines she'd stolen from the coffee table.

"She won't let me sleep!" I wailed. "She won't shut up, and I'll never get to sleep, and I won't be able to do my job, and I'm going to fall asleep at work, and I'm going to get fired, and this was a horrible mistake. We have to send her back."

By now, Dan's gotten used to my pronouncements—which is to say he knows to ignore 99 percent of them. But at the time, he was just my boyfriend, and we had moved in together only a few months earlier. That meant we were still early enough in our relationship for him to take me seriously. All he knew for certain was to be terrified of what would inevitably happen when I couldn't sleep between my shifts: full-on apocalyptic breakdowns.

"Send her back?" he asked. "To where?"

"Back to the store. Maybe they'll take her back!"

"We can't do that," he said, horrified.

"Then maybe we should take her to a shelter. She's cute enough. She'll find a good home," I said with the desperation of a junkie, willing to do anything to get my fix of sleep. "We can't keep her. What were we thinking? A puppy is such an overrated thing."

Dan rubbed his thumb and index finger against his forehead, trying not to lose it entirely.

"We wanted a dog," he said and sighed. "*You* wanted a dog. You wanted *this* dog, and here she is. And now you want to dump her?"

"But she's going to kill me," I screeched, my face hot and swollen as I cried. "And I don't love her. Aren't we supposed to love her?"

"She just got here," he said.

"Do *you* love her?"

"Well," he said, looking at the spiky-haired animal now learning quickly to be silent when there's wailing coming from the humans. "No. Not yet. I mean, what's to love?"

It's true. She was an ugly duckling. Her feathery hair poked out in a variety of wild browns and blacks. Her feet were ungainly on the ends of her wobbly spider legs. She did not make eye contact and hated being picked up or touched at all.

"I hate her," I said, assuming the fetal position on the floor to sob some more.

"No, you don't. You just don't love her. Yet."

With that, Dan mercifully ushered me off to bed and, with monk-like focus, tended to the dog, carrying her in and out of the apartment for frequent bathroom breaks so I wouldn't be awakened by her tiny, cacophonous claws on the hardwood floors.

So the dog stayed.

Within a few days, we settled on her name: Izzie. We named her after the elderly fishmonger at the Jewish deli my father would take me to on Sunday mornings when I was a child. He'd always sneak me a piece of fish or cheese over the glass when no one was looking. The name came to mind because we quickly noticed that this dog always wanted us to sneak her a treat while we ate—that and Izzie rhymes with "frizzy," which is one of her defining physical characteristics.

In the weeks that followed, my diurnal standoffs with Izzie took on a new rhythm. I'd come home from work in the morning and take her on a begrudging sleepwalk around Brooklyn. Occasionally, she'd mercifully reward my efforts by actually doing her business outside. Within a few weeks, she began making eye contact—at first only while she pooped. But when those eye contact–filled poops would happen in the street and not in our apartment, I would cheer out loud for her with delight, showing her how happy it made me to have her choose the sidewalk instead of my floor for this task. It was such a victory that I didn't even care about the strange looks I'd get from construction workers, gawking at the crazy lady in pajamas in the middle of the day, celebrating while her dog shat on the pavement.

I began dividing my daytime sleep into shifts to better meet her needs. After her morning walk, we'd nap for a few hours and wake around 5:00 p.m. to hit the postwork rush hour at the dog run where I'd let her romp unfettered for an hour or two and try not to fall asleep in public.

Izzie learned a lot from these daily trips to the dog run—more than I could ever teach her. She came to know her place in the pack and to understand that while at home, she may rule the roost, in public, she must defer to other dogs, people, and children with their tiny, fragile hands that may sometimes not know their own strength. She quickly learned not to bite and not to antagonize other dogs as, it seemed to me, the canine cast of characters in the park took on the instructive role that her litter-mates might have if she'd been allowed to remain with them into her later puppyhood.

People often compliment Dan and me for Izzie's now-friendly and loving demeanor and her ability to play so well with both children and other dogs. I can take no credit for her gentle nature, and I'm very up front with people when they seek training tips. In Izzie's early months with us, my focused attempts at training only confused her. The best thing I ever did for her, I believe, was showing up at that dog park every day, rain or shine, and letting her be free. Supervised, sure. But not micromanaged. Free to wrestle, play, and even earn a warning nip from an older, wiser dog when she got out of line.

These lessons thankfully have stood her in good stead through the years. To this day, when we encounter aggressive dogs that lunge at her on their leashes and bark in her face during our walks, she never responds in kind, knowing to continue prancing ahead without further engaging their ire. When children toddle up to her without warning to pet her before their parents can stop them and ask if she's friendly, she knows never to nip or startle. No thanks to any tutelage of mine, in all these years, Izzie has never bitten anyone—although with her breath being what it is, we know that her kisses are her best defense, the ultimate chemical weapon. She reserves her rage and her teeth for one thing and one thing alone: the nozzle of my vacuum cleaner, which is now dented and scarred from her wrath and my attempts to keep a passably clean house.

After the dog park, when my early evening second bedtime would arrive, I'd try and further my efforts to tire her out by having her chase a ball around the apartment or by trying to teach her a trick or two before tucking her into her crate. She'd wake me occasionally with her scratching or her soft moans, but with every passing day, she learned to sleep when I slept. Sometimes, she was so well behaved, I'd try and get her to cuddle in bed with me. Every time I tried, however, she'd rebuff my efforts and scuttle away to curl up by herself in a corner. So fine—she was independent. That, and I was certainly not her favorite. She seemed to know that on her first day at home with us, I'd tried to eject her from my Brooklyn love nest with Dan to return to the happy peace of our life *à deux*. When he was home, she tended to gravitate toward him, understanding that he had saved her from my capriciousness and the harsh world outside our door that first night.

After a few months of our new routine, I came home from work one morning to find Izzie quietly crying in the playpen we'd attached to her crate. It was unlike her. Usually, she would at least pop up and paw at the gate when I'd come home—not out of excitement or happiness but rather as a means of acknowledging my existence and an end to her brief but solitary confinement with only the sound of WNYC's Leonard Lopate to keep her company.

I drew closer to her and saw that there were small speckles of dried blood on her paws. I stepped cautiously into the playpen. She retreated into her crate. I tried to coax her toward me, even as she refused. I scratched her behind the ears and stroked her back, quietly cooing to her. Tentatively, she put one paw in front of the other and walked out of the crate and over to my lap. With a heavy puff, she sighed and laid her head—mouth open, tongue out, panting—onto my knee. There, inside, I could see that two tiny teeth were bent at near ninety-degree angles to her bleeding gums. They were ready to fall out in place of her adult teeth to come. She lay there, head voluntarily poised on my lap for the very first time, and waited for me to help. Carefully, knowing all too well her purposeful and sharp warning nips that it seemed she reserved only for me and not Dan, I worked my fingers into her mouth and gently jostled the teeth from their place and into the palm of my hand.

"You're okay," I whispered as she let me kiss the top of her head for the very first time. She smelled like my shampoo. Izzie whimpered, still frightened to find the tools she most trusted wobbling around impotent inside her. "See?"

I held out my hand and showed her the teeth. Her nose bobbed up and down on the end of her snout as she sniffed the things that had just come from inside her. And she stayed with me for what felt like a very long time.

Now, years later, our lives are intertwined, and I would sooner cut off my own hand than let her go. It's only taken half a decade—even longer in dog years—but finally, I've surpassed Dan in Izzie's eyes. I'm very proud to say that I'm her favorite now. Dan is only a little bitter about his reversal of fortune, accusing me of having Stockholmed her. But I sometimes have nightmares about those first days still and try, every day, to do penance for my terrible, early dog-parenting mistakes—for my willingness to toss her aside like a defective toy.

I wonder if Izzie remembers that day that she lost her first teeth. I wonder if somewhere in the back of her bestial brain, she sees that moment as the beginning of us too. I wonder if all the thousands of miles of walks, the hundreds of illicit snacks I've snuck her under the table, the hours I've slept holding her close in our bed have all been built on that first moment we learned to trust each other.

Five years after that first moment of bonding, our lives were beginning to look very different. Dan and I had married, and we'd long since packed our bags to move out west to Denver. Izzie was enjoying on-demand access to our fenced yard and the dog park at the lake at the end of the block. We were spending our summers hiking up fallow ski slopes as Izzie blazed ahead, traipsing through waves of wildflowers. I'd even managed to voice-train her to walk safely off leash as we'd romp through dense trees and creeks. Somehow, we'd turned our neurotic Brooklyn puppy into a confident, Colorado mountain dog.

But Dan and I were also gearing up for fertility treatments and preparing to make some of the most challenging personal, physical, and financial decisions of our life together. With just a few weeks to go before starting the IVF process, I started to feel sick. But sick in a different way than I ever had before.

It was January, and we were in Boca Raton, visiting Dan's grandparents, Ema and Zaida. Izzie was spread-eagle on the floor by Zaida's feet, sleeping off the kugel and salami we'd begged them not to feed her. Zaida could never help himself. *It's a Jewish dog!* he'd always exclaim in his thick accent, as if it were her birthright to enjoy large hunks of Hebrew National. He was born on a dairy farm in Poland before having to flee the war and so had always kept a lifelong soft spot for animals—especially Izzie. He loved to get her riled up and watch her scamper around, barking back at him until she would collapse beside him on a couch with her tongue flopped completely out of her mouth.

Dan and I were bumming around on the couch, watching daytime TV blasting at elderly-person volume levels, also trying to sleep off the haze of kugel and salami on a balmy Floridian afternoon. I texted Dan as he was sitting next to me so no one else would know.

pharmacy run?

we should get a test

Dan just looked at me, puzzled. I shrugged. Worst came to

worst, it would break our lazy spell and get us out of the house into the fresh air for the first time that day.

Off we went, certain we'd be wrong, certain it was impossible. We bought a box of tests, and I hustled off to the bathroom to take the first one alone. I thought it would be so obvious, so black-and-white. But when the timer ran out and the answer was right there in front of me, I didn't understand. I held it to the light. There it was, barely visible on the tiny white window, the faintest pink line I'd ever seen. I ran to get Dan, my face giving nothing away as I didn't even know what it meant. We locked ourselves in the bathroom and squinted at the stick. *Could this really count?* I took three more immediately, all with the same ambiguous result.

"There would be no second line there at all if it were negative," he said, using the special voice he has when discussing matters of science, as if his abandoned premed track in college means that he has special expertise in the workings of pregnancy tests.

"But it's barely there. Like, you have to squint and hold it to the light to see it."

"Barely there is still there. There's a line there. That's a positive test."

I made him vow not to tell Ema and Zaida. I didn't want to break their hearts when this inevitably failed. This was just a line, not a baby.

But with the dozens of tests I repeated in the coming days and weeks at a frenzied pace, that faint pink line got darker and darker. My head was spinning. Most days, I repeated it several times a day. Each time, that second line got darker, and presumably, I got more pregnant. It couldn't be. Me, IVF clinic reject, pregnant? We told no one and began the hunt for an obstetrician.

We rescheduled our appointments with the fertility clinic, pushing them back by a month or two, sure we'd still have to go anyway when this whole pregnancy thing inevitably fell through.

But it didn't. The pregnancy stuck, and every day that passed, I breathed just a tiny bit easier that I might go the distance on this thing. It helped that the obstetrician we ultimately found was more of a prenatal cheerleader than a doctor.

"Wow! How cool is that?" he exclaimed at my first ultrasound to confirm the pregnancy, only six weeks along. With three decades of delivering babies under his belt, he still gushed like it was the very first blurry dot on a sonogram he'd ever seen in his career. I was vulnerable and scared enough to buy it. "That right there is textbook. That's exactly how we want it to look. Amazing!"

But despite my doctor's confidence, I couldn't fully shake my certainty that I shouldn't get my hopes up. We were told this was impossible by some of the most respected experts in their field. So why should we dare to doubt them?

"Can we, you know, tell anyone?" I asked the doctor, hoping a new professional opinion could banish the fears imposed by those from the very recent past.

"Yes," he said warmly. "Go tell your families."

We packed our bags and Izzie's too and booked a trip back to our hometown of Philadelphia to see our families and tell them in person. But how could we tell them?

We've all seen the viral videos of pregnancy announcements or the maternity photo shoots. In them, the woman always looks so confident holding her belly, so sure that everything is going to be just fine and that there will be a baby in her arms at the end of the journey. That wasn't me. We'd been to so many doctors and had had so many disappointments. The whole thing felt unreal.

It didn't feel honest to talk about this invisible force inside of me like it was going to become a person at the end of nine months. It wasn't a baby. It wasn't a little boy or a little girl. It wasn't even a fetus yet. It just was an idea, and a crazy one at that. Something I couldn't see or touch. Something too fragile to be real. To even utter the possibility now flowing into our lives filled me with terror, as if it could end everything we were hoping would be real and permanent and life-altering. I didn't have it in me at this point to say the words *I'm pregnant*. I couldn't even say those words to myself.

On the ground in Philadelphia, I gathered my parents in the formal living room they never use.

"Izzie has a new trick she wants to show you," I said, two heartbeats inside of me but only mine pounding loud enough to throb in my ears.

"That dog can barely give a paw," my mother said, already bored by the prospect of having to pay Izzie any more attention than she already does. She likes Izzie well enough but finds our love of the dog indulgent, excessive, and annoying—at best.

"Well, this is a new trick, and I think you'll really like it," I promised, not having anticipated resistance. "Hang on. I gotta get the prop."

"Props?" my mother wailed. "This trick has props? Kill me now."

I ran off to put on Izzie's tiny T-shirt, custom fit to her long, skinny body. She looked at me skeptically. She hates wearing anything, even a leash.

"Just for a minute," I promised, kissing her between the eyes for reassurance, then sending her back into the living room.

She came scurrying out across the slippery wood floors like a cockroach, tucking her tail, fighting the shirt on her back.

"What's it say?" my parents asked, leaning in for a closer look at the writing on the shirt. "*Shhhh, I have a secret. Rub my tummy to find out*," they read in near-perfect unison.

Dan and I exchanged nervous glances.

They complied and bent down to give Izzie the most important belly rub of our lives. She rolled onto her back, and there it was, written on the front of the shirt: *I'm going to be a big sister!*

My dad looked at me with terror. "You're getting *another* dog?"

We'd actually expected that that's what they'd guess first—that says a lot about us, perhaps.

"No," my mom said, her eyes welling up. Then she started screaming, the happiest sound I've ever heard from her.

I pulled the blurry ultrasound picture from my pocket.

"Really?" she asked, her voice begging it to be true.

"Did you do this all by yourself?" my dad asked.

"Well, Dan helped." I shrugged.

But he was really asking if we'd somehow snuck in a round of IVF without updating them that we'd gone through it. We told him we hadn't, not that it mattered. Now, as improbable as it was, we just had to hope it would stick.

After the crying and hugging and several other rather impertinent questions, my mother gave Izzie—now freed from the bonds of her T-shirt—a loving rub on the head.

"That was a very good trick, Izzie. Your best yet," she said. "But once baby comes, just you wait. They're going to forget all about you!"

Impossible. Baby or no baby, Izzie is irreplaceable, and our bond is unique among all others in my life. As I grow with the baby inside of me, it becomes very clear to me: Izzie is not our child. But that doesn't mean we love her less or will forget about her when the baby comes, because a baby cannot take her place. Izzie is a silent sister, a loyal friend, as much a part of me as a limb.

The counting in weeks becomes counting in months and then trimesters. Soon enough, I don't need to learn to utter the words *I'm pregnant*; my body tells people for me. My daily five-mile hikes with Izzie get whittled down to four, then three, then slow waddles around the block. Where she used to mush ahead, dragging me through the streets by her supposedly antipull harness, now she walks by my side, glancing up at me frequently as we go. As much as I've changed with this pregnancy, so has she, it seems.

But for all the surprise and joy at finding we were pregnant in the first place, the challenges with making it through have become a way of life. Every night, I wake at 3:00 a.m. and can't get back to sleep. Izzie hears me stirring and yawns from her bed on the other side of the room. She knows what I'm thinking in the silent darkness. I grab my iPad and pillow and waddle out of bed. She's waiting for me. I open the door, and she's off, scanning the halls, clearing the way like a celebrity bodyguard as we decamp to the guest room.

In the quiet of our own private bedroom, with no fear of disturbing my sleeping husband, we toss and turn and make Netflix really earn that monthly subscription fee, binge-watching whatever appeals to us until we can pass out. If I get lucky enough to fall asleep first, Izzie slinks to the foot of the bed so that her violent jerks and jabs when dreaming don't whack me in the face or belly.

When you're pregnant and you're notorious among family and friends for letting your dog be the center of your world, people like to ask: *Is the dog getting jealous yet?* My own mother, visiting us just a couple of months before my due date, looks at Izzie yet again with pitying eyes.

"You are going to be so lonely," she coos, cradling Izzie's crusty muzzle in her hands. "They're going to forget all about you."

Other mothers like to recount stories of how their dogs reacted to their pregnancies, either growing protective or envious. One neighborhood mom tells me how her beloved Lab lunged at her newborn with rage in its eyes when she brought her eldest daughter home from the hospital. She had to give the dog up to childless relatives in another city after the incident. My sister-in-law gives us a book on how to prepare the dog for the baby so that everyone is safe and happy. But paging through it, all I find are horror stories of the worst possible scenarios: the toddler who stuck his hand in the dog's bowl and nearly lost it when the territorial creature bit down in retaliation.

So far, I'm not worried about Izzie. She's always loved children—perhaps too much. She's got a nasty habit of darting across the street when she hears one of my neighbor's little girls calling her name. She stares deep into their eyes and leans against their unstable toddler frames as they pet her and try to grab at her frenetic nub of a tail. My pregnancy doesn't factor into much of Izzie's daily routine. She hasn't grown more needy or more protective. She's not withdrawn, sullen, or jealous. If there's any change, she seems only to be more patient and deferential—a shocking transformation from a fiercely independent beast like she is. Well, and maybe she's gotten a little lazy now that we've dramatically downsized our daily hikes.

But there is one thing that has become suddenly apparent to us as we confront our futures with the permanent and awe-inspiring responsibility ahead of us. If everything goes according to the natural order, we will be parents to this baby for the rest of our lives. There will never come a day that we have to live when our child does not. We will perhaps be gone as this baby, once grown, moves forward with a life and new family without us.

But to have a dog is to know and anticipate a different kind of sadness and longing. It means knowing that, in all likelihood, we will have to live without Izzie one day. We will have to watch how time moves mercilessly faster for her than for us, her spark fading and her health declining until we bear witness as she leaves this world. She's the only dog we've ever known. With this pregnancy, the fact that one day we will have to part with her suddenly becomes reality in a way I had never before considered. It's as if until now, we've been living in a fantasy world where she's going to be around forever—our unchangeable little family unit.

While other mothers might imagine their child's first day at school or first time riding a bike, I imagine the day our little one will start bonding with Izzie. When we learn that this baby is going to be a boy, the picture gets clearer. I see our son taking his first steps with one hand on her back for balance. I can see them running through the neighborhood, chasing after the local chicken that roams up and down the block, and seeking grand adventures that I will never be a part of. It fills me with both joy and sadness to think that then, Izzie won't be my dog anymore; she will belong to my son, and she will love him more than anything else until the day she is gone. I can only hope she stays for many years, long enough to find a permanent place in his memory and his imagination, so that he will always remember her with as much love as I will. And maybe that's how she will live on forever: eternally joyful and free in our son's happiest, earliest, safest memories.

But for now, Izzie is still here. She's lying between Dan and me in the bed, her back pressed to my giant belly. I feel myself losing my grip as I look at her sleeping on her own paws.

"Someone should have warned me," I tell my husband, trying desperately not to cry. "No one told me that I shouldn't let myself love her so much."

"Too late," he says.

CHAPTER ELEVEN

We Can't Ignore the Doggie in the Window

IT'S A SINGSONG TUNE WE ALL KNOW: A LILTING VOICE delivering the simple story of a woman in a pet shop seeking a dog to keep her lover company as she travels to California. "How much is that doggie in the window?" Patti Page asks in her now-classic 1952 novelty tune as dogs pleasantly yapped to the beat. It was an undeniable hit, selling two million copies and spurring a spike in registrations for the American Kennel Club.

Today, the song's innocent tone describing a visit to the friendly neighborhood pet shop rings false. So much so that even Patti Page changed her tune. In 2008, she teamed up with the Humane Society to record a new version of the hit, called "Do You See that Doggie in the Shelter?" Instead of inquiring after the "one with the waggly tail," now Page asked for "the one with the take-me-home eyes."

She explained her reason for distancing herself from her most famous hit song more than half a century after it climbed to the top of the charts.

"At the time, 'Doggie in the Window' seemed like a sweet and harmless message, and everyone still thought the corner pet store was just a place to see adorable puppies. And now the puppies in pet stores may still be adorable, but most of them come from puppy mills. I'd never heard before of pet stores having mass breeding places or anything like that. I was just as surprised as I'm sure most people are now," Page said in a video, interspersed with B-roll of terrified dogs in puppy mills. "The original song asks the question 'How much is that doggie in the window?' Today, the answer is 'too much.' And I don't just mean the price tag on the puppies in pet stores. The real cost is in the suffering of the mother dogs back at the puppy mill. That's where most pet store puppies come from. And that kind of cruelty is too high a price to pay."[1]

It's been nearly a decade now since Page officially distanced herself from the original message of the song. She passed away in 2013. But the connection between puppy mills and pet stores has become increasingly understood by the general public thanks, in no small part, to public relations efforts like the Humane Society's work with Page and similar initiatives across the animal welfare advocacy community. However, people—myself shamefully included—continue to buy these animals. Otherwise compassionate, smart, informed people, many of whom would be quick to say they are animal lovers, are still able to mentally distance themselves from the truth of where these dogs are born.

So why is it that we still can't ignore that doggie in the window?

"An adorable puppy is its parent's worst nightmare," Tim Rickey tells me. He's the head of the ASPCA's field investigations team and has shut down hundreds of illegal puppy mills during his long career. You've probably even seen him yourself on the organization's late-night infomercials, scooping dogs out of filth and cradling them against his ASPCA T-shirt as the announcer calls for donations. And while there's no doubt that irresponsible breeding is central to the puppy mill problem, the demand and interest created on the retail side has been keeping these facilities in operation for years.

"When you walk into a pet store and see a cute puppy or a kitten in a cage, it's very hard not to want to take that pet home. There's a very magnetic force when you're staring in the eyes of a ten-week-old puppy. People don't think beyond that. That's one of the central points: the retailers are really helping this industry," Rickey explains.

No demand, no reason to supply.

He recounts to me a recent raid that his team led in Michigan where he discovered wire crates stacked one on top of the other in a dank basement. Bulldogs weighing fifty pounds were crammed into these tiny cages with no room even to move, let alone exercise or glimpse the outside world. In another room nearby, he spotted all the puppies separated out. They were freshly groomed and bathed—ready to go to a pet store, a broker, or a loving and unwitting home that very day, the dark secrets of their birth shampooed away.

"We're looking at adult animals that are living in filthy, disgusting conditions. And we're looking at the puppies that were probably going out that day. You see the difference. They pulled these puppies away from the mothers...and prepared them for the public. People see a beautiful, healthy puppy, and they never think about the conditions that the parents were living in," Rickey says.

To better understand why people are able to purchase dogs they likely know come from inhumane breeding operations, I speak to Russell Belk, distinguished research professor of marketing at York University. He has written extensively about the psychology of ownership, particularly as it relates to humans and their canine companions. Additionally, as a world-renowned expert on consumer behavior, he has a uniquely academic perspective on why puppies fall into an ethical blind spot once they are made available in a retail setting.

"By the time the dog or cat is ready to sell, it is already responding to humans," Belk explains. "It's already jumping up from the cage and saying, in effect, *Take me, take me, choose me, choose me.*"[2]

While they may not have Belk's academic credentials, pet shop salespeople implicitly understand more than you'd think about consumer behavior and psychology.

"There's something called the *endowment effect:* that if we give people something—be it a sample product or a test-drive in a car—the mere fact that they've touched it and held it makes them more attached to it and less willing to give it up. That's a trick that salespeople know," Belk explains.

As a result, the customer who casually walks into a pet shop, thinking he is there only to look and not purchase anything, may find himself on the business end of the endowment effect. Now that he's seen and interacted with a puppy, he's going to want to take it home—better judgment and awareness of the puppy mill problem be damned. When the pet shop offered Dan and I an area where we could interact with Izzie out of her cage, hold her, and pet her, we were unwittingly experiencing this effect in action. This effect also explains why many people are unwilling to part with dogs they've purchased from a pet store that are later found to be sick. Once the dog is in our home for even a short time, Belk says, the animal has become an extension of our self.

"The real bonding and incorporation into our identity is what takes place after we acquire the pet," Belk says. "Initially, it's a matter of indifference—or almost indifference—whether one puppy or another in a litter is the one that goes home with us. But after even just a couple of weeks, that's not the case, because we've started to bond with the animal. We've given it a name. We've fed it, we've begun to train it, and in doing those things, we're putting our mark on it, and it's putting its mark on us with its personality and its smile—if you will—and its response to us. The bonding that takes place after acquisition is probably when we most fully incorporate that animal into our sense of self."

If a dog is purchased from a responsible breeder or from otherwise humane conditions, there should be no problem with the bonding that takes place once everyone is home safe and sound. However, Belk points out, people are more likely to make an impulse purchase of a dog at a pet shop than they would with a breeder, given the amount of time and research the latter process typically involves. As a result, the buyer in the pet store is going to be more likely to find himself emotionally intertwined with, at worst, a sick dog and, at best, a dog sourced from undesirable conditions.

Either way, a puppy is a puppy, and the human psychological response to it is undeniable, no matter where it comes from—and that is part of the danger.

"There may be some specificity to the person that is more susceptible to it. But puppies and kittens, like human babies, have these neonatal features. They have relatively big eyes and relatively big heads compared to the size of their bodies. That makes them cute. That's why we take these same characteristics and put them on cartoon animals," Belk says. "This is, if you will, maybe an evolutionary trait: we take care of baby animals. And humans have to take care of our babies for a long period of time compared to other animals. Partly because they endear themselves in this way from the moment of birth."

Once attached, the human-canine bond can seem unbreakable. It's enough, even, that people can emotionally distance themselves from the truth of their dog's unseemly origin. As the dog becomes an extension of our family and our self, it becomes harder and harder to see the reality.

"Unless [the dog] has some kind of a physical mark—it's limping, or it has an injury that it carries through life—that stigma attached to acquiring it begins to disappear," Belk explains. "There may be a bit of [the pet shop stigma] that clings and doesn't disappear, but for the most part, it gives way to the interactions with the animal and its personality—how it interacts with the family. It does, for the most part, become a family member and gets treated to birthdays and Christmas gifts and perhaps a funeral when it dies. So that context of acquisition ultimately fades into the background."

This effect is so powerful that, surprisingly enough, even animal welfare advocates can fall victim to it. And thanks to the internet, people can now engage with these animals without ever setting foot in a pet shop.

The ASPCA's Tim Rickey has seen lifelong animal lovers allow themselves to be duped by the allure of a cute puppy with an ugly provenance. He recalls a colleague in the animal welfare profession telling him about a puppy his wife had bought from a breeder she found online. The breeder offered to meet her halfway between their homes given that they lived four hours apart. Rickey was floored at what he was hearing from his fellow animal welfare advocate, who should certainly have known better.

"I said, 'You realize that's a strategy within the puppy mill industry?'" Rickey recalls, shocked that his colleague hadn't realized the breeder was trying to keep him from seeing the conditions into which this puppy had been born. "He'd never connected that. He just thought the breeders were being very nice."

But the fact that even animal welfare advocates are able to overlook the true origins of a seemingly perfect puppy speaks to the power of the connection between the buyer and a dog for sale.

"A majority of the public has not really made this connection which is, if you are going to buy an animal from someone breeding it, you should see where that animal is and make sure it's not a puppy mill. But they want to believe people because they've already fallen in love with the animal," Rickey says. "They're already in love and emotionally bonded, and they want that pet. So, oftentimes, the rational thought they might have if they weren't dealing with such a highly emotional issue is gone. They're focused on getting the pet instead of taking a step back and saying, 'I'll drive the other two hours because I want to come visit your facility and see where this animal was born and see how the parents are being taken care of.'"

So how did we get to where we are today? Whose bright idea was it to put the doggie in the window in the first place, so far from the context of its birth?

Most in the industry credit the now-defunct Docktor Pet Centers with spurring the explosion of the commercial dog-breeding industry as we know it today. With more than three hundred stores across the country at its height in the 1980s, Docktor was more than three times larger than Petland, currently the biggest brick-and-mortar retail pet seller in the nation—the other large pet stores like Petco and PetSmart have committed to not selling dogs but rather to hosting adoption events.

Starting in the 1960s, Milton Docktor sought to make his business boom.

"He hired all these MBAs to come in and help…and what they quickly pointed out to him is, as in any business, you need to draw people into your store if you want to sell something. They felt that by selling puppies—putting puppies in the store-front window—you were attracting people into your store," Bob Baker of the Missouri Alliance for Animal Legislation tells me. "People would be walking by the store window, and they would see the cute little puppy and walk in. They quickly realized that once that customer came in the store, they could then sell them pet products. So then there was a demand for these puppies, and that demand grew because they realized that when you made that puppy sale, not only did you make money from selling that puppy, but also you had totally a ready-made market for pet supplies."[3]

Baker recalls reviewing the old Docktor Pet Centers training manuals and finding that salespeople were expected to bring in as much money on pet supplies as they did on the initial cost of the dog itself.

"[Docktor] realized the profitability of selling dogs mostly as an attraction just to get you in the store. But then, later on, [he realized] the profit of selling that dog: you need feed for the dog, you need a leash for the dog, you need a collar, you need a bed. You can just sell so much more with that dog, and it really took off," Baker says.

But puppies have to come from somewhere. And if you're sourcing a supply chain for Docktor Pet Centers' hundreds of franchisees across the country, just like any cost-savvy business, you're going to go for mass production at low prices. Unfortunately for the puppies, responsible breeders didn't fit the bill for Docktor.

"When they went to the responsible breeders, they had two problems. One, the price was way too high for [Docktor's] profit margins," Baker says. "They also had the problem that...no responsible breeder would ever sell a dog in a pet store. Most responsible breeders, they've spent a lot of time raising that dog. They want to make sure it goes into a good home... A good breeder wants their dogs well socialized and doesn't want them stuck in a cage while they are waiting to be sold: that would be anathema to a good dog breeder. They also don't want them coming into contact with other dogs at such a young age. Dogs are very susceptible to disease at that young age. Their immune system doesn't fully develop at that point in time. They would never risk putting their dogs into a pet store environment, where these dogs are going to come in contact with randomly sourced dogs from all over the country."

But just how do these "randomly sourced dogs from all over the country" end up in pet stores? The key element is often the broker: a middleman or a company that is licensed by the USDA and is tasked with buying these puppies from breeders and transporting them to wholesale at pet shops. Today, the nation's largest broker is the Hunte Corporation.

Founded in 1991, the Hunte Corporation operates by the motto *Where puppies come first!* But today, they primarily do business under the name Choice Puppies after exposés from animal advocate groups irrevocably tarnished the Hunte name. It's not surprising that the company would rebrand itself after a 2009 investigation from a Missouri advocacy group revealed that Hunte was dumping hundreds of pounds of dead puppies monthly—enough that the organization called for the Missouri Department of Natural Resources to intervene.[4]

The Hunte Corporation is based in a sprawling 130,000-square-foot facility in southwest Missouri. The company buys up puppies across the heartland from breeders both large and small and then ships them primarily by tractor-trailer to pet shops, typically in big cities across the nation. Many animal welfare advocates agree that the reason puppy mills are so concentrated in the Midwest and in particular Missouri is because of Hunte: the company keeps breeders in business with a steady demand for their dogs.

Naturally, I wanted to learn more about the Hunte Corporation given its central role in connecting pet shops to breeders. I reached out to former Hunte President and CEO Ryan Boyle over the course of nearly a year until he quietly left the company after a fourteen-year tenure in July 2016. My requests for an interview were never answered. I also attempted to reach the company through its frequent ally, farmers' advocacy group Protect the Harvest, as well as through its contact portal—all to no avail.

With no answers from Hunte, I turned to the Humane Society to get a better picture of this puppy brokering behemoth. For starters, I wanted to know exactly how many puppies Hunte transports every year.

The animal advocacy group had successfully obtained Hunte's most recent USDA license renewal applications through a FOIA request. The Humane Society's John Goodwin provided them to me, along with the company's license renewal applications from over a decade ago by way of comparison. These numbers tell a story.

Hunte, the nation's largest broker, wholesaler, and transporter of puppies for sale, is the bellwether for the dog-selling industry. Keep in mind: in 2005, there were few, if any, restrictions on who pet shops could purchase from. Today, there are pet shop restrictions or bans in the state of California and in two hundred municipalities and counting. By contrasting Hunte's numbers from 2005 to 2015, it's clear to see just how effective pet store bans and ordinances restricting purchases from breeders with violations on their USDA inspection reports have been on reining in this industry.

Let's take a look.

In 2005, the Hunte Corporation sold 88,235 puppies. By 2008, it had dropped somewhat to 72,890.

These earlier license renewal forms do not go into much detail on the company's earnings from these puppy sales—an omission that went on to be corrected in more recent forms. Instead, Hunte simply lists its "total gross dollar amount derived from regulated activities" as being over $100,000—certainly an understatement to say the least, as we can be sure these puppies were not selling for just over a dollar apiece.

But by 2013, as more states began regulating which breeders pet shops could purchase from and more municipalities banned pet shops from selling puppies that were not obtained from a rescue, Hunte Corporation had started to feel the pinch. In just five years, the company's number of reported puppies sold had dropped by half, down from 72,890 in 2008 to 37,247 puppies sold in 2013. Also in 2013, the company began reporting a more accurate figure for the total gross amount earned from selling these puppies. In 2013, those 37,247 puppies brought in $16,823,283 to the Hunte Corporation.

In the years that followed, the numbers kept dropping.

In 2015, the company sold 34,038 puppies. But this time, the Hunte Corporation made significantly less money in doing so: $12,330,147. These dipping figures show that the average price per puppy that Hunte was able to command when selling to retailers dropped from being around $450 in 2013 to around $362 by 2015 as the market thinned out.

These numbers speak volumes. First, they show that local and state ordinances restricting or banning the sale of puppies in retail establishments have a very real impact on commercial breeders and the brokers that keep them up and running. Second, the numbers show that the value of a commercially bred puppy is dropping—which suggests to me that consumers are getting the message that's being tirelessly trumpeted by the ASPCA, the Humane Society, and others that a pet shop dog is not worth the money and they would be just as happy with a shelter dog. While animal welfare advocates see this as a win, the pet industry is not surprisingly crying foul.

"I think pet retail bans, in general, are an emotional response and unfortunately an ineffective response to an acknowledged problem, which is illegal, irresponsible breeding," Mike Bober, president and CEO of the Pet Industry Joint Advisory Council (PIJAC) tells me.[5] His Washington, DC–based organization acts as the representative and lobbyist for pet stores, animal distributors, and pet product manufacturers—including Hunte. PIJAC has been vocal about its efforts over the years to raise the standard of care at USDA-licensed breeding facilities and has also published animal care guidelines for pet retailers, which are not required to be inspected by the USDA each year.

But most animal welfare groups are wary of PIJAC because the organization works to protect the existence of retail pet stores as well as their supply chain. To wit, in 2015, PIJAC bestowed upon Hunte's late founder Andrew Hunte its "Vision Award." For what it's worth, I also asked Bober if he could connect me with the Hunte Corporation for an interview. He never followed through on this request despite seeming amenable to doing so in our conversation and despite my follow-up attempts to spur him into action.

But when I spoke to Bober, I asked him why we even need retail pet stores at all. Why can't consumers just adopt dogs and use pet shops for the supplies they will inevitably need? After all, the pet supply business is nothing to sneeze at: we spent $66.75 billion on feeding, clothing, entertaining, and caring for our animals in 2016 according to the American Pet Products Association (APPA).[6] That's billion—with a B. And by the way, those numbers are on the rise even as an increasing number of municipalities restrict the sale of puppies and cut into the profits of breeders and brokers like the Hunte Corporation. Since 2005, our spending on our pets has nearly doubled. But of that nearly $67 billion, only $2.1 billion went to "live animal purchases" according to the APPA—a number that includes all pet purchases, including cats, rabbits, hamsters, fish, lizards, and so on. So surely pet shops could more than stay afloat without selling dogs—or any live animals for that matter.

Bober doesn't think so.

"Pet shops are actually more important to the public than [they are] to the industry." Bober tells me. "I think that one of the key elements of lifelong relationships with pets is finding the ideal companion animal for your particular situation right off the bat rather than having a couple of false starts or, you know, looking for whatever happens to be available. You really owe it to yourself and any animal that you're going to bring into your home to do the research and to identify the best animal for your situation. One of the things that retail pet stores offer is the ability to connect the individuals with breeders to whom they may not otherwise be able to connect, based on either geographic disparity or economic inability to travel to meet the breeder in person. This can be a real limiting factor for lower-income families, as well as families that have very specific needs due to things like allergies. So we feel that pet choice, which is enhanced through the existence of retail pet stores, really is an important part of helping people find that ideal companion animal."

Not only does Bober see retail pet stores as vital to consumers, but he also sees them as necessary to support the USDA-licensed breeders over the illegal bad actors.

"The illegal breeders out there—those who should be licensed but actively flout the existence of federal law—they are the problem that we all need to work to address," Bober says. "Passing a ban on retail sales in a jurisdiction doesn't do anything to do that. It's an emotional response to a legitimate problem, but it doesn't do anything to advance the solution."

I see Bober's point here, and I certainly agree that a black-market puppy trade would be a terrible thing. However, his thinking on the bans on the retail pet shops assumes that dogs purchased from USDA-licensed facilities are being treated humanely. His reasoning is sound if the USDA is adequately enforcing regulations that actually account for the unique needs of these animals we love so much that we lavish billions on them annually.

The trouble is, the USDA is not holding up its end of the bargain.

THE DOGGIE IN THE BROWSER WINDOW

Until 2013, if a breeder sold his dogs online, he did not need to be licensed by the USDA. Consider this fact for just a moment. Until very recently—long after internet commerce was well established—breeders could operate online with no government oversight whatsoever. How? By claiming they were retail pet shops.

When the exemption from retail pet stores from USDA licensure was first created more than forty years ago, the agriculture agency envisioned it applying to brick-and-mortar pet shops or hobby breeders selling directly from their homes or farms. In a fact sheet published by the USDA, the agency explains its original reasoning: "Such establishments were not regulated under the [Animal Welfare Act] because it was assumed that customers were providing public oversight."

Because of this exemption, depending on where you live, your mall's local pet store selling puppies likely holds a business license and needs to stay up to code with the Health Department—not the federal government.

While it's easy to find fault with the Animal Welfare Act's minimal regulations that the USDA does impose upon its licensees, it's even easier to find fault with the fact that breeders selling online were legally exempted from any USDA oversight at all.

Before the rise of the web, breeders were able to sell dogs directly to individual customers via ads in newspapers and magazines and achieve that retail pet store exemption. This, of course, didn't guarantee humane treatment but at least was on a much smaller scale than the internet now facilitates. But as Sara Amundson, executive director of the Humane Society Legislative Fund, tells me with a wry laugh, she's been fighting to end this retail pet store exemption since long before Al Gore invented the internet. However, time and time again, animal welfare advocates were unable to do so. You can hardly blame breeders for taking advantage of the gaping loophole to licensure the internet provides: it was just too good to ignore. By 2010, 80 percent of the worst breeders in the country were those who were freely going unlicensed thanks to this exemption, according to the USDA's own internal investigation.[7]

Before the rise of e-commerce, breeders had been forced to rely on pet shops and brokers like the Hunte Corporation to handle wide distribution. Through the web, dogs could be shipped—for a fee paid by the buyer—unaccompanied on a crate in a plane's cargo hold, and the buyer could then head to his local airport and pick up his brand-new pup. All this without ever meeting a breeder face-to-face, checking out the dog for sale in person, or seeing the place where it was born and bred.

Brick-and-mortar pet shops, already becoming sullied by their reputation as the end point for puppy mills, were no longer even necessary in the puppy purchase transaction. Suddenly, the doggie in the window became the doggie in the internet browser window. And like most things we buy online, there was no guarantee that the dog you clicked on to purchase was, in fact, the dog that you would receive. After all, a beautifully composed stock image of Pomeranian puppies cuddling their mother in a velvet-lined wicker basket is a much easier sell than the real puppies that are actually being offered: traumatized, miserable dogs clinging to each other in a wire cage, their exhausted mother covered in sores and excrement. Now, there was no need to even bother obscuring the truth, because as we all know, on the internet, the truth can be so easily replaced with fantasy.

For years, online sales grew virtually unabated and entirely

unregulated by the USDA. New websites launched to aggre-
gate available puppies for hungry buyers: NextDayPets.com,
PuppyFind.com, MyLittlePuppy.com, to name a few. These
aggregator sites, which effectively operate as brokers, remain
largely unregulated by the USDA to this day.

"By gosh, every one of those [aggregator] websites should be
turned in to the USDA, because they are brokers and they should
be licensed—no ifs, ands, or buts. It is that simple," Amundson of
the Humane Society Legislative Fund says of this ongoing problem.[8]

While of course there could have been responsible breeders
posting on these sites, there was no one to ensure that that was
the case in an official capacity. Finally, in 2013, the USDA was
forced to contend with the issue of online pet sales. At that point,
the USDA revised its definition of what constituted a retail pet
store to exclude anyone selling puppies "sight unseen" to buyers.
Now, to qualify for the exemption from being USDA licensed
as a breeder, three parties must meet in person for every sale: the
buyer, the seller, and the dog. Anything less, and the seller must
obtain a USDA license and undergo routine inspections.

This clarification of what exactly defines a retail pet store was
the most recent change to the Animal Welfare Act concerning
commercial dog breeding, and it did not even require an amendment. Instead, it required Secretary of Agriculture Tom Vilsack
under President Obama to agree to the revision. That's it. Simple
enough, right? Well, not quite.

Amundson says that animal welfare advocates began the battle
to make this change as early as 1997 when the Doris Day Animal
League, a nonprofit now absorbed into the Humane Society,
submitted a petition to the USDA to change the definition of
what constitutes a retail pet store. The secretary of agriculture

at that time, Dan Glickman, declined to change the definition, prompting the Doris Day Animal League to lead the charge up through the nation's judicial system until it landed in the U.S. Supreme Court in late 2002.

In the landmark case *Doris Day Animal League v. Veneman,* the organization fought for then-Secretary of Agriculture Ann Veneman to specifically remove the exemption from any breeder claiming his residence as a pet store. Given that so many breeders live on the property where they work, much as traditional family farmers once did, this change could have had massive implications for the industry.

"The secretary of agriculture had absolute discretion to make a decision to proactively cover those folks on the basis of that retail pet store exemption being written into regulation. It did not require amending the [Animal Welfare Act]. What it did require was a secretary of ag with the will to make that happen," says Amundson, who was working for the Doris Day Animal League during the Supreme Court case.

When the decision came down in early 2003, the Supreme Court allowed the exemption to continue, explaining that the Animal Welfare Act never defines what exactly constitutes a store.

"One usually thinks of a store as a business open to the public and engaged in the sale of goods. But not all stores are open to the public, and not all stores are located in shopping malls or other typical business locations," the decision reads.[9]

With this reasoning handed down from the Supreme Court, it's easy to see how the exemption was allowed to apply to internet sales of dogs for so many years. Although the decision in this case did not specifically mention the internet at all, it did offer one window of hope for animal welfare advocates by reiterating that

the secretary of agriculture has the power to change the definition of a term appearing in the Animal Welfare Act—a power
that the secretary of agriculture at that time, Veneman, declined
to use, citing a lack of resources for what would be a large uptick
in enforcement efforts. The court found the secretary's decision
to focus the agency's resources on wholesale breeding facilities
instead of these other sellers claiming the retail pet store exemption to be in "the best interest of animal welfare."[10]

But even though the Doris Day Animal League did not win
this battle, Amundson saw the hidden opportunity in the decision.
Now she just had to find a secretary of agriculture willing to make
the change.

"We sort of went administration by administration, trying
to make the case that we needed to rally the resources in order
to realize the merits of the case. But that's tough. And it really
was not until serious discussions with the Obama administration
where they said, we may not have 100 percent, we may not have
75 percent, but if we don't start somewhere, we're not going to
be in a position to ever tackle this issue," Amundson says of the
nearly twenty-year journey to change the retail pet store definition. "It's always going to be an excuse that we just don't have the
resources. So [the Obama administration] took a leap of faith to
a certain degree and just made a decision that they were going to
start to regulate these folks. It may be that the [USDA] only had
so many dollars that could be allocated to that function, but at
least they were going to honor the merits of that case."

The effect of this change cannot be understated.

With this new rule finally in place, if a breeder was selling dogs
online without the buyer physically present, he now had to get a
license, keep his facility up to snuff with the USDA, and submit

his facility to unannounced inspections just like everyone else. Brick-and-mortar retail pet stores remain exempt from USDA oversight and regulations even now. As the USDA states, in these cases, the consumer provides his own oversight.

But before we agree that a consumer can provide his own oversight, consider the following example.

A customer walks into a pet shop in New Jersey. The dogs look fine enough. She purchases one and goes home with her puppy, never the wiser. But the store's owner bred this puppy at his own facility more than one thousand miles away to be sold exclusively at this shop. Along the way, the store's owner never needed to be licensed by the USDA or adhere to any of its regulations—even at his remote breeding facility across state lines. In a case like this, it's hard to argue that the customer has provided any oversight into the conditions at the facility where her puppy was bred. But this example still qualifies as a valid exemption from USDA licensure. How? Because all three parties were present at the time of the sale: the buyer, the seller, and the dog. This example is not hypothetical and, in fact, is exactly the way that the now notorious Just Pups operated until its owner, Vincent LoSacco, was charged with hundreds of counts of animal cruelty. But more about LoSacco later.

Not surprisingly, unscrupulous breeders without a brick-and-mortar pet shop have still found loopholes to the new retail sales rule. While the new rule requires licenses for online sellers who transport their dogs to buyers without ever meeting in person, many breeders now circumvent the regulation by selling within driving distance of their facilities. As in the example raised by the ASPCA's Rickey, often these breeders offer to drive to a mutually convenient, neutral location to finalize the sale of the dog. I've seen parking lots as the most frequent site of choice for these transactions: outside a Walmart, a Cracker Barrel, a motel, or a strip mall. To my eyes, none of these locations look like a retail pet store, but hey, according to the USDA exemption, that's what they are. These dogs, purchased online, are not then being sold sight unseen. All are present and accounted for: breeder, buyer, and dog. As Rickey mentioned, this tactic is a classic red flag that a buyer is likely working with a puppy mill and not a responsible breeder. A responsible breeder should have no qualms about allowing a prospective buyer to visit his facility and decide for himself if it is maintained in acceptable conditions. A puppy mill operator will be less comfortable allowing a buyer to see his facility with his own eyes. But these perfectly legal transactions give the consumer no ability to come to his own conclusions about the condition of the dogs at these unlicensed operations.

But leaving this troubling loophole aside, the glaring question remains: Why did it take so long for the USDA to address the rampant issue of unlicensed internet puppy sales? To only enact a revision in 2013 seems a bit late given that e-commerce is nothing new. As early as 2009, the USDA had already stated publicly that internet sales constituted a "massive loophole" for breeders looking to cash in on that retail pet store exemption to the Animal Welfare Act.[11] So what was the hold up?

In large part, it took the agency's internal Office of the Inspector General (OIG) audit in 2010 to finally make it clear that action on this issue was overdue. In addition to showing that 80 percent of the problematic breeders included in the investigation were enjoying the retail pet store exemption, the audit report found a number of glaring deficiencies in the department's handling of "problematic dealers." Among them, the internal

investigation found that the "enforcement process was ineffective," "inspectors did not cite or document violations properly
to support enforcement actions," and—of course—"some large
breeders circumvented the Animal Welfare Act by selling animals
over the internet."

Three years and a stalled legislative act in Congress later,
Secretary Vilsack finally closed the loophole on his own by revising the definition of what constitutes a retail pet store.

So I asked the USDA directly: Why did it take so long to rein
in the issue of unlicensed breeders selling on the internet?

"I have no idea. No idea," Gibbens says. "The process itself
is long. When you're in the animal welfare world, to propose a
rule…it can be a matter of years. Because the animal world is so
controversial—or maybe not controversial. Maybe that's a bad
word. It's that you've got really strong feelings on polar sides of
the issue that you're writing the regulation for. And so, it takes a
while to get it through the political system."[12]

═══

"Hi there! My name is Rex, and I just know that we are meant
to be."

It's a pickup line that immediately draws me into Rex's online
profile. Rex is family-oriented, loving, and more than ready and
willing to settle down for a lifetime commitment. But no, Rex
isn't the man of anyone's dreams, and this isn't an online dating
profile. Rex is a six-week-old Morkie—a cross between a Maltese
and a Yorkshire terrier—posted for sale on internet puppy seller
PuppySpot.com. And Rex can be yours for $1,995 as soon as he's
eight weeks old.

"I have been dreaming of coming home to my new family, and I sure hope that it is you! I promise that we will have lots of fun together. We can spend all day playing if you'd like. Whenever you get tired, I will be right there to cuddle up by your side," Rex's profile continues, again making promises that go far above and beyond what most online daters could ever hope for.

But it's this little endnote that makes one promise I'm not sure Rex can really stick to.

"I'll be healthy too, so I will be ready for anything that you have planned."

I guess when it comes to buying dogs, there's no *in sickness and in health* kind of vow required. But then again, with Rex, you shouldn't need it, right? He's healthy. He promises.

Rex is puppy #487643 on PuppySpot.com. The site was formerly known as Purebred Breeders, LLC, until Greg Liberman took over as CEO in 2015. If PuppySpot feels like a dating website, it's no accident. Prior to taking over PuppySpot, Liberman was the CEO and president of Spark Networks, the parent company of a gaggle of dating websites including JDate.com and ChristianMingle.com. In 2014, he left his former role and began assembling his dream team to be the executive leaders at his new venture, the updated, renamed, and much more consumer-friendly PuppySpot. Also from Spark Networks are his chief marketing officer and his chief information officer— the latter perhaps accounting for the website's design that feels uncannily like an online dating site. Even PuppySpot's new chief financial officer has worked in the online dating biz at eHarmony.

Given their successes in the online dating world, this new executive team knew they had a branding problem on their hands with Purebred Breeders, LLC. In 2011, the company had already been criticized on national television by the *Today Show.* The morning show had aired a damning feature on the Humane Society's investigation into the broker. The investigation found that Purebred Breeders, LLC, at the time the largest online dog seller in the country, was selling sick puppies across eight hundred websites that it operated under a variety of names, misleading customers into believing that they were buying from local breeders in their area. In conjunction with the investigation, the Humane Society filed suit against Purebred Breeders on behalf of customers who received sick or dying dogs.[13] Purebred Breeders sent a response to NBC News refuting the report, saying, "Of the hundreds of excellent breeders we deal with regularly, only six are identified in the complaint sponsored by the Humane Society. After determining that the issues raised with these breeders had merit, they were immediately terminated from our network."[14]

Purebred Breeders simultaneously issued a press release that was much more forceful:

> The NBC *Today Show* report on Purebred Breeders grossly misrepresented our company and the work we do, day in and day out to ensure that only the healthiest and best-bred puppies reach our families. The story did not reflect the overwhelming majority of our breeders who are animal lovers and do their best to raise healthy puppies. The Humane Society of the U.S. (HSUS), who is behind the story, is a lobbying group that has a history of attacking organizations that are involved in the business of breeding and selling pets.[15] *

---

*   Although I was working at the *Today Show* when this story aired, I was not involved in its reporting.

Undeterred, the Humane Society continued mounting its case and found the number of customers looking to join the lawsuit growing. Ultimately, however, the case was dismissed in 2012 when a Florida judge ruled that the Humane Society had failed to back up its claims.

By 2014, however, the Cooper City, Florida–based puppy seller was subject to another investigation, this time by the local NBC News affiliate.[16] A woman complained that she'd paid Purebred Breeders $2,600 for a Labradoodle puppy and instead received a sick dog that was a poodle–cocker spaniel mix. At the time, reporters spoke to the Better Business Bureau, which said that they had received seventy-five complaints about Purebred Breeders in just the last few years. Meanwhile, the Humane Society lobbied with the USDA to push Purebred Breeders to get licensed as a broker. Purebred Breeders released another statement in response to the matter, saying it had refunded the buyer. The company also said that it was working with the USDA to be in compliance.

Either way, when Liberman and his band of online dating executives took over a year later, they knew they had to make some serious changes. After all, googling "Purebred Breeders" wouldn't lead a prospective buyer to a very pretty scene.

So first things first, Liberman's team filed documents with the Florida State Department to change the company's name to PuppySpot as of October 2016. When I inquired as to why Liberman and his executive team wanted anything to do with Purebred Breeders and didn't simply start an online dog-selling company fresh, the media team sent me the following response:

We made the decision to use that preexisting company's infrastructure as the basis for a reinvented company with a new leadership team, a different operating plan, and most importantly, a strong corporate culture founded on transparency and accountability.[17]

With the name changed from the sullied Purebred Breeders, LLC, to PuppySpot, the team relaunched the website with their new brand. In conjunction with PuppySpot's relaunch, the company announced that it would celebrate that October is Adopt-a-Dog Month by making a donation to the National Animal Interest Alliance's Shelter Project.[18]

While it may sound like this donation is going to directly help dogs in shelters, it is not. For starters, the National Animal Interest Alliance (NAIA) is not an animal welfare group. It is, by its own description, "an educational organization that was founded in 1991 to support and promote responsible animal ownership and use, and to oppose animal rights extremism."[19] Counted as animal rights extremists according to NAIA are—you guessed it—the Humane Society and the Animal Welfare Institute, among others.[20] NAIA also has an advocacy arm that works to lobby on behalf of the group's interests. Perhaps not surprisingly, NAIA and its president Patti Strand spoke out ardently against the change to the definition of retail pet stores in the Animal Welfare Act, closing the exemption for breeders selling online without a USDA license.

As for the shelter project that PuppySpot was offering a donation for? NAIA's Shelter Project does not actually benefit dogs in shelters directly, despite the name. Rather, it is a project that collects data on dogs in shelters. In 2015, the project released data finding that purebreds were scarce in animal shelters.[21] No surprise there. But the organization used this data to show that breeders are doing an excellent job of preventing overpopulation and poor health outcomes—points that are both heavily in question by animal welfare groups.

When I asked PuppySpot to explain why this project was their chosen charity, the company responded that they support the NAIA Shelter Project's mission of "reducing animal euthanasia."

But PuppySpot changed tack in one remarkable way from its predecessor. As of May 2015, the company became fully licensed as a broker by the USDA. As CEO Liberman tells me, this was a voluntary measure to be in full support of the USDA's work— even though he believes the company technically does not need to be licensed for what it's currently doing. The USDA told me that PuppySpot obtained this license due to the updated rule on retail pet shops that would allow breeders to sell to consumers over the internet. As of this writing, records showed that PuppySpot had no violations on its license. The company's new consumer-friendly design also takes on the specter of puppy mills directly with a "No Puppy Mill Promise" heralded prominently on the site: "PuppySpot Guarantees Its Breeders Are NOT Puppy Mills."

At this point, I'm less naïve than I was when I bought Izzie, believing her pet shop's pronouncement that it only sourced dogs from USDA-licensed breeders, not puppy mills. As I've found, those terms are not mutually exclusive. So I asked Liberman how he ensures that he isn't wholesaling dogs from puppy mills.

Liberman tells me that PuppySpot has a proprietary screening process—above and beyond all state and federal requirements— that breeders must pass in order to list their puppies on the site. While his website says that only 15 percent of breeders actually make the grade, Liberman tells me that in 2016 that number actually dipped to an even more selective 10 percent.[22] In our interview, I asked Liberman several times to give me some specific examples of what PuppySpot requires of breeders in this proprietary process. Does it include demonstrated efforts to ensure psychological well-being, daily exercise, limits on how often the females breed, increased cage sizes? Any of the above? He wouldn't budge. His media relations team would not either, despite Liberman's repeated insistence that he is in the business to bring transparency to the industry. The only insights they would provide are that the standards are "rigorous" and most breeders don't make the grade.

"There's a ton that goes into our screening process. It differs from the USDA process—it differs from every other screening standard out there," Liberman says, again unwilling to get into any specifics. "There are a bunch of different standards out there that we can look at and make sure that we always have the best in class."

Once the breeder is deemed acceptable by whatever those PuppySpot standards are, the dogs are then administered the company's specific vaccination and health protocol—complete with yet another proprietary health exam, the details of which cannot be revealed to me.

I should pause here to say that I can respect trade secrets. I realize the value of keeping certain information proprietary. However, when the trade secret is screening whether a puppy is born and raised humanely, it seems that there should be some information given to the consumer beyond the statistics of how many breeders make the cut. Especially given CEO Liberman's feelings about transparency.

"We're fully committed to transparency in what we do, and I think that's one of the things that drew me to this industry," he says, jumping to this topic of transparency before I can even ask him about it. "I think this is an industry where transparency in a lot of ways is lacking... We are still building a transparent business where there aren't so many X factors with finding a puppy."

He made a similar statement in the press release at the company's relaunch: "At its core, PuppySpot is a service, but it is far more than just a service. It's a community where dogs are celebrated and where trust, confidence, and transparency are paramount."

Trust, confidence, and transparency. These are buzzwords for the pet retail industry, because it is well understood that all three have been eroded by bad actors in the breeding world. As a journalist, I'm particularly a sucker for transparency—a word that, by now, you may be noticing is a theme in conversations with Liberman and PuppySpot. If, in fact, transparency is one company's core brand promises, I wanted to dig down a little further on it.

Let's go back to our Morkie dream date, Rex.

His profile page offers some useful information: his birth date, the weights of each of his parents, his color markings, and the fact that he is unregistered with any pedigree like the AKC because he is a designer hybrid and not a pure breed. And of course—front and center—his price and the number to call seven days a week to purchase him.

That's all useful information to have, but I wouldn't call these facts a win for transparency. Nowhere on Rex's profile does it tell me where he was bred and presumably is living until he is purchased. Unlike the online dating sites that Liberman and his cohort used to run, I cannot search on PuppySpot for potential dogs in my area. If I fall in love with Rex, he may be living at a breeder's facility just down the road or on the other side of the country. I can't be sure if he's from a state with added protections or just the minimal federal regulations and weed him out of my search accordingly. I can't even submit a FOIA request to obtain the inspection reports of his breeder, because there's no name or USDA number for whoever bred this puppy. Instead, I must trust fully in PuppySpot to do everything for me—including my due diligence. This stands in sharp contrast to brick-and-mortar pet shops in an increasing number of municipalities that are now required to provide cage cards detailing who the breeder is for each dog. Here, no such luck. Liberman says that once a buyer begins the process, however, he is connected with the dog's breeder and given all his or her information.

Still, I ask Liberman why a buyer should not be able to search by location—as one would do on a dating website—and then follow the tips he's given by the ASPCA or the Humane Society to go see a breeding operation in person for himself and determine whether it is a puppy mill. He quickly dismisses the idea.

"That can often be a very reckless way to find a good breeder. Someone can look like a good breeder, and they're not. And so we have our own standards to do all the vetting, to do all the qualifying," he says, emphasizing the value of allowing his company's "puppy concierge" to do the due diligence for the customer—despite not revealing what that due diligence entails.

"Historically, it's been a very local business, and we saw the opportunity to come in here and say, okay, we want people to find the perfect puppy for their family, no matter where they are, no matter where the breeder is, and to have confidence that they were getting it from a responsible source. And that's what we do. So much of what we do is focused on the compliance side of things," he says.

However, PuppySpot is not alone in this space of connecting buyers with dogs. There's also PuppyFind.com. As Liberman will be the first to tell you, sites like PuppyFind are more of an online classified ad section than a service that evaluates breeders and connects them with customers accordingly. Fair enough. PuppyFind's site is slightly less visually appealing and consumer friendly, more of a catalog than an online dating site. But here, there is somewhat more transparency: each dog has his breeder's name, phone number, and website listed below him so that a prospective buyer can at least attempt to do some light googling to kick the tires. Again, the value of having a breeder's name has dropped significantly since the once publicly available USDA inspection-report database was pulled from the web under the Trump administration. Still, if I wanted to limit my search for a dog to a breeder in my area who I could personally visit and vet for myself, I could do that with the information provided on PuppyFind and not Liberman's PuppySpot. However, this doesn't mean that PuppyFind is, by any stretch of the imagination, a one-way ticket to a responsibly sourced dog.

For its part, the Humane Society has been advocating on behalf of consumers over at PuppyFind. In October 2016, the organization had a law firm file suit in Arizona, where the site is based, on behalf of consumers who say they unknowingly were led to purchase sick puppy mill dogs from the site. The complaint accused PuppyFind of inflating ratings and deleting negative reviews in an effort to mislead customers. The Humane Society was also able to trace puppies posted on PuppyFind to known commercial breeders who had made the Horrible Hundred list for their numerous violations with the USDA.

Unlike Liberman's PuppySpot, PuppyFind does not have a

USDA license. Nor does it need to. It operates merely as a match-maker and middleman, connecting buyers to breeders. This is likely why PuppyFind offers up breeder contact information to buyers: ultimately, it's up to the breeder to arrange for shipping and transportation. PuppyFind is not licensed to do any of that. PuppySpot, on the other hand, manages the transaction, from finding the dog, to shipping it to the consumer through its team of travel agents, to making it possible for the consumer to poten-tially never even know the name of the dog's breeder. While Liberman tells me that "the breeder will interface with the buyer as much as the buyer wants to interface with the breeder," his site does make it awfully easy to never have to.

As far as the Humane Society Legislative Fund's Amundson sees it, both types of online aggregators should have to be licensed by the USDA.

"Here's the shtick: if they serve as a go-between [for] the breeder and the ultimate consumer and they never take posses-sion of that dog, they are a broker, and I want these folks turned in. I want them to know the role they play carries responsibil-ity," Amundson says. "It's almost worse than what some of the breeders are doing, because [the websites] never see these living, breathing puppies that they are part of a transaction on, and it just blows my mind. This is not a broker who is selling reduced-price washers and dryers. These are living, breathing puppies that they are making a business of. And they have no [interaction with] the animal welfare side because nobody has tackled this issue of turning them in to the USDA... Certainly at the federal level, they operate with impunity... And I don't care if they are innocent in the whole situation, because they don't know what they're doing. Somebody has got to educate them, and because it's interstate commerce, they should be brought under the Animal Welfare Act specifications on the definition of broker."

But not every puppy that crosses state lines for sale comes through a broker.

Now we arrive at Vincent LoSacco, the owner of Just Pups, a notorious chain of New York and New Jersey pet stores. For years, LoSacco used Missouri breeders Randy and Kandy Hale as his primary suppliers. But when the Hales faced dozens of violations from the USDA and the state of Missouri, they relinquished their licenses and turned over the business to LoSacco to run in his own name, even as they remained the designated local agents running the show on the ground.

So in 2015, LoSacco became his own breeder, supplying his pet shops. This as the people who were actually running the day-to-day operations were the very same folks who the USDA and the state had put out of business after years of violations. But with this move, LoSacco could operate without a USDA license, because he was breeding and transporting his own animals to sell in person more than twelve hundred miles from where they were born, qualifying for the retail pet store exemption. So much for the customer being able to provide his own oversight at a pet shop.

However, over the course of 2016, mounting animal cruelty charges and health code violations forcing LoSacco's stores to close left him with a problem: lots of dogs and nowhere to sell them. So in July 2016, despite all the charges against him, LoSacco managed to obtain a USDA license that would enable him to sell online or to other retailers. In fact, he has since sold his dogs to the American Dog Club store in Long Island where I purchased Izzie, according to a cage card provided to me by the

Companion Animal Protection Society (CAPS). The owner of the American Dog Club, Elliot Gordon, did not respond to my repeated requests for an interview.

But being able to sell dogs online was not an expedient enough solution for Vincent LoSacco. With his legal fees mounting and his sales numbers slumping, LoSacco set about cashing in by selling off hundreds of his breeding-stock dogs at an auction in August 2016. When I heard about it, I jumped on the next flight to Missouri to see it for myself.

CHAPTER TWELVE

On the Auction Block

I'M BIDDER NUMBER 51 AT THE JUST PUPS KENNEL
Dispersal dog auction in Milan, Missouri. I take my badge and
my catalog and try to blend in under the wood rafters of the
livestock pavilion. It's uncommonly hot and humid, so I slip off
my cardigan—after all, there's no hiding my growing baby bump
anymore. There are more than 450 dogs here from LoSacco's
facility, and they will cycle through the auction block over the
next eight hours. Maybe my pregnancy has heightened my senses,
but I swear that over the pungent scent of wet hay lining the
floors, I can smell the anxiety of the dogs. It's a scent I know well
from Izzie, like something slightly burned and bitter.

The smaller breeds yap in their crates, elevated from the
ground to be nearly at eye level for inspection before they go
up for bidding. Each cage bears a number corresponding to an
entry in the thick catalog. Here's Just Pups Yosha, lot number
128, female. Born September 17, 2010. She's got to be the tiniest
Yorkshire terrier of the bunch. Her teeth interlace with each

other horizontally like a Venus flytrap. She growls at me when I approach even as I coo gently *it's okay, it's okay* at the front of her cage. The other Yorkie in her cage, M's Ann, lot 127, also a six-year-old female but at least three times her size, stands on top of Yosha, protecting her from me. I back away to avoid adding to their distress. I've never had a dog perceive me as a threat before, and it's a very strange and uncomfortable feeling.

About a dozen teens and preteens are hustling around the event, wearing shirts bearing the logo of Just Pups, Vincent LoSacco's pet store chain in New Jersey. I ask a boy who looks to be about fifteen why he's wearing the shirt, asking if he and his cohort flew in all the way from New Jersey to work the auction today. He shrugs and says no, it was just what he was given to wear to work the auction. But there, in the background, behind the auctioneers, I spot LoSacco himself, all the way out here in rural, northeast Missouri, his cell phone earpiece glowing neon blue next to his salt-and-pepper widow's peak.

At the time of this auction, Just Pups owner LoSacco is facing hundreds of animal cruelty charges on the other side of the country. Over the past eight months, he's been forced to shut four of his five stores, and the state of New Jersey is trying to stop him from ever selling or even advertising another animal there again, armed with consumer fraud charges. And yet today, with a green light from the USDA, he's about to be rewarded by making tens of thousands of dollars selling off dogs from his breeding facilities. And yes, folks, it's all perfectly legal.

From May 16, 2015, to July 28, 2016, LoSacco ran his Missouri-based breeding facility housing upward of seven hundred dogs without a USDA license—a move that was also entirely legal. His vertically integrated operation was a brilliant play, if using the USDA's own loophole to avoid inspection is your game. Because he was breeding the dogs to be sold at his own stores, he qualified for the retail pet store exemption and was perfectly within his rights to breed his own dogs for sale without federal oversight, even with his breeding operation halfway across the country from his stores.

But because in Missouri LoSacco still needed a state license to breed even if he was USDA exempt, I was able to obtain the records showing what the LoSacco operation looked like over the course of that year, legally out of the reach of the USDA.

In March 2015, LoSacco's company, Just Pups, officially took possession of all dogs previously belonging to the breeders Randy and Kandy Hale. While LoSacco could have gotten away with escaping any state or federal oversight outside of Missouri, the Show-Me State was where he had already set up his puppy pipeline through the Hales. They had been LoSacco's main supplier but were buckling under pressure from the USDA after years of serious violations documenting problems like frozen dog cages and untreated open wounds. Within several weeks, the Hales would see their USDA license lapse. Still, Missouri records show that in April 2015, Randy Hale became the local agent for LoSacco's Just Pups.

On April 15, 2015, a Missouri Department of Agriculture inspector completed LoSacco's first state report on the property and found no noncompliant items. With the stroke of a pen, 463 adult dogs and 249 puppies went from being the property of the Hales to being that of LoSacco. Suddenly, the slate was wiped clean: LoSacco was able to start fresh, the business now under a new name. Now, a buyer searching LoSacco's new reports would never know the truth of the past years—there is no mention of the Hales in any of his state inspection reports. As far as a person searching LoSacco's records would know, he started a brand-new breeding facility on that day. Of course, the 712 dogs on the premises had no idea that they were now in a new facility. Same cages, same treatment, same story, same people running the show as the day before—changing owners changing nothing.

But just a year after the Hales turned their dogs over to LoSacco on paper, the situation was starting to deteriorate for the dogs, now 744 in number, at the facility within its rights to be unlicensed by the USDA. And keep in mind, with lapsed USDA-licensee Randy Hale running the show, it's unlikely the operation ran much differently from before LoSacco signed his name to it.

For example, on May 4, 2016, a state inspector slapped LoSacco with a direct violation—the highest level of noncompliance available to assign. On this visit, the state inspector brought along a veterinarian who found a female Rottweiler to be suffering from "hair loss, scaly dermatitis, and excoriations of the neck and back." A follow-up visit on May 31, 2016, found that the dog had been treated, and the item was corrected.

This violation, among dozens only state inspectors documented, demonstrates exactly why USDA licensure and inspections—while imperfect—are necessary for large-scale breeders. If LoSacco were licensed by the USDA, this violation of the Animal Welfare Act would be marked as a direct noncompliance on his records and would have barred him from selling to pet shops in any of the seven states that regulate breeders based on their USDA inspection reports. Significantly, the majority of LoSacco's stores were in New Jersey, which is one of those seven states. New Jersey's Pet Purchase Protection Act bans breeders with one direct violation on the past two years of records from selling to pet shops. But that legislation—and similar laws in other states and municipalities—only applies to federal inspection reports. So even though the breeding facility had Animal Welfare Act violations on its state inspection report, LoSacco was allowed to keep on churning out puppies for sale unabated. Of course, for the dog that was unquestionably harmed by this violation, it didn't matter which agency documented it. The damage was done.

Meanwhile, on the other side of the country, what was becoming of these dogs that LoSacco was allowed to breed and transport without any federal oversight from the USDA?

VALHALLA, NEW YORK

On January 19, 2016, the New York Department of Agriculture and Markets denied LoSacco's application to renew his business license. Between October and December of 2015, the department said that his store failed four inspections due to "critical deficiencies."[1]

The Just Pups location in Valhalla, New York, was forced to close in February 2016.

EAST BRUNSWICK, NEW JERSEY

In February 2016, New Jersey SPCA inspectors announced that they have found the bodies of three dead dogs in the freezer of LoSacco's East Brunswick Just Pups store. LoSacco admitted to the finding and says he had no idea how long they had been in there—maybe eight months, maybe a year, maybe more. In an interview with local news site Patch.com, LoSacco said that his staff was just following protocol: when a dog in the pet shop dies, it goes into the freezer before being taken to the vet for cremation.

"There are one hundred dogs in the store at any time," LoSacco told Patch.com. "Dogs in pet stores die. That's a fact. If people don't want to admit it, they're lying. Puppies, when they are born—30 percent don't make it to twelve weeks old."[2]

On March 28, 2016, LoSacco's business license in East Brunswick, New Jersey, was officially revoked. He was charged with 267 counts of animal cruelty by the New Jersey SPCA, and the Just Pups location in East Brunswick closed its doors for good.[3]

PARAMUS, NEW JERSEY

On April 4, 2016, sixty-seven dogs were found in a freezing van outside LoSacco's Paramus shop where they have been left unattended overnight. Police said they were stuffed in cages too small for them to stand and not given adequate food or water.[4] This charge violates the Animal Welfare Act's transportation regulations and would have to be documented by USDA inspectors if LoSacco had a valid Class B license to operate as a dealer and broker—the exact type of license he was granted by the USDA just three months later. LoSacco's brother admitted the dogs were left in the van unattended after being transported in from out of state—more than likely from his Missouri facility. The store was forced to close until further notice.

The county prosecutor's office charged LoSacco with 134 counts of animal cruelty.[5] Additionally, the Paramus Board of Health issued 403 summonses to LoSacco for other violations associated with this store.[6] LoSacco was vocal, denying any wrongdoing in these cases and fighting the charges in court.

On May 2, 2016, LoSacco relinquished his business license to operate the Paramus location of Just Pups, and it closed permanently.

EMERSON, NEW JERSEY

On July 13, 2016, LoSacco agreed to shut down his Emerson, New Jersey, store after the borough council denied his license renewal application. He said he would transfer all unsold dogs to shelters or the last store standing in East Hanover, New Jersey.

Amid all these charges calling for the humane treatment of his dogs, pressure was simultaneously mounting for the protection of LoSacco's human customers. On July 5, 2016, the New Jersey State attorney general teamed up with the state division of Consumer Affairs to charge LoSacco with deceiving customers into purchasing sick puppies and dogs at all four of his stores in the state. They issued a press release detailing the charges, stating that they were now trying to keep him from ever advertising or selling animals in New Jersey again. They were also seeking civil penalties of up to $10,000 for each of the dozens of violations in the complaint.[7]

Meanwhile, back in Missouri, after all these instances of animal cruelty had been blasted in the press…

On July 25, 2016, the USDA stopped by LoSacco's facility to conduct a prelicense inspection for him obtain a Class B USDA license allowing him both to breed and transport dogs. If no violations were found, he would be able to sell his animals online or to other retailers. Sure enough, two USDA Animal Care inspectors wrote in their report that they had found no noncompliant items at the facility. For what it's worth, prelicense inspections are announced—meaning that LoSacco was able to prepare the facility before federal agents poked around that day.

Just two days later, on July 27, 2016, a Missouri state inspector's unannounced inspection found a very different scene than the USDA did. He slapped LoSacco with yet another direct violation. The state veterinarian found a long-haired dachshund to be lethargic, with lacerations on her front limb. He also noted that she appeared to be in heat. The vet ordered the dog to be taken immediately to a veterinarian for treatment.[8]

The very next day, July 28, 2016, the USDA inexplicably gave LoSacco the golden ticket: a Class B license enabling him to act as a breeder, dealer, or broker of dogs. The dead dogs in the freezer, the van left packed with puppies overnight in the cold, the consumer fraud charges: these all came down on LoSacco before July 28, 2016—the date he was awarded that USDA license. Thanks to our federal government, from that day forward, he would be licensed to breed, sell, and transport dogs anywhere in the country or on the internet. And unless you're buying in one of the states or municipalities with additional restrictions on pet shop sales, you would never even know that you're buying a dog from LoSacco.

Right or wrong, LoSacco passed the test. Now, with his pet store business in New Jersey tanking amid consumer and animal advocate outrage, LoSacco is apparently changing tack on his vertically integrated operation. With his USDA license in hand, he does not need to sell his dogs in his own stores—he can now sell them to anyone. But first, he needs to cash in. Legal fees aren't cheap, you know.

I walk toward the auction block to get a better view. It's been just ten days since a scheduled USDA inspection unsurprisingly failed to turn up any violations at LoSacco's kennel and effectively green-lit this entire event. A crowd of about 150 breeders sits in risers and foldout chairs around two separate podiums as simultaneous auctions are called in two rings. There are clear factions here: half of those gathered here are the usual, rural breeder crowd, and the other half are Amish, the men in their straw hats and brightly colored shirts under suspenders, the women in their thin, papery bonnets and long, dark dresses. The Amish men gather around in small hubs on the side of the auction ring, discussing the dogs on the block in their hushed German dialect. After all, agriculture and livestock are the foundation of what the Amish do, and dogs are just one more animal they can farm.

A handful of Shiba Inus are put on the block. The biggest of the bunch has her head cocked back in terror, and her lips are curled in a snarl.

"She's real nervous but she's bred," the auctioneer says, meaning that the crowd should not worry about her temperament, because she has successfully born litters in the past. Of course, temperament can matter an awful lot when determining the quality of care she's received in her life and the temperament she will likely pass on to her future litters. She eventually sells for $1,775.

Next up are the toy poodles. The auctioneer lists their lot numbers and starts calling them. He's assisted by two men in front of the podium pointing to bidders—many of whom the auctioneers know by name. They edge the bidding higher and higher. For an apricot-colored poodle, bidding notches above $1,200 and slows. The auctioneer pauses his rapid-fire calling to do a little salesmanship.

"Those are real reds," he says. "I haven't seen anything like them in three, four years. Come on!"

The bidding resumes. She sells for $2,050.

A crowd of Amish men is gathering over in the large-breed section of the cages. I stroll over to see what they're staring at. I should have guessed: it's the stars of the show, a large cage with about a dozen fluffy golden retriever puppies dozing and playing on sawdust. They look to be in good health, and their coats are all puffed out and bright.

"How much you think they're worth?" a kind-faced, elderly breeder asks me.

"No idea. But they're clearly interested," I say, nodding toward the Amish men on the other side of the cage.

The breeder makes a face.

"They're terrible," he says. "Treat their dogs like crap and have tons of money to spend at these things."

I shrug.

"You breed goldens?" I ask.

"Trying to get into it a little," he says. "Just looking for a male for my female."

He crouches down to get a better look.

"That little guy looks damn near dead," he says of one lying facedown in the sawdust, motionless as its littermates scuffle and play. Later, I'll circle back and find that the pup is very much alive, but in that moment, the thought chills me.

I ask a worker feeding a crate full of German shepherd puppies if he knows where the wheaten terriers are.

"They're over there with the rest of the big dogs," he says.

"The big dogs?" I'm stunned. Only in this context would a wheaten be considered one of the big ones. In the commercial breeding operations, smaller dogs like Yorkies and teacup breeds are generally the most common and most profitable.

They're more cost efficient as they take up less space to house and feed.

The wheatens are in the very back of the pavilion, the last row of crates facing out toward the parking lot. To my untrained eye, they appear to range in health and disposition more than any other breed present today.

On the corner is lot number 443, Just Pups Winnie. Female, born July 21, 2007. She's alone in her crate bearing a sign alerting prospective buyers that she's in heat. Nine years old and still breeding. That seems like an awfully long life in a cage to me. Her protracted fertility has clearly extended her sentence.

Winnie is small, maybe half the size of Izzie—and Izzie is generally seen as a runt for the breed. Two metal paint cans are zip-tied to the wire enclosing her cage: one is filled with kibble, the other is presumably filled with water, but the liquid inside is so deeply rust-colored that it looks like it could be wine. She cowers in the back of her cage when I approach, revealing one eye that is oozing brown down the side of her face to her jaw, staining her hair. Her nipples are heavy and black in crooked rows down her belly. I try cooing to her, to convey that I'm not a threat. She presses her tiny body even harder against the back wall of the cage and never takes her eyes off me.

The next cage holds lot number 446, Top-of-the-Line Bob. Male, born May 16, 2013. The sign on the cage says that lot number 442 should be in this cage too, but she's pregnant and due any time. Her puppies will be sold off with her later this morning. Top-of-the-Line Bob is shaved and distressed, cowering away from me as well.

I move to the next cage and am shocked by what I see in lot number 444, Just Pups Dozer. Male, born April 15, 2014.

He is thrilled to see me, attempting to prance around his cage, wagging his tiny nub of a tail. His cinnamon coat is in excellent shape, and when he tries to get as close to me as possible through the cage, I can see that his teeth look perfect as well. He bows into a playful puppy pose that I know well from Izzie when she's looking to wrestle. Then he attempts to jump up in a wheaten greetin' onto the front of his cage. I can see some redness and a few sores between the pads of his paws. But otherwise, this would appear to be a happy, healthy dog that could easily make himself at home in any person's living room today. And yet, the contrast between his health and demeanor and his neighbors is striking and ominous—they all come from the same facility.

I move on to the next cage. Lots number 438 and 439 are here, both female, Just Pups Lilly and Just Pups Tera respectively. They share a birthday with friendly Dozer in the next cage of April 15, 2014. I'm guessing they were littermates. They share Dozer's excellent coat quality. But psychologically, they don't seem to have Dozer's bounce. One is nervously eating her own feces from the bottom of the cage. The other hides in the back, avoiding eye contact with me.

I circle back to the auction block to check on the latest lot up for bid. Standing off to the side, anxiously smoking a cigarette is Theresa Strader, the founder of the National Mill Dog Rescue who took me on her rescue trip across the heartland several months back. I'm not surprised to run into her here: the dog that first inspired her to start her rescue operation came from an auction like this back in 2007. She tells me in a low voice that there are several other rescues represented here today in addition to hers. We part ways quickly—being seen talking to a well-known rescuer could raise suspicion about my presence and see me booted from the premises. Theresa's a known quantity around here, and her longstanding relationships with breeders allow her to avoid the typical ire they hold for rescuers. But I can't bank on being able to share in the goodwill she has cultivated.

Later, Theresa will demand that I strike her quotes and rescue from my story, angry that I spoke with breeders on her trip and thereafter despite my insistence from our earliest conversations—in person and in writing—that interviewing both sides was an essential part of my investigation. However, it is not within the standards of my profession as a journalist to strike quotes after they've been knowingly and willingly offered on the record. Still, her change of heart reflects the challenge of covering this story—I've run into people on both sides who are not comfortable with a fair investigation. Both sides often wish to be accepted and supported without question.

Here at the auction, I take a seat in the back bleachers to get a better view. A pair of women sitting nearby start lobbing rapid-fire questions at me. They ask what I'm bidding on and what I think of the much-hyped golden retriever puppies in the large-dog area.

"Not sure. I don't know much about golden breeding," I say.

"You buying anything else then?" the younger one asks. Her teeth are red from years of chewing tobacco.

"I don't think so."

I mention that I may be heading off after this to visit another breeder, and they pounce.

"Does she have goldens?"

"I don't know," I say truthfully.

The older one leans in close. "Well, we're rescuers. But we only do goldens. But don't tell anyone that we're rescuers."

"Doesn't bother me," I say.

"How much you think they'll go for?" the red-toothed younger one asks me.

I shrug.

"Do you have Facebook?" the older one asks a little too brightly. "What's your full name? I'd love to add you."

I excuse myself abruptly but as politely as possible to get away from the conversation. I'm doubtful that they're actually rescuers. I get the sense that they're baiting me to see if I'll out myself as a rescuer because they're breeders who know who Theresa is and saw me talking to her. Or because I just don't seem to fit in. I'm not sure which.

If, in fact, they are rescuers, I feel a twinge of annoyance at the notion that they "only do goldens." I understand breed affinity, as I was guilty of it myself in purchasing Izzie. However, I personally find the notion of saving only a certain breed to be a bit at odds with the philosophy of a rescue. Besides, if they're dead set on walking out of here with a golden, they're going to be paying thousands of dollars to "rescue" one of the ones here today.

The Southwest Auction Service is running today's show. The Hughes family has operated the company since 1988. It's one of the last auction houses in the country that serves the dog-breeding community and has long roots in the industry going back generations. Ultimately, they deny my requests for an interview. But Southwest Auction Service's own promotional materials tell at least part of the story. On its website, the company boasts that it has sold many dogs for more than $5,000 and once even sold a single dog for $12,600.[9] With all the attention that the goldens are getting today, it's clear they won't go cheap. Rescue operations, particularly breed-specific rescues, have been known to show up at auctions like this one, paying hundreds or even thousands of dollars for the dogs on the block. To her credit, Theresa says that when she goes to auctions, she only ever pays small pittances for the dogs that are not attracting any breeder's interest: the sick, the malformed, the dying. In short, the ones who will be put down if they can't fetch a few bucks on the block. But according to Pete, my undercover puppy mill investigator contact, rescuers who buy up the unwanted ones are in the minority among those who go to these auctions. He has witnessed the odd ecosystem in which the rescues pay the breeders for their stock at auction—often at top dollar, funded by the donations of well-meaning supporters. This then funds the breeders looking to replace their old dogs, purchase new ones, and continue their operations.

"I have watched the rescues bid against each other, whether it was knowingly or not," Pete tells me. "Half of the people who go to these auctions are activists who are buying the old, spent breeding stock. And they are filling the pockets of puppy millers to be able to replace their breeding stock. So as a breeder, you know that once a dog is done, the people who hate you are going to pay you to replace them."

Seems like any way you slice it, an auction block is no place for a dog. If only the Animal Welfare Act mandated a cap on breeding frequency and cycles and created a path to adoption. Then maybe breeding would be a lot less lucrative for bad actors to get into. And less of a breeding ground for side industries like the auction trade. As I'm seeing, as round after round of dogs are called to the auction block and sold, when breeding becomes a profit-driven business, the dogs will always suffer.

In early November 2016, several months after I attend the kennel dispersal auction in Missouri, LoSacco pleads guilty in a Paramus, New Jersey, courtroom to four health code violations. These violations stemmed from the sixty-seven puppies found stuffed in a freezing van outside his Paramus store in April 2016. While he originally faced hundreds of charges for this violation, the vast majority are dropped in a plea deal. He is ordered to pay $19,000 over the course of two and a half years to an animal control contract service as restitution.[10]

A week after this, a New Jersey couple sues LoSacco for selling them a dog that was unfit for sale. The Cavalier King Charles Spaniel named Cuddles died within a month of having been purchased from Just Pups and spent more time in the veterinary hospital than it ever got to spend at home. The plaintiffs seek reimbursement for the $10,000 they spent on the dog's medical bills plus damages.[11]

But with hundreds of dogs sold at the auction I attended for well north of $1,000 each, LoSacco could easily have earned the money within an hour or two to pay off both of those sums.

On February 3, 2017, a red sign appears on the door of LoSacco's East Hanover Just Pups, indicating that the New Jersey State Department of Health has shut it down for failing a sanitation inspection. This East Hanover location is LoSacco's last remaining brick-and-mortar pet shop. The Health Department launches a probe, the results of which will determine whether LoSacco can ever reopen. Interestingly, a coalition of other pet shop owners bands together to formally distance themselves from LoSacco, issuing a statement through trade group PIJAC calling his actions "extremely disturbing" and not reflective of the industry as a whole.[12]

On March 6, 2017, the East Hanover township council unanimously votes to revoke LoSacco's operating license.[13]

I attempt to contact LoSacco through his attorney, seeking comment or an interview. My requests to connect are never answered. While I wish I could have heard LoSacco's side of the story, I think that the most uncomfortable questions that I have to ask aren't for him at all—they're for the USDA.

Namely, why in the world did the USDA green-light LoSacco's license in July 2016?

Once again, I meet with Dr. Gibbens at the USDA campus. This time, I bring with me a stack of LoSacco's Missouri state inspection reports along with printouts of the news stories documenting the charges against him—including the New Jersey State attorney general's fraud complaint against him, along with its companion press release time-stamped just days before the USDA granted LoSacco his license. Before I can even present it to him, Gibbens begins talking about how rigorous his department's prelicense inspection protocol is and how much time his agents spend with license applicants to educate them before granting them their paperwork.

"If we find that there's been an animal cruelty charge—we've found that before and then denied the license," Gibbens explains. "Or if we've found that [the license applicant has] broken some other state law or county law, we've just denied their application. We have to go through court to do that too, but we've successfully done that. Do I wish we could do more? Sure."[14]

I pull out the LoSacco file I've compiled, hand it over to him, and walk him through the timeline of events: the hundreds of charges against him, the dead dogs in the freezer, all the forced store closings that took place before the USDA granted him his license. Gibbens explains that LoSacco must have had a clean inspection report on the day that the announced prelicense inspection was conducted, even though state agents found multiple critical violations on their unannounced inspections within days of this visit. But, he concedes, that discrepancy does not surprise him, because all prelicense inspections are announced. Gibbens even offers that it would be foolish for a bad applicant to not hide any wrongdoing before federal inspectors show up.

He excuses himself to search his computer for more information. He pulls up LoSacco's file and then informs me that LoSacco is now under investigation by the agency, so he cannot comment on it further. Of course, Gibbens acknowledges, this investigation had to have been opened sometime after the license was granted.

So again, why was this person given a license in the first place?

"If we'd had some of this information and this had taken place before we issued the license, we would have pursued rejecting the application," Gibbens says simply, paging through the file I've given him—including stacks of Missouri state inspection reports, replete with horrible violations.

"But these stories made headlines," I remind him, showing him, yet again, the dates on all the news items and state inspection reports, predating his department granting LoSacco a license.

"It may point out a problem with our system," he says. "We get a license application for somebody in Missouri, our default is not going to be to go to New York to see if there are any problems."

"But put this guy's name into a Google search—that's it," I say, incredulous. "There's nothing good that pops up. Just even of his name. Immediately, it's all there, that's all, it's blanketed."

Gibbens returns to the stack of news stories I've handed him. He points out that at the time when the USDA granted LoSacco a license, the hundreds of animal cruelty charges against him had not yet been tried in court and adjudicated. Without that final, legal determination, his agency has not typically been successful in pulling a license.

So why not just delay granting the license? What was the rush? Why not hold the application until the courts decide? Then, once they do, either accept or deny the license application?

Gibbens agrees that his agency does have the authority to delay the licensing process until more information comes in. He says that the USDA has done this in the past. So why didn't the agency at least try to delay licensing of Vincent LoSacco, perhaps the most publicized, infamous pet store owner in the country at the time?

"We didn't have the information," Gibbens says. "I wouldn't be the person who researched it. That would be our licensing staff. At the time, I don't know who did what. But whatever was done, we obviously didn't have this information when we processed his application."

We can argue that the USDA is understaffed. We can argue that it is bureaucratic. We can even argue that it's difficult to coordinate with the state agencies to find out what they have on the record. But it's terribly hard to argue in favor of an agency that failed to run a simple Google search on an applicant's name before granting his license.

As of this writing, all LoSacco's stores are shuttered. But through it all, he still holds onto his USDA license under the Just Pups business name, allowing him to keep breeding and selling to anyone in the country.

CHAPTER THIRTEEN

Pet Shop Problems

MOST OF THE TIME, WHEN DAN AND I LOOK AT IZZIE, WE
feel that we've dodged a bullet. Especially knowing what I know
now. There's no denying that she's been far from perfect through
the years. Her health has had its ups and downs, but thankfully—
thus far—she hasn't presented with anything that can't be fixed
with a course of antibiotics or a change of diet.

As loving as she is, Izzie is quite neurotic—but then again, so
are my husband and I. It's hard to blame her personality flaws
on anyone but us. But as Dr. Overall has suggested, some of
Izzie's anxieties may also be genetic or inborn—damage done to
her mother before she was even conceived. It's just one example
of how, in purchasing a dog from a breeder, Dan and I and
everyone else who shells out cash for puppies are taking a high
stakes gamble.

"Risk is the flaw in the puppy mill thing. It's what everyone
counts on and what the consumer counts on without knowing
it. What [commercial breeders] are doing is they're doing risk

[assessments], and they don't understand risk." Overall explains of the way that large-scale breeders play with the genetics of their dogs without fully understanding the game. "The average human does not understand risk and randomness. They want a guarantee. They don't understand that there is uncertainty involved in everything... So you could get a perfectly good puppy mill dog. We may not know what those distributions of dogs look like. But somebody's going to get a great one. Because somewhere, there is a dog that's going to survive that and excel. And some [humans] have come out of horrendous experiences and done brilliantly. Because we're resilient, and we're survivors, and we're overachievers, and we do that. Dogs exist like that as well."[1]

But of course, these special dogs who can survive the trauma of birth in a puppy mill and go on to thrive are few and far between. As consumers, we cannot bank on the fact that the puppy we purchase from a pet store or online will be that special dog. And as we know, even Izzie has apparently not emerged unscathed— her noise phobia a case in point.

But this is an animal that was so important to us that my maid of honor snuck her into our black-tie wedding. The reception hall had even warned us in advance that we'd be in violation of the health code if Izzie tried to crash the party—but just a moment of her paws on our dance floor was worth the admonishment. Her flaws are now just a part of the dog that we love, and we unconditionally accept them. We even mold our lives around them, so I guess she's trained us. But we are lucky. The marks of her breeding could have been much uglier: a life of disease or even a life cut short in puppyhood. A pet-store puppy purchase remains a risky investment. So far, we have nothing but happiness to show for ours, while others have had nothing but heartache.

NANCY AND LOLA

Nancy Sasso had never owned a dog before in her life. She was a part-time store manager living in Holmdel, New Jersey, fifty miles south of New York City. Her husband had just retired as a lieutenant after forty-one years as a police officer. It was in spring 2012 that she got a call from her college-aged son Michael who was at the American Puppy Club in nearby Middletown with his girlfriend. They'd spotted a Chihuahua, and it was love at first sight.

"He says 'Mom, come down here. I need a credit card to pay for her,'" Nancy recalls. "So I went over there. I knew nothing about this store. We'd never had a dog before. And [the pet shop staff] started throwing all these papers at me. I'm going 'What am I signing here?' And they're going 'Oh, don't worry about it. It's just for the care of your dog. No big deal.'"[2]

Nancy estimates that she paid a little over $1,200 for the tiny puppy that day. They took the dog home and named her Lola. She weighed less than a pound. Immediately, the problems began.

"She starts coughing, hacking, throwing up. I'm like, 'What's wrong?'" Nancy says.

She took Lola to the veterinarian and was given a diagnosis of kennel cough, also known as infectious canine tracheobronchitis. It's a common but treatable respiratory ailment typically seen in dogs kept in close quarters—hence the name. Nancy brought Lola home, but the puppy could not shake her cough. She took the puppy to three more veterinarians, some of whom Nancy was referred to by the pet store. Meanwhile, Nancy's son began to get curious about the American Puppy Club. He searched online and found a flurry of negative reviews.

"There were all these people who bought dogs from this store, and they were writing about all the problems they had with their dogs, and I'm like 'Oh my God,'" Nancy recalls.

While the American Puppy Club has since closed, I reached out to the store's owner, Lorin Kislak, through his new pet shop: the Breeders Club of America, just half a mile down the road in Middletown, New Jersey. My request for comment was never returned.

In the meantime, for Lola, things were getting worse.

Lola began to behave very strangely, thrusting her head onto the carpet and darting around the room with her skull pinned to the floor. Nancy knew that was terribly wrong.

"I had this gut feeling that something was really wrong with her," Nancy says. "In one respect, I was in denial, because I didn't want her to be sick or lose her. Then in the next respect, I was like, 'Just come on. Something is wrong with her.' She was a beautiful Chihuahua. But she would rub her face so hard, she would rub all the fur off."

Back to the vet.

Now, the doctor told Nancy that four-month-old Lola's tear ducts were drying up, an affliction the vet says she'd never seen before in a dog so young. Nancy followed the prescribed treatment: the pills and the eye drops. But soon, she began to realize the awful truth.

"She would run in the room, and we'd go, 'Hi Lola!' And she'd turn her head all over the place. I'd say to my husband 'What is she doing?'"

Lola was going blind.

A few more months went by without answers from the veterinarian. All the while, she says, the pet store refused to listen to their plight or help with the mounting medical bills. Nancy and her son tried to get what's known as an unfit letter from their first veterinarian, documenting that Lola was not healthy enough for the American Puppy Club to sell in the first place. Under New Jersey's Pet Purchase Protection Act, a purchaser of a "defective" companion animal that receives an unfit letter from a veterinarian within two weeks of sale is eligible for refund or exchange from the pet store that sold it. Or the purchaser could be reimbursed for medical bills totaling up to twice the original sale price of the companion animal. The time window is somewhat longer for cases where the owner can prove the dog died of a congenital cause. As of this writing, there are twenty-one states with so-called puppy lemon laws that offer similar guarantees for health.[3]

But unfortunately for Nancy, it's common practice for the pet shop to refer buyers to veterinarians with whom they have a relationship—our first vet for Izzie was one we were sent to in this way. In Nancy's case, she says that this vet that she had been referred to by the pet store had unsurprisingly refused to write an unfit letter for Lola. By the time she'd gotten a handle on the situation, that two-week window from the date of sale had long since closed.

By Christmas 2012, Lola's health crisis had escalated yet again.

"I'm wrapping gifts, and Rory, all of a sudden, she spun around and slammed her head into the wall," Nancy says. "I screamed bloody murder, and she ran over to the door, into the corner, and she hid. I ran right over and grabbed her. My husband was downstairs, and I started screaming to him 'Something's wrong with Lola!' We picked her up, and we ran right back to the vet."

The vet ran a series of blood tests and referred Nancy to a nearby animal hospital. There, she put Lola on the floor, and in front of a team of veterinary neurosurgeons, the tiny puppy began manically circling. The doctors watched and delivered a damning diagnosis: necrotizing encephalitis.

"I just went, 'Oh dear God, what the heck is that?'" Nancy recalls of her shock and bewilderment. "[The doctor] looked at me, and she said, 'Your dog is dying. You'll be lucky if you have four months with her.' And I had an out-of-body experience. 'I was like what the heck is going on here? I can't even believe this is all happening to us.'"

The vets told her that the encephalitis was caused by a parasite called *Neospora caninum*, most often found to have been contracted from cows. The doctors told Nancy they believed that Lola had been infected when her mother ingested cattle feces at the breeding operation where she was likely born. While the parasite can often be treated if caught early enough, by the time it was diagnosed in Lola, it was far too late—both to save her and to get her declared unfit for sale under state law.

"The encephalitis eats away at the brain," Nancy says. "She just got progressively worse. She started having seizures even on her seizure medicine. Then her back legs were locked up, and she walked with a really bad gait. It was all different things. It was the seizures, it was the blindness… So they put her in intensive care."

By this time, Nancy says she was $6,000 deep in medical bills for Lola, and the dog was barely nine months old. The doctors offered to do an MRI, but with the diagnosis already clear and unequivocally terminal, the Sassos decided that another $2,000 to $3,000 for the test was not worth it.

"So we brought her back home, and we tried to make her comfortable. She had her little pink bed, and we took shifts on the couch. And my poor husband, he'd just retired, and we spent months trying to care for this poor dog. I think the worst part was having to call my son up at college and tell him that his poor little puppy was dying. The poor kid, he was crying his eyes out. I mean, it affected everybody."

By March 2013, it was clear to Nancy that the only humane option was to put Lola down.

"We didn't want to put her down on her birthday," Nancy says.

So they waited an extra week and then had the vet euthanize her.

"I told the vet that we want her [body] back. We want to bring her back [home]."

Nancy starts to weep.

"I'm so sorry," she says, trying to get through her tears to finish recounting Lola's story to me. "My son carried her in the backyard, and we buried her there. It was terrible. I'm sorry. It was really awful. We went through a lot with this poor dog."

But while Lola's short and painful life had ended, Nancy's crusade had just begun.

"[The American Puppy Club] messed with the wrong person. I don't back down. It affected my kid and my family. You know? And I saw what this dog went through and how much it hurt us. I was going to go to the end. And that's what I did. That's what I did."

When I purchased Izzie, her paperwork gave me her breeder's name and address along with the names of the dogs who sired her. Nancy, however, still has yet to learn who exactly Lola's breeder was, and she will probably never have a definitive answer to that question. Instead, Lola's paperwork bears only the name Abe Miller of Quail Creek Kennel in Ohio. And while he is listed in the document as "breeder," Miller is in fact a USDA-licensed broker, meaning that his operation also moves puppies from breeder to buyer or pet store. As a result, it's entirely possible he brokered Lola to the American Puppy Club and was not, in fact, her breeder. To wit, he is listed on the Humane Society's 2016 Horrible Hundred list for buying "more than one hundred puppies from unlicensed breeders."[4]

In 2012, just a month after Lola was sold to Nancy, a USDA inspector cited Miller for several violations. For one, he was found to be falsifying the birth dates of puppies so that he could ship them before the age of eight weeks, which the USDA prohibits. In that same USDA report, he was found to be acquiring puppies from unlicensed breeders.[5] This information was uncovered in a 2015 investigation from CBS Philadelphia, which also found that Miller had been slapped with several other violations when operating his business under the name DML Kennel.[6] But he wrote the USDA in 2012 asking to change his company's name so it could continue on a better path, obscuring the document trail under the former business name. The request was granted, and Quail Creek Kennel was born.[7]

As for Nancy, she says that Miller had much better luck working with the USDA than she did.

"I've called the USDA on him numerous times, and they did nothing. Absolutely nothing. I talked to the directors at the USDA. I went up as far as you could go on the ladder. And they did nothing. They sent investigators. They said, 'We're pretty sure we know your dog came from him but...we can't track exactly what puppy mill she came from,'" she says.

I asked the USDA about Nancy and Lola's case, and the agency's public affairs specialist, Tanya Espinoza, said it was not possible for the department to shut down a licensee like Abe Miller.

"If we receive a complaint, we look into that complaint to determine if there is an Animal Welfare Act noncompliance," Espinoza told me in an email. "While it is unfortunate that [Lola] died, the death of a puppy would not necessarily be an Animal Welfare Act noncompliance."[8]

As for giving Miller the green light to change the name of his business to potentially hide past dirty dealings, Espinoza says that's permissible.

"Facilities are allowed to change the name of their business, as long as the entity that holds the license does not change, as there is no restriction in the Animal Welfare Act that prevents them from doing so," Espinoza explained. "A name change does not obscure previous dealings, as the inspection reports are still listed for three years regardless of the name of the facility."

The trouble is, if someone has only ever dealt with the renamed company, he won't know to search for the inspection reports of the old one.

Naturally, Nancy was left feeling that her options with the USDA were exhausted. Perhaps that explains why Nancy was more than happy to help animal welfare groups throw down the gauntlet on the legislative side. When one group asked her to testify to help pass New Jersey Senate Bill 1870 to amend the Pet Purchase Protection Act, she was eager to do so in memory of Lola.

"It passed unanimously through the senate and the assembly," Nancy says with pride. She recalls one animal welfare advocate telling her that state legislators had gotten sick of seeing the same organizations showing up to testify. Hearing the personal story of someone who had previously no notion of the battle to fight puppy mills was able to wake them up. "She said to me 'Nance, if you didn't come testify, this would have never flew... When you got up and spoke, they all were just staring at you. Your whole story made a difference.'"

The bill passed in early 2015 and was signed into law, prohibiting stores from purchasing animals from breeders who had received one direct violation or three lesser, nondirect violations on past USDA inspections. Similar legislation was also passed in six other states, New York City, and a few surrounding counties. The hard-won law Nancy fought for in Lola's name also mandated that pet stores put placards on the cages of cats and dogs for sale listing the names, addresses, phone numbers, and USDA license numbers for the breeders they came from along with instructions on how to visit the USDA inspection report database online— making it yet another state law that was severely handicapped by the Trump administration's deactivation of the public database.

As for Nancy, she holds Lola's legacy of unconditional love close to her heart. She remembers her as a dog who adored her human companions despite the pain that our species had inflicted upon her.

"All she wanted to do was be with us. She curled up in a ball on top of us every night. She was the sweetest, the cutest—you would have loved her. She was a doll," Nancy says, her voice breaking. "I have a niece who's handicapped. She can't walk. And when we first brought Lola in, Lola jumped right in her lap and curled up in a ball. My niece loved her. Lola would just lick her to death, and we'd all be laughing. She licked everybody. She loved everybody."

CHAPTER FOURTEEN

Science vs. Common Sense

IT'S A QUESTION MANY DOG OWNERS TAKE FOR granted: What's the best way to care for a dog?

Izzie has a certain level of care that Dan and I maintain on a daily basis. She gets a minimum of three walks a day. Her food bowl is always clean and full of hypoallergenic (read: expensive), prescription kibble that must be purchased through her vet to keep her from having stomach distress. Her water bowl is always full, often with crushed ice, which she seems to enjoy. She has her own bed in every room of the house, although she prefers to sit in Dan's recliner or to sleep in our bed. Small baskets of her toys are kept in tidy corners, always available to her day and night should inspiration strike her. If we have to leave the house for a few hours, she receives a treat to distract her as we dart out the door and lock up. In the evenings, after her dinner sends a jolt of energy through her scrawny frame, my husband or I will indulge her in a game of tug-of-war or catch, depending on which of her favorite toys she wishes to abuse on any given day.

This is our standard of care. Through some trial and error, these are the things Dan and I have learned make for the healthiest, happiest—and hopefully longest-lived—Izzie.

Throughout our neighborhood of dog lovers here in Denver, there is a wide range of care for animals that I observe daily. Our neighbors, for example, used to keep their dogs largely outdoors and unattended. This was distressing to us when we first moved in. The dogs, though large boxer–pit bull mixes of some sort, have very short hair and barked and brayed day and night when forced to remain outdoors for hours on end, even in the snow. While eventually we had to plead with them to do something about these dogs being outside all day—and to their credit, they did—it's clear that they love these animals. Would Izzie survive even a day in the snow, locked outside in our yard? No. Both mentally and physically, she is not equipped for that type of feat. But our neighbors' dogs ultimately seemed physically no worse for wear—although they appear to be much less anxious and bark significantly less when they are allowed to come and go as they please through a doggie door on the back of the house.

Other dog owners have different priorities. There are the tattooed CrossFitters who complete two long daily runs past my door with their dogs, rain or shine. There is the pair of retirees who dress their Airedale terrier in a little red jacket when it's cold out. There's the mother who strolls her baby in a carriage while her three-legged dog hops along off-leash up and down our block so the pup can enjoy a little bit of freedom after cancer robbed her of a limb. Izzie doesn't discriminate and still gives the dog a gentle chase when she spots her.

Still, as I've learned, dog parents can be no less judgmental of other dog parents than human parents can be of other mothers and fathers.

But who's right?

The quality of care that a dog receives as a companion animal in a home is generally not policed unless it falls into the territory of animal hoarding or cruelty. In Denver County, where Izzie and I live, the rules are fairly open to interpretation. It's against the law to "needlessly beat, inflict violence upon or kill, overwork, torture or mutilate, or to otherwise treat in a cruel, dangerous, or inhumane manner, any animal, or to cause such acts."[1] I have to wonder who decides when beating a dog is or is not done "needlessly" and what circumstances would ever necessitate beating a dog.

Other rules ban leaving dogs in unventilated cars unattended and give the city the right to impound any animal showing signs of neglect, but beyond the example of malnourishment, the rules do not further specify what qualifies as neglect. The most black-and-white rule among them all is the ban on owning more than three domestic dogs per household. Not much room for interpretation there.

These are local laws and are enforced by the police or animal control, not the USDA. They're fairly standard with some minor variations for most of the country. But according to these laws that define what constitutes cruelty to animals in my neck of the woods, it's fairly plain to see that if I were to keep Izzie in conditions identical to those upheld by the USDA standards that govern commercial breeders, a Denver police officer could either arrest me, fine me, or confiscate my animal—or all of the above.

This divide between how most of us would treat our dogs and how the animals are treated in a breeding facility is at the heart of the debate on how to regulate the industry. There's the common sense camp: those who believe that regulations for dog breeding should take into account what seems obvious about dogs and their needs. Then there's the side that insists that more science is needed to determine exactly what is best for the dogs.

Gibbens at the USDA is one of those on the proscience side, as is Mike Bober, president and CEO of the Pet Industry Joint Advisory Council (PIJAC). Firmly on the other side of the debate are those often lumped into the category of animal welfare advocates who say that many in the commercial pet industry are hiding behind science as a way to avoid making the kinds of common sense changes that would easily alleviate pain and suffering for dogs in breeding facilities. After all, Dan and I are no dog experts. We ourselves have come to our conclusions on how to care for Izzie based on simple observations and common sense. The same goes for most domestic dog owners in this country; these animals don't exactly come with a training manual.

For the pet breeding and selling industry, common sense regulations incite concern. Because here's the problem with common sense: it tells us without a shred of hesitation that a dog does not belong in a cage without any human contact. And of course, large-scale commercial breeders can't make a business on lovingly breeding litters whenever a pair of dogs chooses to mate.

John Goodwin at the Humane Society is one of these voices calling for the industry to make immediate changes without waiting for peer-reviewed studies to tell them what is already apparent.

"I think research and studies can be insightful, good, and useful provided that they're correct. So that's good. Though I don't need science to tell me that a dog should be able to put her paws on solid ground and take a run around a backyard,"

Goodwin tells me. "And I am put off by some in the pet industry who seem to take a page out of the tobacco industry's playbook in that they won't make any reforms until the science is more clear. That's the exact same thing that cigarette companies said. *We have to see more science to be sure that smoking causes cancer. We have to see more science that says that dogs need a cage size that's more than just six inches larger than their bodies.* You don't need science for that. You just need three brain cells to figure that out."[2]

Gibbens at the USDA, who is himself the owner of several pet dogs and cats, still finds that there is an essential role for science to play in the determining of national standards that his agency can enforce. I asked him to explain his proscience position.

"It's the society that we live in, I think, that directs this. We're at a point now in society where things are not really going to get changed without some science," Gibbens says. "We can put our qualities and how we feel about ourselves and how we feel about our golden retriever at home on dogs, because that's how we would think about them. But from a commercial standpoint, I think the best thing to do is to have some science, and that will withstand a lot of challenges. You may say, 'It's intuitive, dogs need ten hours of sunshine a day.' And your neighbor may say 'No, six is fine.' So I think science is important."[3]

But herein lies the hypocrisy: the regulations in the Animal Welfare Act that the USDA is enforcing have admittedly little to no science behind them.

"There isn't science that was used for the basis for the previous requirements. So to me, to some extent, there has to be some arbitrariness to what is developed in the way of standards, and to me, it ought to be erring on ensuring the welfare of the animals. I mean, having an enclosure that's just six inches higher than the head of the dog is absurd," Cathy Liss of the Animal Welfare Institute says.[4]

"Where does that number even come from?" I ask her, trying to probe into the USDA's precise calculations for kennel sizing.

"That's why I say it was arbitrary," she says. "Again, that's what was proposed through regulation, not based on science, and that's what [the USDA] went with. So heaven forbid a dog should try to jump, which we would consider a normal behavior."

When I ask Gibbens the same question, he concedes that the Animal Welfare Act's regulations are not based on science.

At the eye of the storm of the science versus common sense debate is Dr. Candace Croney, the head of the Center for Animal Welfare Science at Purdue University. Since she was appointed to her position in 2014, she has taken on a challenge that few would ever want to touch: researching the welfare of dogs in commercial breeding operations to determine, scientifically, what new standards can and should be put in place. While her work has certainly attracted the interest of the industry and advocacy groups alike, she has, more importantly, won the support of the USDA, PIJAC, and even the nation's largest chain of pet stores—Petland—in her efforts.

"We support raising the standards of care, providing they are standards that are backed with sound science. That's why we're supportive of the efforts that are underway at Purdue University," Bober of PIJAC tells me. "Because the reality is, a lot of what's out there, unfortunately, is not based on science. It's either based on gut instinct or, in some cases, raw emotion."[5]

Brian Winslow, vice president of animal welfare and franchisee services at Petland, is also quick to tell me he supports Dr. Croney's efforts to create new breeder standards.

"We have been advocates of the Purdue program because it isn't based on any state standard... It goes across all state lines," he says.[6]

From Winslow's business-savvy perspective, higher levels of care for breeding dogs could mean commanding higher prices from customers who are happy to pay for the peace of mind that their puppy came from a responsible breeder.

But support from the likes of Petland, PIJAC, and the USDA has led to concern from animal welfare watchdogs like the Humane Society.

"They're using the Purdue research to not endorse reforms that are common sense," Goodwin says. "That's not an indictment of Purdue or Candace Croney—she may be doing excellent work. It is an indictment of people who are using her work as an excuse to not take action."

But Dr. Croney, firmly wedged in the middle of this debate and attracting both praise and rage from both sides, could not be more delighted to address the question of whether common sense should or should not outweigh science.

"I wish more people would ask the question, because it's a little bit of an elephant in the room," she says. "I will tell you, I kind of agree that there are some areas where you really do know what you're looking at when you see it. What is difficult is that there are other areas where people don't know what they don't know... And I will tell you, it frustrates me to no end when I hear scientists and others—including those who sometimes use it as a defense to not really do anything different—say 'Well, we can't do anything, because we don't have science.' Then, promptly, the answer becomes 'Well, there's no science, and there's no signs of science, so we'll just stay in a holding pattern here, and we'll never have to do anything different, right?'"[7]

Croney then gamely provides me with a concrete example of a science versus common sense debate she's had to navigate: the troublesome question of what is the best type of flooring for commercial dog-breeding kennels.

For most of us who are dog owners, the fact that this issue is at the forefront of the debate over the welfare of breeding canines may come as a surprise—after all, even as dog owners fret over what food is healthiest or how much exercise is needed, none of us ever consider what type of flooring is safest for our dogs' paws. And for good reason: the average companion animal will experience a variety of surfaces in the course of a day, from carpets to hardwood floors to concrete sidewalks to mud or grass. But when confined to a crate for years, without any mandates that a dog be given time to pace or roam on any other surface, the question of the safety of flooring becomes an essential one.

Having personally seen some of the sores and foot problems that can arise in breeding dogs who live their entire life on wire mesh or pea gravel, I can attest to the fact that flooring matters. But what kind of flooring is best?

"I can't believe we have more science on what's safe, comfortable flooring for farm animals than we do for dogs," Croney tells me. "That's shocking."

But perhaps what is most telling of Croney's position in the science versus common sense debate is her decision to exclude one type of flooring from her study right from the get-go.

"We did not study dogs on chicken wire," she says. Some breeders do attempt to keep their dogs on this thin, painful surface, although some state regulations explicitly ban it. "I can tell you that with the anatomy of the dog's foot and what chicken wire looks like...common sense says that that doesn't work."

For what it's worth, most chicken wire is too thin to meet the standards of the Animal Welfare Act.

But with common sense as her starting point, Croney used science to investigate the several types of flooring that are used most often in kennels, including coated metal, slatted plastic, and concrete—all of which are permissible under the Animal Welfare Act.

"What we found is absolutely no significant foot health movement or other problems in these types of floors," she concludes.

But other veterinarians do not agree with Croney's conclusion. Overall, for one, asserts that wire–mesh flooring of any kind can damage the anatomy of the dog's foot and also runs contrary to the dog's natural preference for other surfaces. When Overall assessed Izzie, she noted that my dog does not engage her own feet in exploration frequently and does not like having them touched—a trait that she pointed out is often seen in dogs who spent their earliest development period on wire mesh.

Croney, however, says that cage flooring materials are only part of the equation. Instead, she says that all dogs should have access to the outside and not be confined to a cage for life—even though there is nothing in the Animal Welfare Act to prohibit breeders from doing so. She acknowledges that in her research finding no significant problems in the feet of dogs kept on a variety of surfaces, the subjects were not solely confined to a single surface despite the fact that many breeders do keep dogs in this fashion.

"All these dogs [in the study] had access to outdoor runs that had solid flooring on there, and most if not all of them had access to exercise areas, runs, and so on. So it's entirely possible that in addition to that really good management of their feet, you know, access to these other surfaces may have provided them some protection," Croney says.

However, access to outdoor runs is not mandated by the USDA, and in large, commercial breeding operations, dogs often lack that critical access.

It is also worth noting that Croney did not bring her canine test subjects into her lab for years on end to explore her hypotheses. Instead, she went out to real, USDA-licensed kennels to conduct her experiments and collect her data. I asked her if she has encountered criticism of selection bias—after all, the worst breeders out there, even with a USDA license, would be very unlikely to allow a group of scientists onto their property to investigate their animals.

"We thought it was important to get a sense of where people were with the physical health of these dogs out in the real world," Croney says of why her team did not bring dogs into their own controlled lab for these tests. "But like you said, people who are not doing so great of a job are probably not going to be the first ones to volunteer [for our studies], right? So here's what's interesting. There are times when people volunteer because they really do think they are doing a great job... I was taken aback, because they really think they are doing a brilliant job," she says. "So how do we tactfully convey that [they're not]?"

Croney then dives down to one of the points she sees at the heart of the science versus common sense debate: forget the semantics, forget the data—just look at the dogs.

"Dogs are beautiful. They can't lie to us," she says. "They can't change their body condition. They can't change their behavior just because, you know, someone says the pesky scientists are showing up today."

Overall, Croney found that physical health problems were not nearly as dire as the behavioral problems she observed in breeding dogs. Even in the large-scale commercial breeding operations that are frequently blamed with being the worst for the dogs, she says that behavioral development was the biggest area of opportunity.

"I need you to know that when I did this research, I did not know anything about this industry," Croney admits. Her long career in animal welfare has included extensive research into animal behavior and bioethics surrounding the use of animals in agriculture and other endeavors. She has worked as a scientific advisor on issues of animal welfare to numerous and diverse groups including the American Humane Association, the National Pork Board, Merck, Target, and Bob Evans Farms. But when it came to commercial dog breeding, she confesses that she had a lot to learn. "I had exactly the same concerns and perceptions that the average person did: that commercial breeding is the same thing as being a puppy mill, and they are all bad, and the dogs are in bad conditions, and the people don't care about their dogs… Honestly, that's where I started. And for me, I sort of had to put aside my own bias, because one of the things I teach [at Purdue] in addition to animal behavior and welfare is ethics."

She describes her personal process in approaching the project as requiring her to set aside her own opinions to avoid trying to be the "moral police." Instead, she sought out the opportunities where she could best make a difference in the lives of the animals involved in the industry.

"I have to tell you, it's been hard," she says frankly.

She also admits that it has been hard to convey to breeders that they need to change their ways. Often, breeders regard Croney and her team as egg-headed outsiders who could not possibly understand the ins and outs of their livelihood.

"The beauty of it, again, is we go back to the dogs. The dogs are the answer to everything. So when we show them what the dogs are showing in their behavior, when we show them what the dogs are showing in terms of their overall physical health, the beauty of it is that even if the breeders resist that information, now they can see it too. So now, the onus is on them to do something about that."

By the same token, the animals themselves cannot speak to the political wrangling behind the scenes that has dogged Croney's project with Purdue.

In September 2015, the Humane Society, the ASPCA, and the Humane Society Veterinary Medical Association joined forces to issue a formal petition to raise the USDA's federal standards of care for dogs in breeding facilities. The proposed standards called for restrictions on wire flooring in kennels and the frequency of breeding. They pushed the USDA to mandate that breeders provide their dogs with exercise outside of their cages, yearly veterinary visits, constant access to clean drinking water, and larger cage sizes. The proposal also called for a new requirement that breeders make an effort to adopt out their retired breeding dogs to rescue groups rather than simply euthanizing or abandoning them.

In his statement at the time, Wayne Pacelle, president and CEO of the Humane Society, returned to the need for common sense to dictate how these dogs are treated.

"It's common sense that dogs should have water, space, exercise, and other basic care, and responsible dog breeders and pet industry groups should welcome these improved standards to restore consumer confidence and deal with the outliers who cut corners and treat puppies like products. The current standards are insufficient and outdated and need to be fortified to crack down on abusive puppy mills."[8]

The petition was, however, rebuffed by the USDA and the pet industry.

"We would be concerned about any such petition that is based on either hearsay or anecdote, as opposed to say based on well-defined and tested principles," Bober of pet industry group PIJAC tells me of the reason why his influential organization has failed to support the petition.

The USDA's Gibbens tells me that his agency is now seeing many petitions, of which the Humane Society's effort is just one. Taking action on any one petition, he says, would set a poor precedent.

"We're a creature of the federal government and a creature of the law. So we've got to be open to changes," Gibbens says. "Petitions seem to be the new thing. We've gotten eight or ten of those in the last year or two, and we don't have a regulatory requirement to do stuff with them. But we want to get input. We don't want to sit there with blinders on. You know, if there is good science or something that will clearly improve the welfare of the lives of animals, I say yeah, we're open to it. But we have to be careful as a federal agency about actively—proactively—pursuing something that might be outside the restraints of the law."

The Humane Society's Goodwin is not impressed. He fears that with industry funding and backing from the USDA, the Purdue standards could create a situation in which the "fox is guarding the hen house."

"These groups that are funding the Purdue research, they have refused to this point to endorse the petition we've submitted to the USDA that calls for overhaul of the regulations to all these commercial operations. They say they won't endorse it until they see what Purdue comes up with on the off chance that it's even higher than what we've called for. That's not an excuse. That's not a reason to refuse to endorse it," he says. "The industry is refusing to endorse the one effort that would actually raise the standards for the government inspectors."

Dr. Croney is well aware of the Humane Society's petition. While her group has yet to issue its final recommendations, she tells me that her standards address the same areas of concern and go even further than those in that petition.

Croney acknowledges that PIJAC provided some of the seed funding for her research and has been "conceptually support-ive" of her team's work. The USDA, while providing no actual funding, she credits with being "very, very supportive" of her work by providing her with a research fellow to assist in the study.

"But [the USDA has] had nothing to do with developing the actual standards. They've had no input in them. They don't even know what's in there," she says.

Croney insists that in spite of this support, it is not the goal of her research to create new laws or provide instructions to the USDA.

"They will take a good, hard look at the research itself, and if they think there is something they need to change, then they'll make the decision to do that," she says. However, dealing with criticism is part of the job when you're at the center of a highly emotional debate like dog breeding. Croney is not immune to it and even welcomes it, acknowledging that she's heard it and thinks it's fair. In fact, she points out that if she were not the one conducting and overseeing the research herself, she would likely be just as skeptical of the program. But with her long background in the study of the ethics of using animals for industry, she believes that she brings more than just a scientific mind to the table.

"The science may support it, but there are some valid ethical questions here that we should be thinking about," she says. "That's always been how I've run my program and so, to be honest, it doesn't really matter who supports the program conceptually or not. We set this up so that even people who provided funding for the standards and for the research will get the research when everybody else gets the research. None of them have even seen the [recommended] standards themselves. That's because there absolutely needs to be a separation of church and state when it comes to industry-funded research—which this was, to be really clear. But the beauty of it is, no one needs to believe us. The dogs cannot tell a story other than truth."

CANINE CARE CERTIFIED

In August 2016, Purdue released its first voluntary program for breeders who want to go the extra mile. Dubbed Canine Care Certified, the program is run by an independent auditing company and is now out of Dr. Croney's hands but is using her research as its guide. I find it interesting that a scientist whose work is championed by the USDA has given her research to a third-party company that exists to shore up the gaps left by our federal government's licensing apparatus. However, as that research is now being used by an independent auditing service, the nitty-gritty of what it precisely calls for is considered proprietary information and cannot be shared with the public beyond a few overarching principles. This makes it frustratingly difficult for those of us who would like to see the much-anticipated new standards and evaluate them. But at its core, what the Canine Care Certified program is intended to do is provide breeders with an opportunity to voluntarily submit their facilities to a third-party inspector who can give them a mark of distinction that goes above and beyond the USDA seal of approval.

"Ideally, there are a couple of things that should motivate the breeders," Croney says. "I think you want the pride and the ability to prove that you're not just doing what you're required to do, you are going far above and beyond."

Croney then goes on to explain that the other key component in motivating breeders to submit to the inspectors for the Canine Care Certified program is to elevate the value of the dogs they are selling. "If you are going to get a dog, everybody wants a physically healthy dog. You want a dog that is behaviorally sound, or at least one that you know is set up in life to succeed as opposed to running into issues down the line, right? And while there is no way to guarantee a perfectly and behaviorally healthy dog that doesn't have any problems, if you're a consumer, you probably want to pick the dog that comes with something that lets you know they were well taken care of [and] their parents were well taken care of, so that the risk of running into these problems is lower than the dog that doesn't come with this type of certification process behind it."

Personally, I agree with Croney. I believe that if someone is going to purchase a dog instead of adopt, he should be willing to pay a premium to ensure that dog was humanely bred. Like a fair-trade sticker on a bag of coffee or a "pasture-raised" label on a carton of eggs, so too could the exemplary dog breeders out there demonstrate that they are worthy of an extra investment—particularly on an animal that the average American spends more than $1,500 to care for annually.[9]

Croney believes that there is a desire among commercial breeders who run responsible operations to differentiate themselves from those who oversee facilities that could easily be labeled as puppy mills. Same goes for retailers who wish to show consumers that their dogs, while they may be for sale and are not rescues, truly do not come from puppy mills. Then, with the Canine Care Certified mark of distinction, these breeders can command a higher price for their dogs as they come with a stronger value proposition.

"Doing all this extra stuff [to become Canine Care Certified] actually costs money. And frankly, their dogs are worth more because they've had more work and more effort put into raising them to a much higher standard of care that can actually be documented," Croney says.

This is a point that particularly interests Petland's Winslow. Even as pet stores are closing or ending their puppy sales operations around the country, Petland persists. I asked Winslow how many dogs the company sells each year, and he replied that the company does not disclose the numbers of puppies they sell because "animal rights advocates will take any number and twist it to their advantage. Animal rights advocates think that no animals should be sold, and broadcasting numbers gives them ammunition."[10]

As for those animal rights advocates, the Humane Society estimates that Petland sells tens of thousands of puppies every year across the United States. And just as Winslow mentioned, the chain has been a frequent target of scrutiny and even outrage from animal advocacy groups. Notably, in 2008, the Humane Society published the results of an investigation into Petland that labeled the store "the nation's largest retail supporter of puppy mills."[11] While these animal welfare advocates may fight any sales of puppies by Petland or any retailer, it's obvious that the chain holds immense influence over the industry where there remains a demand for pet store puppies. To have Petland's support for reform at a national level and the company's commitment to only purchase from breeders who obtain the imprimatur of the Canine Care Certified program could be a game changer.

"Our goal is, at some point in time, that every puppy that goes through a Petland store comes from a breeder that is Canine Care Certified," Winslow says. "Based on a lot of variables outside of our control, we can't mandate the speed [at] which the [Canine Care Certified] program expands, meaning that we're not third-party inspectors. We're not in charge of the marketing of the program. But what we can control is our influence on breeders for one, to join, and two, to compensate them on doing a job that would be recognized by a third-party auditor."

While Winslow stopped short of telling me that Petland would commit to only purchasing from these certified breeders, he said it is the company's "desire" to do so someday. Winslow says that Petland is working consistently to improve and has increased its efforts to personally visit and evaluate as many of the breeders in its supply chain as possible. Having a third party that can be trusted with performing these evaluations would save the company time and money while also helping to restore public trust—all around, it would be good business.

So far, similar efforts to provide additional certification to the best dog breeders in the business have been attempted at the state level. But with each state conforming to different standards, the national impact has been minimal.

"A couple of states have, within their borders, programs that not only go above the Animal Welfare Act [but also above] their own state regulations," Winslow acknowledges. "Kansas has this program called KEEP, Missouri has Blue Ribbon, Pennsylvania has [the Kennel Assurance Program] KAP... All of them are voluntary. All of them are things that raise standards...but if you ask the average person who walks down the street or comes in one of our stores... it's not transparent enough. Because it never makes its way outside of that state's boundaries. I'm pretty confident because of the legs that the [Purdue] Canine Care Certification program already has, and it's bolted onto a prominent veterinary school, and doctors of animal welfare are signing their name to it... This program has the ability to go beyond the borders of Indiana. And it will reach a level of transparency that meets demand, and as you create demand, you increase prices."

But for now, the Canine Care Certified program is rolling out slowly and does not offer the transparency of showing exactly what it requires from breeders. Furthermore, the certification program costs $1,500 a year plus $10 for every dog a facility has over a head count of fifty.[12] For the bad actors out there who are only in the business to make money, I'm skeptical that paying these fees will ever seem like a worth investment—especially when it costs so little just to get a USDA license and nothing more. In the meantime, well-meaning consumers are still purchasing dogs that—either intentionally or unintentionally—are falling through the massive gaps in regulation and enforcement.

So what is the best way to care for a dog? The answer is still being decided by the government and by the pet industry—even if the common sense of pet owners would beg to differ. But it's human nature to be horrified when we catch a glimpse of how the pet dog is treated in a breeding facility. And when a pet owner comes to realize how her dog was treated in its previous, agricultural context, the outrage can be life altering.

CHAPTER FIFTEEN

When Big Breeders Have Big Friends

KRISTIN AKIN IS THE FIRST TO ADMIT THAT SHE SHOULD have known better when she fell head over heels for Lovey.

She and her husband, Justin, had already gone through the process of taking two dogs into their St. Louis home. First, it was a wheaten terrier named Gilligan that they adopted from a breed-specific rescue when they were first married. Kristin filled out a lengthy application and then opened the doors to her home for an inspection from the rescue group. But the rescue almost threw the brakes on Gilligan's adoption because the Akins did not yet have a fence for their yard. The couple signed a contract promising to erect one within a year. The rescue was satisfied, and Gilligan came home.

One happy dog–lifetime later, Gilligan passed away, and the Akins were ready for another dog. Now parents of a young child, the family returned to the same rescue. But at the time, the rescue could not find them a wheaten that would be good with their son. So Kristin set her sights on a goldendoodle. She found a small, local breeder to work with.

She patiently filled out another lengthy application describing the size of her house and yard, detailing her family's schedules to demonstrate whether they'd have sufficient time to walk their new pup, how many children they had in the household, whether she had already engaged a veterinarian for its care, and what her family's history with dogs had been. The Akinses passed muster, and off they went to personally pick up their next dog, Skipper, from the breeder's kennels in person.

After living with Skipper for a couple of years, Kristin and her husband started thinking that bringing a second goldendoodle into the family might help with some of his hyperactivity.

"We kept talking over the last two years that we've had him that maybe if we get him a friend, he'll chill out," Kristin recalls.[1]

So Kristin and her husband began their search the way most consumers do: online. She found the aptly named NextDayPets. com and began idly searching its roster of available dogs. Sooner than they could have ever planned, Kristin was struck. She found a dog for sale that immediately she knew she had to have.

"Part of what we liked is that the dog was already four months old, so that seemed really appealing. She wasn't a brand-new puppy… It was kind of a knee-jerk reaction," Kristin says, trying—but failing, as most people do—to explain why she was so intensely certain this was the exact dog for her family.

This type of impulse purchase is common, even among well-intentioned buyers like Kristin. In fact, people who have gone through reputable breeders or shelters in the past can be particularly vulnerable to the lure of a click-to-buy puppy—after all, they know just how time-consuming the process of doing it right can be. To them, an easy purchase can seem like a harmless shortcut. However, as Kristin would go on to discover, these easily purchased dogs more often than not go on to be anything but easy in the long run.

For Kristin, that click-to-buy dog would turn out to be Lovey. And from the very beginning, Lovey was different from the dogs Kristin had in the past.

BUYING LOVEY

On June 3, 2016, Kristin sent an inquiry to purchase Lovey—then named online as Kylee—from the breeder. She texted the breeder's phone number posted on NextDayPets and got a quick response the very same day telling her that the dog was still available and ready to go home right away. To secure the dog, she was told to pay a $300 deposit and fill out the application.

"I take full ownership in that I was not thinking through it all after the previous things that I had to go through to get the other two dogs," Kristin says. "It wasn't until I was filling out the application that I did kinda make a mental note, like, this isn't really an application. It's just name, address, city, state."

With the deposit paid, Kristin looked up the breeder online: Debra Ritter of Cornerstone Farms in Curryville, Missouri. Kristin found her website. The page is typical of many other breeders I've encountered: frilly web graphics that might have seemed high-tech over a decade ago, stock images of fluffy puppies, and lengthy references to the Bible and the God-driven mission of their work with animals. Their landing page features the following welcome message:

We are Cornerstone Farms, home of the Ritter Family! We've been showing, training, and breeding for over 30 yrs. We offer references and a lifetime of puppy support. We are State, AKC, USDA, and Vet inspected yearly... As a Missouri State licensed breeder we are held to the highest standard of care for our companions. We very firmly advocate against such places where animals are kept in unsanitary, often unsafe conditions and used only as tools for profit... We love our dogs and they are our pets, every one of them!

We love Jesus too!!![2]

On another part of the site, explaining the process of how they will fly or ship a dog anywhere in the country for a fee, the Ritters again emphasize their faith and their dedication:

Purchasing a companion from anyplace around the world can be fun and exciting! We do our best to make the whole thing a lot of fun for the kids, peaceful and trouble-free for Dad and Mom. All of the Ritters love Jesus, so if you do as well then faith helps the whole process be stress free!

When reading through the website, Kristin noted all these religious references and also saw the breeder's list of accreditations running down the left side of the screen, including their pronouncement that they are "proud to be members" of the Missouri Department of Agriculture and the USDA. Neither the Missouri Department of Agriculture nor the USDA have members—only licensees.

"I noticed the accreditations, and they seemed legit to me. I did not dig any further or do any [additional] googling," Kristin says regretfully.

She began emailing back and forth with Ritter. Kristin asked why Lovey was a bit older than the majority of the dogs posted online for sale—most of the other listed puppies average between eight and twelve weeks.

"[Ritter] said, 'Oh, we keep all our puppies… If they don't all get a home right away, then we keep them until they get placed,'" Kristin recalls.

Next, Kristin asked how big the dog was. Ritter responded that the puppy was twenty pounds. This answer was acceptable for Kristin who did the rough math that a dog weighing twenty pounds at four months should mature to be around twice that size once fully grown. She also took heart to hear from Ritter that the dog was already socialized and had been living with her family in her home as a pet. The wheels were now in motion; Kristin was instructed to pay $1,250 for the dog via PayPal. She immediately ponied it up.

Ritter then mentioned that she would be driving into Kristin's part of town the next day to deliver puppies to a few other families in the St. Louis area.

"I was expecting that I would drive to Curryville [Missouri]—wherever the hell that was—and that was fine," Kristin says, expecting that she would repeat her experience of purchasing her dog Skipper from a breeder, when she had traveled to the kennel where he was born to pick him up in person. But the convenience seemed harmless at the time. Why not just pick up her new dog the next day in the parking lot of a local shopping center and spare herself the one-hundred-mile drive from St. Louis to rural Curryville?

"I'm embarrassed because now I've read all this stuff on puppy mills," Kristin concedes, referring to the fact that groups like the

Humane Society and the ASPCA often list it as a red flag when a breeder offers to meet a buyer in a neutral location as opposed to letting her view the property where they breed and raise dogs for herself.

As it turns out, NextDayPets.com lived up to its name and brand promise. Sure as Kristin had found her dog on the site on June 3, she was sitting in a shopping center parking lot near her home, waiting to pick up the pup on June 4. A dusty brown conversion van pulled up, and one of Ritter's daughters emerged with Lovey. Debra Ritter herself had stayed behind in Curryville and was not present for the handoff.

Ritter's daughter put a leash around the dog's neck. Kristin says the dog seemed to be on tranquilizers: barely moving and zoned out. Believing that this dog had been kept as the Ritter family pet, Kristin assumed it was just scared to be somewhere unfamiliar and so far from home.

"I crept over, and I'm like *Hiiii!* in my sweet, baby voice. I put my hand out, and she's just totally withdrawn from me and from everybody. It wasn't like when you take your dog to the groomer and they don't want to leave you and they're like clawing on you and trying to hold on and stay in your arms. It wasn't like she was connected to them and not wanting to leave them. She just stood there like she was a zombie…she wasn't cowering. Her head was down. She just was standing there like 'I got nothing.' You know what I mean? Like, 'I'm a beat-down person who just doesn't have anything to give you. I mean, I'm not sad to leave these people, but I'm definitely not glad to see you, because all the people I've seen are shitheads.' Excuse my French."

But Lovey's demeanor wasn't the only remarkable thing about her at that first meeting in the parking lot: the goldendoodle that

had been promised to be twenty pounds just the day before was
clearly more than twice that weight.

"I said to [the Ritters' daughter], 'Wow, she's a lot bigger than
we were expecting.' She was like, 'Yeah, we weighed her today.
She's actually like forty-five [pounds].'"

But the money was already paid, and the deal was already done.
Kristin signed the dog's USDA disposition forms and managed
to scoop the suspiciously large puppy into her car and take her
home. As she drove, she couldn't help panicking that this four-
month-old puppy already tipping the scales at forty-five pounds
would potentially double in size when it reached adulthood, an
eventuality she and her husband had simply not envisioned or
mentally prepared for. But all the same, Lovey was her dog now,
and that was that.

But with Lovey came more problems and more questions.

Immediately, Kristin discovered that Lovey had constant
diarrhea. When she wasn't evacuating her bowels, she was
compulsively scratching herself with maniacal vigor. Seeking a
remedy, Kristin tried to bathe her, expecting to find bugs or fleas
on her body. Instead, she found scabs all over her skin, concentrated around Lovey's joints. In the tub, she pulled back Lovey's
ears in horror.

"I lift up the flap, you know, and it's dirty, dirty, dirty, stinky,
stinky, stinky, oily, greasy, filled with dirt, horrible. I used a half
a bag of cotton balls and hydrogen peroxide trying to clean them
out the best I could. They were just filthy," she says, the self-
described clean freak still cringing at the memory.

Meanwhile, Lovey's demeanor remained troubling. Kristin
lives in a two-story home with stairs. But for Lovey, these stairs
were a physical impossibility and an unfamiliar mental puzzle. She

simply could not climb them, not even the single step required to enter the main floor. Kristin and her husband reasoned that this dog had never seen a stair before in her life.

"She'd probably never been inside a house," Kristin recalls, once again uncertain how this dog could have possibly been raised as a pet in the warm and loving home environment that Ritter had described to her. "For probably the first week to ten days, to go upstairs to bed at night, we would just carry her. Carry her up and down."

Things became even stranger once Kristin's vet took a look at Lovey.

"He's immediately running his hands over her and looking at her. [He says], 'Oh, she's really pretty. Where did you get her?' And I tell him, and he's like, 'Okay, so how old is she?' And I say four months. And he's like, 'Oh no, this dog is not anywhere near four months.'"

Kristin was stunned.

"I'm standing there like a total dingbat. [I asked], 'What do you mean?'"

The vet, who Kristin had known for years as he cared for her previous dogs, pulled back Lovey's gums to show Kristin her teeth—fully descended, not a baby tooth or gap in sight. He explained to her that a dog's full, adult teeth typically descend between seven or eight months of age. In Lovey's case, he pointed out, they were all in, and they had already accrued signs of significant wear and tear, with tartar building up on her molars. He estimated that Lovey was between a year and two years old at least.

Kristin asked her vet why the breeder would possibly lie about Lovey's age.

"[He said] 'If I were to guess, she probably didn't go into heat.

So they decided she's no use if she can't be bred. They probably thought they'd try to sell her, and if they can, great. If not, then they'd probably shoot her,'" she recalls him saying, assuring her that, in the breeding world, it's relatively common practice.

Kristin and her vet decided to revaccinate Lovey just in case her paperwork turned out to be incorrect, as its credibility was already in question over her age alone.

The good news was that in spite of the diarrhea, her stool samples tested negative for any parasites or infections. They ran comprehensive blood tests and were able to rule out any serious issues other than severe allergies. They put Lovey on a new, hypoallergenic food and shampoo regimen that, in the days and weeks to follow, cleared up her skin and digestive problems. The vet consoled Kristin by explaining that all of Lovey's problems seemed fixable and were likely due simply to neglect. He also chalked up the dog's zombielike malaise to fear. It seemed to him that she'd likely never been around people before and was terrified but should eventually warm up.

After a two-hour vet visit and a bill topping $800 on her brand-new dog, Kristin started digging online in earnest. Very quickly, she was able to find numerous customer complaints against Cornerstone Farms despite its then-A+ rating with the Better Business Bureau.[3] The cherry on top was the breeder's inclusion in the Humane Society's Horrible Hundred list of the worst puppy mills in the country. Significantly, the Humane Society notes that Cornerstone Farms is a "repeat offender" and confirmed to me that the organization has received reports in years past that were so exigent, they had to be passed on to local law enforcement.[4]

"I'm just crying. I am so mad at myself, like, I can't believe I fell [for this]. I would never want to support a puppy mill, and I know Missouri's known for them, and I just didn't do enough homework. I didn't stop and think. In hindsight now, I'm comparing [the process] to the other two: the good breeder and the adoption," Kristin says. "It made me really sick inside."

Kristin continued in her attempts to seek information directly from the Ritters. She texted them that she loved the dog and had no interest in being refunded or in returning her but wanted to know how old she was really so she could appropriately care for her. She says that the messages went unanswered with the exception of one in which she asked what size crate to purchase for Lovey.

YOUR WORD AGAINST THEIRS

As the silence persisted from the Ritters, Kristin became increasingly incensed. She filed an official animal welfare complaint with the USDA. She also reached out to the Missouri Department of Agriculture to file a Bark Alert, a program the state founded back in 1992, primarily to crack down on unlicensed facilities.

"I'm telling the lady [at the Missouri Department of Agriculture] everything. She's like, 'Yeah, I hear you. But really, it's your word against theirs. So unless you have it documented, there's really not much we can do.'"

This conversation with the Missouri Department of Agriculture, as Kristin recounts it, is particularly puzzling to me. For its part, the agency refused to respond to any of my specific questions regarding Kristin's case. But thanks to Missouri's Sunshine Law, which allows me to request official records from the state similar to a FOIA request, I know for a fact that the Missouri Department of Agriculture has its own records explicitly documenting repeated, serious violations at Cornerstone Farms going back more than a decade. So what's the point of all that record keeping if a consumer filing a complaint is going to be told it's her word against the breeder's?

But of course, Kristin had no idea what the state had on the Ritters, if anything at all. Unlike the USDA, the Missouri Department of Agriculture has never kept even a recent, partial database of breeder-inspection records online for the public to peruse on demand before buying. Instead, it's up to a consumer to file a formal Sunshine request, pay a small fee, and wait several weeks or even months to receive these inspection reports and become fully informed before buying. For an average puppy buyer, this is a high bar for entry to learn about a breeder.

I filed my own Sunshine request on the Ritters with the Missouri Department of Agriculture. After several weeks of back-and-forth, I was instructed to mail a check to their office for their efforts. Soon after, a thick file on Cornerstone Farms arrived at my door. It was more than one hundred pages long with up to five violations per page in some cases. As I held it in my hands, I couldn't understand how the state—in good conscience or in good service to its taxpayers—could tell Kristin that it was her word against the Ritters.

As tedious as it may have been, even this vital process aimed at transparency has come under fire. In July 2016, the Missouri House of Representatives passed a bill that would have eliminated the Sunshine Law on animal welfare and environmental issues. If it had passed the state senate, the bill would have taken away the public's right to request reports on all factory farms including commercial dog breeders. Without it, neither Kristin nor I would know the full extent of the Ritters' history of violations.

"The state legislature has tried to take away the Sunshine reports on health provisions for animals and the environment for the last four years...because [the state government] is controlled by rural legislators," Bob Baker at the Missouri Alliance for Animal Legislation explains. "[The breeders] don't let people in to see the facilities, and then they want to cover up their inspection reports... This industry survives in the dark shadows."[5]

While the bill had the votes to pass through the state senate, Baker and other advocates for transparency managed to fight it until it was amended to save the Sunshine Law.

But challenges to transparency remain an issue when it comes to regulating dog breeders. Baker points out that at a breeder conference he attended in the summer of 2016, the USDA's Gibbens told the attendees that they were free to use post office box addresses on the then-publicly-available online USDA database so long as they kept their physical address privately on file with the agency and its inspectors.

I tried to attend this meeting for myself but was rebuffed by the USDA, told there were simply no available seats left—even as I informed them I was more than happy to stand. After the conference, Baker laughed when I told him why I hadn't been allowed to attend. He reported to me that there were dozens of empty seats available.

So I went straight to the source and asked Gibbens about his comments to breeders that they may keep their physical addresses hidden from the public and inquired whether this allowance further impedes industry transparency.

"We try to be as transparent as we can, and that's the reason for that search engine being online," Gibbens said, back in August 2016. "And would the breeding industry prefer that the search engine not be online? Probably a lot of them would prefer that they not be online. But I think that kind of transparency helps hold the industry accountable. Any industry like that that's going to succeed is going to have to look acceptable to the public. And if the public can find out what they look like, then they can demonstrate their acceptability… I think we're doing a good job of being transparent."[6]

Six months later, as we know, the Trump administration pulled the entire database of publicly available USDA inspection reports from the web.

While the federal inspection report database was imperfect, it was still better than nothing at all. As of summer 2016, when Kristin was purchasing Lovey, the database was still up and running. But Cornerstone Farms had no violations on its year-old USDA license available for all to see—despite what state inspection reports clearly showed.

In documents provided to me by the Humane Society, I learned that the Ritters had only obtained their federal license in 2015 after receiving an official USDA warning for eleven instances of selling dogs without a license. For decades, they'd been able to operate with only state oversight until the USDA updated its retail sale rules in 2013 so that a breeder would need a federal license to sell to a customer without the buyer meeting the dog face-to-face. As of this writing, the Ritters are licensed by the USDA, allowing them to sell their dogs online to anyone nationwide.

As she launched her complaint against Cornerstone Farms to the USDA, Kristin had been making records of her own, keeping track of every text, email, phone call, and piece of paperwork, going far above and beyond what most average consumers would do. She compiled the documents and submitted them. After all that, she was informed that in order to receive the agency's ruling on the complaint, she'd have to write a letter and mail it to the USDA's FOIA office, then wait another sixty days. She did so, and the waiting game began.

"I can see why most people probably don't do it," she says of the lengthy, confusing, and arduous process.

Around this time, news of Kristin's challenges with Lovey began to circulate around her group of friends. One friend, who volunteers as an anti-puppy-mill advocate, had done some digging on Cornerstone Farms in the past and handily dropped a stack of Missouri Department of Agriculture inspection reports on the operation into Kristin's lap—the same ones that I obtained and verified through my own Sunshine request. They were disturbing to say the least.

On October 20, 2014, an inspector from the Missouri Department of Agriculture found a female standard poodle tattooed with the name "Brooke" at Cornerstone Farms to be compulsively shaking her head. The inspector checked her right ear to find "a buildup of brown/black substance."[7] The Ritters were ordered to take the dog for treatment with a licensed veterinarian. That same day, the state found two other female poodle mixes with "open sores in the ear, eye, and throat regions." The inspectors learned from the Ritters that these wounds were caused by a dog fight.

"Licensee stated that she was treating these sores but the sores were not healing progressively," the report reads.

On February 9, 2015, the same state inspector returned to Cornerstone Farms and marked eleven previously noncompliant items from the October 20, 2014, inspection had been corrected. However, the inspector found seven new noncompliant items to document.

In an enclosure housing Shiba Inu puppies with their mother, the inspector found the flooring to be violating state regulations. "One of the puppies was observed with all four feet passing through the wire flooring. Licensee shall provide proper sized flooring so that puppy's feet will not pass through the flooring and so that the puppy can walk in a normal manner."

The inspector returned on January 21, 2016, and found nine new noncompliant items, two of which were repeats that had already been found and identified on past inspections.[8]

As Kristin pored through these state reports, her blood began to boil.

"You make the Humane Society's [Horrible Hundred] every year, you have continual repetitive, multiple [offenses], but you have the same inspector... It's just very incestuous," she says, infuriated that the same inspector has been assigned to investigate the Ritters' farm since at least 2002. "So this lady comes out, she writes you up on some violations, that's her job. It looks like she is doing her job, because her job is to inspect you... In the meantime, nobody is paying [attention to] the dogs... She comes back six months later, and says 'Yup, you're compliant, and let me write you up on a few new ones.'... This just repeats. How long do you get to be not compliant?"

Kristin asked the Missouri Department of Agriculture this very question: how this cycle of finding violations, giving the Ritters time to correct them, and then adding new ones could be allowed to continue. She was told that the state regulators were working with the Ritters to help them achieve compliance. But when Kristin pressed to find out how many years the back-and-forth could be allowed to continue, she says she received no response.

I asked the department the same question and several others.

While the state declined to respond to my specific questions, it did issue a written statement to me that included this remark: "The department's goal is to get licensees back in compliance. If the department revokes a breeder's license, then it has no regulatory authority at all. The department has a protocol by which repeat offenders are referred to the attorney general's office."[9]

Bob Baker has tried for years to involve the state attorney general and spur the office to file charges against Cornerstone Farms for their repeated violations, most recently with Lovey's case. He says he has gotten nowhere as the Missouri Department of Agriculture has refused to refer Lovey's case to the state attorney general.

MEANWHILE AT THE USDA…

Now that we know what horrors state inspectors were documenting at Cornerstone Farms, let's come back to the federal inspection reports. They had nothing. USDA inspectors failed to notice or document a single violation at Cornerstone Farms even when they went to the facility on the exact same day that state inspectors found and documented a dozen.

On August 4, 2016, state inspectors found and documented thirteen violations, including a Labradoodle puppy and three standard poodle puppies with bright-red blood in their stool. The violations on this date also included two directs, the most severe class of violations, on the books for a male standard poodle with dark blood in its stool and a female standard poodle named Lacy with "dark discharge coming from the right ear" and a live flea in her coat.[10]

On August 8, 2016, state inspectors returned to check up on

these serious cases and found another twelve violations, including several from prior reports that had not yet been corrected.[11]

But on August 8, 2016—that very same day—the USDA also sent out two animal care inspectors of its own to visit the Ritters. While some of the twelve violations that the state inspectors recorded that day would not be in conflict with federal law and only violate Missouri's more restrictive regulations, several concerning the sick dogs recorded by the state would certainly run afoul of the Animal Welfare Act that the USDA is charged with upholding. However, two USDA inspectors visiting the property that day report that they found no noncompliant items during their visit. This, I reiterate, on the very same day that state inspectors found multiple violations.[12]

I couldn't believe the difference between the state and federal inspection reports from the same facility on the same day. I decided to give the USDA the benefit of the doubt. Perhaps the federal agents knew that the state inspectors had been out to see the Ritters that same day and had already documented the violations. Perhaps the federal inspectors chose simply to keep their notes off the official, then-publicly-available record. Given that the USDA has a policy of issuing teachable moments to help breeders improve without sullying their record, I figured that this might be where these inspectors had filed their observations on the Ritters. So I submitted a FOIA request for any "teachable moments" that might have been issued to the Ritters on that date. The USDA responded stating that no, there were no teachable moments for the Ritters issued during the time frame I had specified.[13]

These same federal inspectors who failed to document a single noncompliance or even to educate the Ritters with a teachable moment had also visited the Cornerstone Farms earlier in the year, on May 23, 2016, and recorded yet again that they found no noncompliant items at the facility, even as state inspectors had found nine violations on January 21, 2016—including evidence of dogs with diarrhea and a Dogue de Bordeaux with dark blood in his stool. Again, my FOIA request found that the USDA inspectors failed to issue even an off-the-record teachable moment for this visit as well.

Considering that the USDA had to order the Ritters to obtain their federal license in the first place for selling dogs unlawfully without it, one would think that the agency would be interested in applying a little extra scrutiny to the facility's operations during routine inspections.

Put it this way: State inspectors have never given the Ritters a clean report card. Federal inspectors, as of this writing, have yet to note a single violation.

With state and federal records in my hands from the very same day showing that the USDA was not documenting what Missouri inspectors were, I headed back up to meet with Gibbens at his Fort Collins office. It's worth noting, I was never granted the opportunity to personally witness a USDA inspection despite my requests with the agency to do so. So instead, I had to rely on Gibbens to explain how federal records could paint such a different picture from what state inspectors found. I started by asking how the USDA works with states that have inspection protocols of their own. He said that each state varies but that in Missouri, federal and state inspectors communicate on a weekly basis and often do joint inspections.

"So let's say a Missouri state inspector goes out with a federal inspector together," I begin. "They're there on the same day, and

I've seen some records on the same day. And there are big animal welfare violations: sick dogs, for example. If the state inspector sees it, does the federal inspector also have to document it on his file?"

"Each inspector does his own inspection report," Gibbens replies.

"So the USDA inspector wouldn't say to the state inspector: 'Oh, you've got this. I'm just going to leave it off here.'"

"No," Gibbens answers. "If it's not on one inspector's report, either the requirement was different, or they didn't agree with each other."

I reiterate that the inspection reports sitting in front of him indicate that we are talking about violations to the Animal Welfare Act, things that the federal agents must document: sick and wounded dogs. I put the Ritters' documents side by side in front of him, showing exactly how state inspectors meticulously documented violations on the same day that Gibbens's agents failed to note anything. I also hand him his own response to Kristin's complaint, bearing his signature, asserting that there were no noncompliant items found at the facility. He pauses for a long time, his eyes scanning the reports I've assembled in front of him.

"I wasn't there, and it wouldn't be fair for me to comment on what our inspectors did or didn't do or what the Missouri inspectors did or didn't do. Because I don't know. I know that I have full confidence in those inspectors to determine whether a facility is in compliance with our standards or not. And when they go, it's a snapshot of what they see, while they're there that day. If they were to go back a week later, a few days later, the snapshot's going to be different," says Gibbens.

There's another long pause.

"And I don't know what else to say, Rory," he says with a sigh. "We can't help [Kristin]. We can't get her money back. We can't get her a new puppy. Our laws aren't written that way. Our law is written to see if the licensee is following the requirements of the Animal Welfare Act."

But if inspectors were able to give the Ritters a clean report on the same day that state inspectors found multiple violations to the Animal Welfare Act, it seems that they are not carrying out even the most basic part of the agency's duty of enforcement.

———

Once she had all the facts, Kristin called Debra Ritter directly.

"She's clearly defensive, right off the bat," Kristin says, recalling that Ritter refused to trust the opinion of her vet that the dog was not, in fact, four months old. Then she pushed to take the dog back, although, to Kristin's recollection, Ritter did not offer a refund or replacement. "She's like, 'Do you want to give the dog back? You want the dog?'"

Either way, at this point, returning Lovey was an unthinkable proposition. Lovey was now an inextricable part of Kristin's family.

After the call ended in a contentious standoff, Ritter circled back with Kristin to admit that there had been an error in Lovey's paperwork. Online, the dog had been listed as four months old. Now, Ritter was saying that Lovey's actual date of birth was November 24, 2015, making Lovey seven months old at the time of purchase. Ritter pointed out that this error still did not back up the claims from Kristin's vet that Lovey was likely more than a year old.

Ritter sent the new paperwork to Kristin in the mail bearing the revised birth date but also listing a different dam, or mother dog, from what was originally detailed on Lovey's forms. It should be noted that the state inspection reports also show that violations for missing paperwork and inadequate identification of dogs have been repeated problems for years at the Ritters' operation. Significantly, when they visited the property in August 2016, state inspectors cited the Ritters for failing to list in their inventory a dog of unspecified breed born on November 24, 2015, and sold on June 4, 2016. Lovey's revised paperwork notes her birth date as November 24, 2015. Kristin purchased her on June 4, 2016.

These discrepancies on Lovey's paperwork might have seemed minor compared to the more serious violations found at the Ritters', but they were still chilling to Kristin. She tracked down the veterinarian in Curryville, Missouri, who had signed off on Lovey the day she was purchased, giving her a vaccination report and a clean bill of health.

"I talked to the vet, and he said he only saw one dog that day from Cornerstone Farms. It was clearly a puppy, and it had no ear or skin issues. And this is the most important part: it was not tagged. It wasn't [micro] chipped," Kristin says. "I said 'Oh, well, my dog's chipped. And so you're saying you only saw one dog from [Cornerstone Farms] that day? Then you obviously didn't see my dog, because my dog is chipped, and we can debate all day about ears and skin and [whether she's a] puppy, right? But let's pretend that's not even an issue. There's nothing to debate about if the dog's chipped.'"

I reached out to the veterinarian who certified Lovey's health and vaccinations that day and requested an interview. My request was never answered.

While the veterinarian in Curryville never responded to my inquiry, the Humane Society notes that the relationships between commercial breeders and the often-rural veterinarians they work with can be problematic.

"The vets are paid by the breeders, so they're very unlikely to say anything that contradicts them, because that would affect their future ability to get business from these types of operations," Kathleen Summers, the director of outreach and research for the Humane Society's puppy mills campaign, tells me. She has been following the Ritters' operation and others like it for years in compiling the organization's annual Horrible Hundred list of the nation's worst commercial dog-breeding operations. "We do find a lot of vets in Missouri who work with puppy mills and essentially rubber-stamp their paperwork... They often don't see the dogs until they produce that one certificate of veterinary inspection that's required for the dog to leave the state."[14]

After mounting frustration in trying to deal directly with Ritter and the Curryville veterinarian, Kristin allowed her anti-puppy-mill advocate friend to reach out to local news reporter Chris Hayes at the St. Louis Fox affiliate. Hayes had previously reported on puppy mills in the state, and as a result, he seemed to be a natural fit for the story. He took on Lovey's case and began his reporting by driving out to Curryville to visit the Ritters in person, seeking comment. He never made it onto the property itself and was shooed away after a brief confrontation on the road with the Ritters that he later televised. Shortly after the reporter's visit, Debra Ritter shot Kristin a fiery email saying that she couldn't understand why she was siccing reporters on her after she offered to refund or replace the dog.

"That was never said in my one and only phone call [with

Debra Ritter]," Kristin insists. "It was never 'Let me refund your money.' It was always, 'We'll take the dog back.' And I always was like 'No, I'm not giving the dog back.'"

I reached out to the Ritters to get their side of the story. Initially, they responded by email that they would be happy to discuss Lovey's case but were wondering how I had obtained the dog's information and microchip number, inquiring whether I had purchased her for myself. I reiterated that I was not in possession of the dog and that I was simply a journalist writing about the case. Over the course of several emails that followed, where I attempted to arrange an interview, the Ritters asked me repeatedly why I was interested in the story and who told me about it, urging me to be honest in exchange for their honesty. They did not respond to my specific questions about the sale of Lovey and remained admittedly wary in our brief, written interactions.

Kristin, for her part, never responded to the Ritters' last email, and the Fox reporter continued working the story, preparing to air it a few weeks later. But before the story could make it to the St. Louis airwaves, it took an unexpected turn.

A HIGHER POWER INTERVENES

In August 2016, Kristin began receiving calls on her cell phone from a local number in St. Louis. It wasn't anyone she recognized from her contacts, so she let it go to voicemail the first few times. Initially, the caller left no messages. But then, after about a week of this, Kristin was surprised to find that her mystery caller had finally left a voicemail. When she opened the message, she was shocked to find that the caller was none other than former Missouri congressman Todd Akin.

A bit of background on Akin is necessary here. I should start by saying that Kristin is adamant that he is of no relation to her and her family despite the odd coincidence of their shared last names.

Todd Akin was a six-term Republican congressman for the state of Missouri. His career came to a grinding halt in 2012 when he ran for Senate in a challenge to incumbent Democrat Claire McCaskill. Early on, everything was coming up Akin: he won a heated Republican primary and was leading McCaskill in the polls ahead of the election. But an interview with the very same St. Louis Fox affiliate now investigating the Ritters brought his political ambitions to a very visible end that culminated with his castigation from his own party in the national spotlight.

On August 19, 2012, Akin, a longtime antiabortion advocate with a strong conservative track record, sat for a televised interview with local Fox reporter Charles Jaco to discuss his position on a number of topics relating to the Senate race. When Jaco asked Akin if he stood by his antiabortion stance even in the case of rape, the former congressman made the following—now-infamous—remarks:

> First of all, from what I understand from doctors, that's really rare. If it's a legitimate rape, the female body has ways to try to shut that whole thing down. But let's assume that maybe that didn't work or something. I think there should be some punishment, but the punishment ought to be on the rapist and not attacking the child.[15]

Akin's interview immediately went viral.

First, he was blasted by his opponent, McCaskill. But then, seeing as how 2012 was an election year, the presidential candidates chimed in as well. President Obama condemned the notorious "legitimate rape" comments.[16] Even then-Republican nominee Mitt Romney called Akin's words "inexcusable."[17] Other prominent Republican leaders and pundits pushed for Akin to step out of the Senate race. Akin initially apologized for his comments but stood by his antiabortion stance and refused to pull out of the race.[18] A few months later, he lost to McCaskill. In 2014, he wrote a book accusing the Republican party of throwing him under the bus and letting McCaskill win. In his book, he also recanted his apology and doubled down on his original comments about "legitimate rape," writing that he was referring to the negative impact of stress on a woman's fertility.[19]

Now, almost four years to the day after his very public downfall, here was *the* Todd Akin, calling St. Louis stay-at-home mom Kristin Akin. His voicemail was all folksy cheer and Missouri charm:

> Hello, Kristin! This is Todd Akin. Possibly a long-lost relation of Justin Akin—I assume your husband. And if you had a moment, I'd appreciate it if you could give me a call on my cell phone… Thanks so very much, and hope you have a nice day!

Kristin was astonished to say the least.

"I get this voicemail, and I'm like 'Todd Akin, as in *Todd Akin?*' What in the universe? The cat put himself out of the politics business when he made that horrible comment [about legitimate rape]. He's not getting reelected, so why's he calling me?"

At this point, it didn't even remotely cross Kristin's mind that Akin might be calling about her dog Lovey. After all, why would he?

So, curiosity adequately piqued, Kristin called him back. Akin began by, again, suggesting that perhaps he and Kristin shared a common relative, even getting into how unusual it was for them both to spell their last name the same way. Kristin, however, did not want to waste time with chitchat and genealogy. She asked him why he was calling her.

"[He said] 'Well, I was calling on behalf of my good friends Tom and Debra Ritter.' In my head, I was like, are you kidding me right now? Is this for real?"

Kristin then thought about it for a moment, realizing that the connection made some sense given that the Ritters hold themselves out to be very religious, Evangelical Christians both on their website and in their conversations with Kristin, a background that they share with the former congressman. The conversation continued.

"[He said] 'So my friend said that you bought a puppy from them recently and that, you know, there was a little mistake about the birth date but that they got you the new papers... I was just wondering what really happened. What's your side of the story?'"

Kristin told Akin that she did not want to discuss the matter with him.

"[He said], 'So are you saying that that didn't happen?'"

Again, Kristin refused to discuss Lovey's case with Akin and attempted to beg off the call, citing the fact that her young son was home from school for summer break and needed her attention. Once again, Akin persisted.

"He's like, 'So let me get this right. I mean, they said that you bought a puppy and that they made a mistake. But they sent you the revised papers, and yet you're not letting this go, and they just can't figure out why.'"

One final time, Kristin refused to discuss the matter with Akin, and the call ended.

About a week after Akin spoke with Kristin, I gave him a call. He answered his own phone warmly. I informed him that I was a journalist writing a book about commercial dog breeding. Before I could get any further, he interjected with surprise.[20]

"Oh, I don't know anything about dog breeding at all," he said, seeming perplexed as to why I could possibly be reaching out on the topic.

I clarified that I was looking for more information on his relationship with the Ritters. I reminded him of his call to Kristin on their behalf, saying he was a "good friend" of theirs, asking her about the issues with Lovey and why she would not drop it.

"It was just a mere favor to somebody that I know of. It was because I used to be a congressman. People have asked me to do all kinds of different things. It's just that I thought it'd be nice," he said. "I don't know any of them really, not that well."

"So you don't know the Ritters personally? They're not close friends of yours?" I asked.

"No, not particularly," he said again, still friendly but seeming to become ill at ease with my line of questioning. "You come in contact with a lot of people as a congressman. You don't really get to know them very much."

I asked then how he heard about the Ritters' situation with Kristin and how they'd gotten in touch with him. He said that was a private matter and he was not open to discussing it. I accepted that he wasn't going to budge on this issue and returned to why he would want to get involved at all.

"If I can help somebody, I usually try," Akin told me affably. "I mean, I don't even know you, but I'll talk to you. I try to help people out. But I don't know anything about the situation. Then it was made clear to me that [Kristin] didn't want to talk about it, and that was just fine. I did what I said I'd do, I'd give [Kristin] a call, and that's that."

I then began to list some of the Ritters' violations at Cornerstone Farms: their repeated inclusion in the Humane Society's Horrible Hundred, their warning letter from the USDA for selling dogs sight unseen without a federal license, their pages upon pages of Missouri State Department of Agriculture violations that are also on the official record. I asked him if he knew of these issues when he reached out on the Ritters' behalf. The line cut out. Akin was gone.

I was bewildered. A six-term congressman, even one with a very humiliating end to his career, had to be media savvy enough to not simply hang up on a journalist when the questions got tough. Giving him the benefit of the doubt, I called back immediately. He answered and apologized for being in an area with poor reception, although our call thus far had seemed crystal clear on my end and continued to be without issue until we concluded. But mysteries of cell phone technology aside, I resumed where I left off and repeated my question, asking if he was aware of the Ritters' track record, listing once again the documented violations at the state and national level.

"If that were true—and I don't know that it's true—if that were true, I knew nothing about that," he said.

"So the violations weren't something you'd ever heard of?" I pressed.

"Well, I don't know that it's true," he repeated, refusing to acknowledge the veracity of the inspections or even their existence, rather than just denying knowledge of them. "Maybe you've heard that it's true, but I don't know anything about that. I didn't consider it my business. I'm not in law enforcement. I'm just a citizen."

I reminded him that these violations are well documented with the state of Missouri, that they are not rumors or allegations but rather the result of years of inspections filed on record with the very state he represented in our nation's capital.

"Well, let me stop you right there," he said, clearly growing impatient. "I don't know anything about it, and I don't feel qualified to talk about it. So I think we should just drop it. No, I didn't know anything about it—if that's true. I don't really particularly want to discuss it. I mean, I don't mind talking about stuff I know something about."

He then asked me not to quote him on this topic. I reminded him that up until his saying as much, we were speaking on the record but that I was happy to respect his decision to not proceed if he so chose. He grumbled that as a reporter, I'd probably write whatever I wanted anyway. Then he wished me well, and we both hung up.

When I asked the Ritters how they got the former congressman to call Kristin on their behalf, they wouldn't give me a direct answer. "Our family is known in the Capital for our efforts with…agriculture. We are know [sic] for honesty, kindness, and our Christian stand on life," they wrote.[21]

Ultimately, I was unable to get them to agree to a full interview.

But still, I remained as perplexed as Kristin to learn of the former congressman's interest in her case. I returned to Bob Baker of the Missouri Alliance for Animal Legislation. I wanted to see if he could shed some light on how Todd Akin could possibly be tied to the Ritters. While Baker was dismayed to hear that the former congressman had attempted to involve himself directly in Kristin's case, he was certainly not surprised.

"Believe it or not, during our Proposition B ballot initiative on puppy mills, Missouri Right to Life came out in opposition," Baker recalls of his initial shock when Christian conservative groups joined forces to shoot down the voter-passed legislation to shutter puppy mills. Missouri Right to Life would later come out in strong support of Akin during his political spiral following the "legitimate rape" comments back in 2012 and stood by its PAC endorsement of his Senate bid. "We see this time and again up in the legislature, where these so-called Christian groups or family-values groups are opposing legislation to help the animals. And I can't quite figure it out."

When Baker and other animal advocates attempted to hammer out the compromise on Proposition B that would go on to become the Canine Cruelty Prevention Act in 2011, he asked the Missouri Right to Life leadership why they would oppose humane conditions in dog-breeding facilities.

"We're talking about dog breeders who are raising dogs in inhumane conditions. How does helping breeders continue to raise dogs inhumanely help your cause of right to life?" he recalls asking at the time to no satisfying response. Eventually, he believes his question spooked the group into dropping its public opposition to reforming dog-breeding facilities, leaving the leadership to pursue their beliefs on the topic privately as opposed to using the mouthpiece of the organization.

"I did say, 'I have a lot of friends that are very, very much pro-life and love animals. I mean, why are you crossing these issues?'" Baker recalls of his conversations with the Missouri Right to Life leadership. "But it does have a hold. And so it

doesn't even shock me that [former congressman] Akin—
because he's very much a Christian conservative—that he would
take this stance also. And it's a shame at how the animal abusers
have won over these Christian conservatives. It's beyond me. I
mean, it just doesn't make sense. It's not even consistent with
Christian values to mistreat God's creatures, and this is what I
try to argue with them."[22]

But answering the question as to why Todd Akin had agreed
to take up the crusade of the Ritters was only one part of the
mystery, as far as I could see it. I wanted to know how the Ritters,
dog breeders in a town with a population of 222 in rural Missouri,
were able to get the attention of a six-term former congressman
who had run for Senate. Public downfall or not, Akin was a
powerful ally to have. Again, Baker was not surprised that a rural
dog breeder was able to bend a powerful politician's ear. He has
seen it many times before.

"There is no doubt, [dog breeders] have great political connec-
tions," Baker says. "They're very effective lobbyists. They go
in and they tell them [that reform] is going to lose them their
business…that these laws are going to put them out of business.
And I think they make a very compelling argument. Especially
the rural legislators, they don't have people clamoring the other
way, so they [side with the breeders]… I think they use this to
get the small farmers back who they've sold out over the years,
by representing Smithfield Foods and the other big corporate
[agriculture] groups. So this is the way of endearing themselves to
the small farmers."

Baker also notes that many of these breeders are closely tied in
with the Missouri Farm Bureau.

"The Farm Bureau believes that if they draw the line in the

sand on the dogs, the animal welfare people will never get around to attacking them on how they treat their farm animals," Baker says. "And I think they much prefer to have the fight over the dogs than to have the fight over farm animal issues. Because they feel that if [legislation] does make it to the dog-breeding industry, you're going to do the same to us on our farm animals."

———

In the months since Lovey came home with Kristin's family, the goldendoodle has not grown, topping out at forty-two pounds—right around the same weight she was the day Kristin first picked her up. Kristin sees this as yet another sign that the dog she purchased was, in fact, no puppy but rather a fully grown adult canine. But Lovey has shown marked emotional improvement. Now, Lovey sleeps with her head on Kristin's pillow every night and has even inspired a bit of harmless jealousy in Skipper, the dog she was originally supposed to help keep company. But perhaps the most telling sign that Lovey is recovering is that she has finally started doing something most dog owners would take for granted.

"I didn't notice her tail wagging for probably [the first] two and a half weeks. It did not wag at all," Kristin recalls. "It was funny because one day, I was playing with her, and then her tail starts wagging. Like, it was thumping. She was lying on the couch or the floor or the bed, and I remember distinctly thinking 'Oh my gosh, I think this is the first time I've seen your tail wag.' You know, it just kind of hit me."

With Lovey on the mend, I ask Kristin a question that both former congressman Todd Akin and Debra Ritter have asked her several times: Why not just drop it? Why keep pushing and dealing with all the time-consuming aggravation?

"I was always taught that when you know better, you do better. I know now that these people are doing this—and not just [to] me," Kristin says of her decision to push for a change.

She says that even if the Ritters refunded her for every penny that went into purchasing and caring for Lovey, she would donate it all to an animal charity. Her fight isn't about the money.

"Do you honestly think [Debra Ritter] believes in her mind… that every one of those dogs out there is totally fabulous, being totally cared for in the best condition…that they're happy, healthy, [that she] couldn't do any better? Could she really believe that?"

Kristin pauses for a moment and gathers her thoughts.

"There are plenty of people who breed dogs…and the dogs have a good life too," Kristin says. "It can be done. Because it is done, and I've seen it done."

And I've seen it too.

CHAPTER SIXTEEN

Raise Them Right

GLADYS AND DELANEY DASH TO THE FRONT DOOR WITH a clatter of nails on linoleum to welcome me in. They pirouette and leap with their front paws in the air, jumping up to my thighs. I guess it's true: the so-called wheaten greetin' is universal with this breed. No wonder I haven't been able to train Izzie not to jump up after all these years. But other than that and a passing physical resemblance, there is not much else these purebred wheaten terriers have in common with my Izzie. They're clearly born of a thicker, heartier stock, their frames so square, as mandated by breed standards, that I could use their backs for coffee tables. Their coats are long and wavy, their hair lush and full where Izzie's is thinner and more feathery, prone to mats, and sparse at the knees. The girls buzz around the kitchen, parading their tails, docked at least three inches longer than Izzie's tight nub. They stick up straight behind them like the poles on the backs of amusement-park bumper cars.

Patrice Chevalier and Robert Bergman push past the retired

dogs to welcome me into their home in Centennial, Colorado. They are the owners of Heirloom Wheatens, a small breeding operation that produces an average of one to two litters a year. They run the business right here from their home on a sprawling property in a rural subdivision with views of rolling hills, mountains, and the city of Denver far off in the distance. The house is spacious but cozy, filled with plenty of hints that true wheaten terrier aficionados live here: from the bronze statuettes of two wheatens at play on an entryway table to the sign in the garage that reads SECURITY PROVIDED BY WHEATEN TERRIER.

Patrice welcomes to me to sit out on their patio, overlooking a large, grassy expanse where Gladys and Delaney are chasing each other. A dog barks in the distance from a neighbor's house. The girls stand at attention but do not bark back. I'm impressed: with Izzie's hair trigger, that kind of distant but unseen barking would raise a ruckus and send my house into chaos. When we settle in to chat, the dogs freely dart back up to the patio to eavesdrop and steal a pinecone before cycling back down to their fenced, open space so they can run.

Patrice and Robert initiated their work with wheaten terriers back in 1985 when they began showing their first female in dog shows. Back then, they were more interested in training and obedience competitions with no inkling that breeding would be in the cards for them. But by 1990, they took on a second female and began working with other colleagues in the wheaten terrier show world to co-own and source studs and begin breeding. Since then, they have bred and placed around 150 puppies for owners throughout Colorado and nationwide. Of those, they estimate only four have been returned to their operation for rehoming.

"It's a pure passion project," Patrice says simply of her nearly three decades breeding and showing wheatens. "We got into the breeding aspect as much to experience it and to be able to get an understanding of what creates a dog for obedience and agility."[1]

"You can study all the genetics you want. But if you breed and see the outcome of that, it teaches you a lot afterward," Robert says, picking up Patrice's thread as he often does—the two speak as one much of the time. "I'll say, 'Okay, I thought that we might see that trait in these puppies,' and we sure did. You know, something that maybe was passed down from the stud, you see it come to fruition."

"Are we talking about physical traits? Personality traits? Both?" I ask as Gladys insists I stroke the top of her head, positioning her jawbone purposefully on my thigh.

"Both," Robert says.

"It's personality. It's their thinking process," Patrice continues. "It's their attitude toward new things, different things, strange things. It's how they think through problems: Are they persistent? So they give up easy? How quick do they catch on—"

"How driven are they to please? Versus can they just be themselves—" Robert jumps in.

"Are they real needy? Are they independent?" Patrice says. "So [breeding] was an extension of wanting to understand the dogs better."

This self-described passion project, while clearly quite consuming and fulfilling for them both, has not been the focus of their careers: Patrice is a project manager for Denver Health, and Robert is a retired consultant for PricewaterhouseCoopers and also worked for IBM. For them, their breeding operation is no get-rich-quick scheme or even a lucrative side gig. Given that they typically sell their puppies for around $2,000 each, I figure it can't be too hard to eke out a living from it. I ask them if this passion project could have been their full-time source of income if they'd so chosen. They look at each other and laugh.

"Doing it like we do?" Robert says incredulously. "No. It's a loss."

"So don't go into breeding for the money?" I ask again.

"Not at all." Patrice is emphatic. "We've put more money into this than we've ever gotten out. Even when we've had a litter of ten and a litter of nine."

By way of example, she details a litter she had last year of only two puppies. Just to get those two puppies, she had to pay a $2,500 stud fee to another breeder whose stock she knows and trusts, have that frozen semen shipped in at a cost of $800, and then pay an additional $500 to have her female inseminated. The year before, she'd gone through the same process with the same female and the same stud—with the same hefty costs—and the female did not produce a litter at all. Selling each of the two puppies sold from this pairing for $2,000 a pop, Patrice could barely recover even half of her costs.

"Puppy mills don't do the testing. They don't do any of the health stuff, you know," Robert says. "People always ask me. 'God, you must be making a ton of money, selling a dog for $2,000.' So then I send them a list of all the costs that go into breeding, testing, and all the way through the process."

Patrice continues. "And people will say, 'Oh, but you had seven puppies!' Well, last time, we had one. Time before that, we had two. We've had three, we've had four. You know, you gotta average it out."

Even if Patrice and Robert have made peace with the fact that Heirloom Wheatens is not a cash cow, they say they are proud to be thoughtfully developing a healthy and happy line of wheaten terriers for the posterity of the breed and for their ability to compete across various types of obedience and training shows.

Beyond the meticulous and expensive process of breeding these dogs, the work that goes into vetting and choosing the right buyers for their puppies is almost equally painstaking.

"You're always looking for the correct homes. As breeders, we have a two- or three-page questionnaire that people fill out—it's not just that you come and pick your puppy. And Rory, I don't know how you got your [wheaten terrier], but you have to come meet us. We let our dogs do crazy things when people are here, you know, jumping up on them," Patrice explains of how she scrutinizes potential customers to see how they'll react to the breed's natural exuberance. "It has to be someone we feel comfortable with long term, because we want to know if [the dogs] develop problems. We want to know if they're lost. We want to know those sorts of things, because it all goes into the computer; it all goes into understanding what the heck we have besides what you can see. We're looking for patterns. Part of it is for health, because not everything we have in the breed has a genetic test."

Patrice and Robert have devoted years of their lives to breeding responsibly. They've traveled the world to attend conferences and shows as far away as New Zealand and have even brought back a new breeding dog from Finland to enhance their line and extend their educations into breeding.

But just as it can be with humans, even an obsessively watchful eye to the lineage may not be enough to ensure perfect health. While Patrice says she's been able to breed for health and temperament in her wheatens over the years, sometimes health problems pop up all the same. Cheerio, a fifteen-month-old puppy, is currently still living in the home, unable to be sold after Patrice and Robert discovered she had a rare, genetic skin condition that they say had never before been documented in any wheaten terrier. When I meet her, she is a new and impressive burst of energy now that Gladys and Delaney have gotten used to my presence. She jumps and flirts with me, begging for my constant affection. Her bold eyes and pink tongue are so bright and vivid, she looks like a cartoon puppy, too happy and lovely to even be real. But after traipsing around behind Patrice and me for a bit, she stops dead in her tracks to scratch ferociously at something hidden beneath her flowing, honey-colored coat.

"We're still deciding whether we're going to have to put her down," Patrice says quietly, as if Cheerio might hear us. Cheerio just keeps scratching at her skin lesions. Her discomfort is so acute, it's as if both Patrice and I have completely disappeared. When she's able to return to us from her scratching spell, I pet her, and I can feel the lesions lurking under her hair, a rippling threat just below the surface.

It's clear in talking to Patrice that Cheerio's case distresses her. However, when she speaks about it, her frustration manifests analytically, as if it is a math problem she should have gotten right but could not have possibly accounted for some unknown variable.

Patrice takes me on a tour of her combination home and breeding facility with Gladys and Delaney tagging along. Because she and Robert are not currently expecting any imminent litters, many of the areas that would usually be devoted entirely to breeding now lie fallow or have been overtaken by human activities. In a small side room of the home's den is the birthing room. It used to be Robert's beer-brewing room, Patrice tells me. But when a litter is due, Patrice and Robert sterilize it and shut it down to the other retired dogs like Gladys and Delaney, who have happily followed us in to inspect it. Both were born right here, eight and eleven years ago respectively. Patrice shows me drawers filled with medical equipment in sterile pouches, identical to much of what I recognize from Izzie's vet visits with the exception of several apparatuses that are aimed at helping mother dogs nurse.

"I sleep on the floor in here when a litter is due," Patrice says with good-natured exhaustion. "Because they always seem to give birth in the middle of the night."

For the first three weeks of their lives, the puppies are kept in this small, sterile space with their mother to nurse.

"Once they're born, you've got to get them through the first twenty-four hours, and then you're down here, checking constantly, even after being up all night to deliver. It's like being a new mom," Patrice says.

"We really try to quarantine them for three weeks," Robert says.

"So you're changing bedding, because the bitch is still dripping, you know, from delivery," Patrice says. "You're checking the puppies, putting warm compresses on their [docked] tails or whatever, so they don't get infected—"

"And you have to be watching the female all the time, to see if she's showing any signs of anything going on," Robert continues, detailing the round-the-clock efforts that go into birthing these litters.

But Patrice takes particular pride in describing the painstaking work she begins with her new puppies at just three days old, providing them with special neurological stimulation exercises she learned at a conference with AKC judge and puppy-development researcher Dr. Carmen Battaglia.

"We do these stimulation puppy exercises to develop their ability to handle stress. So it stimulates the vascular system and the neurological system, the brain, and all kinds of nerves," Patrice says.

These exercises are derived from Dr. Battaglia's research into the so-called Super Dog program pioneered by the U.S. military in the 1970s. The Super Dog program—also known as the Bio Sensor program—found that these early stimulation exercises could hold a range of benefits for the lifespan of the dog, including an improved cardiovascular system and a higher resistance to stress. While not universally accepted as being the one-size-fits-all solution to creating healthy, socialized animals, the Super Dog exercises certainly involve plenty of human, hands-on care, attention, and socialization at the earliest stages of life and, at the very least, demonstrate a studied and enthusiastic approach to thoughtful breeding practices.

"Besides handling the puppies every day, you take each puppy—and it's right between this specific age time frame [of three to sixteen days old]—you pick up the puppy, and you hold it head over butt," Patrice explains, detailing the exercises she does with each litter, miming the motions with a puppy-sized empty space between her hands. She keeps detailed diagrams in the room where the puppies are born to ensure that she does it right every time. "And you do that for five seconds. No more. It's very specific—you don't overdo it. Then you turn it upside down so it's tail over head."

"And they're not freaking out?" I ask, shocked, imagining myself trying to swing Izzie upside down at any age.

"Oh yeah, they're squirming and everything else," Patrice says.

"But you're holding them. You aren't moving them. You're just holding them there," Robert clarifies.

From there, they tickle the puppies' feet with different objects like a Q-tip or a pencil eraser. Then they have them stand on a wet cloth for a few seconds.

In these early days, Patrice holds vigil, tracking the puppies' feedings and plotting their growing weights on a chart.

"I pick them up, make sure to handle them, give them kisses on their little heads," she says.

"You gotta give them kisses on their little heads," Robert interjects with mock seriousness, as if prescribing a lifesaving medication. Even though he's joking, he's not wrong: the dogs in large-scale commercial breeding operations almost always lack this kind of positive and gentle intimacy with humans altogether.

From three to five weeks old, the puppies are moved upstairs onto the main floor of the house, into what would typically serve as a laundry room adjacent to the kitchen. There, Patrice and Robert erect a small baby gate so that the tiny puppies can safely observe the goings-on of the household and begin learning not to fear the various daily activities and noises they will be seeing and hearing once they are placed in a home.

At five weeks, the puppies are then relocated to large pens overlooking the couple's formal living room. There, Patrice has access to her home's sound system and plays the puppies special CDs to help prevent them from developing phobias of the typical noise triggers that upset most dogs: sirens, crying babies, honking horns, airplanes. She plies them with baby toys to help them develop early motor skills and approaches them wearing different hats or disguises so they can experience what other people may look like without barking or scurrying away.

At six weeks, the real fun begins as Patrice invites into her home any prospective puppy buyers as well as her circle of friends to come help socialize the newest litter—often with a side of margaritas, Robert makes sure to add for the record. Patrice instructs the gathered crowd to touch the puppies' toes, to put their fingers gently into their mouths, to tug lightly on their ears, all in an effort to help the dogs continue to grow accustomed to human touch.

Between eight and ten weeks, it's time for the puppies to go to their new homes. After weeks of socialization and mingling, the puppies are finally ready. But Patrice and Robert play matchmaker, deciding which human will get which puppy—or, more often, which humans will go home empty-handed. They have several criteria they look for in an owner. For one, they will rarely, if ever, sell a puppy to a home with a child under the age of seven. In other cases where the children are of age, Patrice and Robert watch in their interviews to see if the children listen to their parents and are respectful. They cringe to remember one family where the children came to the home to meet the puppies and were jumping on top of their tables. They went home sans terrier. Robert, for his part, likes to investigate exactly why any given family wants a puppy at that particular time while inquiring into exactly how much research they have put into this specific breed.

"Look at it this way: there are cats, dogs, and then there are terriers. They are very, very different," Robert cautions.

With me, he's preaching to the choir. Dan and I often joke when we see other dogs happily jogging along with their masters or chasing and retrieving tennis balls or rolling in the grass that those are *real dogs*. Izzie is our little imposter, some sort of strange creature that has her own agenda, which may not involve returning any tennis balls, and will do what she sees fit when she sees fit, thank you very much.

But of course, most buyers are more naïve to this breed than I am after years living side by side with a terrier of my own. Robert recalls one prospective buyer he turned away based on the type of personality the man was seeking in a puppy. "I said, 'You need to get a golden retriever.' He wanted a dog that was going to be there when he wanted to interface with it and would otherwise go and lie down in the corner. I said, 'No, you're not going to get that here.'"

When Dan and I bought Izzie from a pet store back in early 2011, there was no interview process of any kind. No one asked us any questions about why we'd selected this breed (allergies) or whether we'd ever even owned a dog before (we hadn't). No one needed to know if we had a backyard where the puppy could play (we didn't). In fact, Dan and I had been the ones asking all the questions then. Thinking back on it now, most of our naïve and clueless questions would have been a red flag to a breeder like Patrice or Robert that we were woefully unprepared to take on a puppy at all, let alone one from a breed that is known to be a bit, shall we say, high maintenance. The pet store was a far easier experience: we showed up and walked out with Izzie after relinquishing $1,000 for her purchase, all within an hour or so. Perhaps the only question we heard was "Visa or MasterCard?" But I'm coming to see that buying a dog should not be quick, easy, and convenient. There should be questions. There should be barriers to entry. This isn't a pair of sunglasses or even a car. This is a creature that you are committing to for the span of its entire life.

I can't help myself: I have to know if Dan and I would have made the cut to be owners of a responsibly bred wheaten when we first set out to get Izzie back in 2011. I lay it all on the table for

Patrice and Robert, how our life was back then: the one-bedroom we shared in a Brooklyn apartment building, my night shift for the *Today Show* leaving only one of us home at any given time, the fact that neither of us had ever owned a dog before, the challenge that we'd only been living together a few short months as boyfriend and girlfriend when we made the commitment to take this animal into our home for the full extent of its life before even committing to each other for life. Patrice and Robert listen and render judgment. Robert launches in first with a hearty *no*. Patrice throws on the brakes and shoots him a look.

"Well, you would be very low on the list," Robert says.

"Oh, I don't know about that," Patrice says, hoping not to offend.

"Oh, I do," Robert insists. "That's where I would put you. And I work the list."

Patrice disagrees, citing the fact that our lack of a backyard at that time meant that any dog we took home would have to get dedicated time walking with us and bonding with us. In some ways, she believes this can be preferable to an owner who simply opens the back door and lets the dog wander off without any time to socialize or develop a personal relationship with its humans. Either way, the two are split on whether I would have gone home empty-handed or become a newly minted dog owner with one of their pups.

When I explain to Patrice and Robert that Izzie came from a pet store, it's like a light bulb goes off in their heads: of course that's how I was able to get a wheaten terrier puppy, no questions asked. Although they don't seem to judge the choice we made at the time, they are very quick to agree that they would never sell to a pet store or over the internet to a buyer they did not personally vet. In the few instances where they have sold one of their dogs to someone out of state, they have been sure to conduct meticulous phone interviews with the buyer and subject them to the same lengthy questionnaire as all their other prospective customers. They often go to the lengths of securing a reference from a local breeder in the buyer's area who could not sell to them because they did not have a litter on deck. When the time has come to finalize the purchase, Robert or another family member has personally driven or flown the puppy to the buyer.

But it's not just the lives of these dogs up until purchase that interests me. A major component of responsible breeding comes down to when and how the females are retired. In most breeding operations, the worst-case scenario is that they're shot or otherwise put down. In other cases, they might be sent to a rescue like Theresa Strader's to be adopted out, hopefully while they still have a few more good years left in them to enjoy. But that's not how Patrice and Robert do things. Whenever a female is no longer able to produce a healthy litter—no matter her age—they retire her but never put her down, sell her, or adopt her out. She lives out the rest of her life in their home just as Gladys and Delaney are doing as we speak. As pets.

"They're our family," Patrice says, almost horrified by my question of whether they'd retire their dogs to another home when they can no longer produce new litters. "I mean, we can't find anybody who would take as good of care of our dogs… You know what I mean. Because by then, we know their quirks. They like running down to the bedroom. They know who sleeps where every night. They know which kennel is theirs."

However, it is worth noting that there is no government inspector looking over Patrice's and Robert's shoulders to ensure that they uphold their breeding operation to the levels they do. While they are certified as an AKC Breeder of Merit and could be subject to inspections from that group, they are not required to hold a USDA license, because they have fewer than four breeding females in their operation. They are also not required to be inspected by the state of Colorado, because they are considered backyard or hobby breeders, of too small a scale to mandate adherence to state regulations. Their commitment to the health and welfare of the breed is a personal mandate.

When I ask Patrice if she can recommend any of her colleagues who, unlike herself and Robert, do this kind of work full-time as a livelihood but manage to do so with excellence, she demurs.

"Sorry to say, I do not know of any colleagues who breed full-time for a living and do an excellent and responsible job of it," Patrice tells me. "My sentiment is [that] once one makes decisions about one's canines based on making a living, the decisions made are no longer focused on the best intent for the animal."[2]

Robert adds, "We have seen breeders who have transitioned from responsible breeders to running a business, and their ethics and judgment [are] very much clouded by [money] and profits."

As the evening begins to darken into dusk, Patrice and Robert take me to the back of the house to tour their kennels and an expansive dog run with children's playground equipment arranged for agility exercises. A male dog is hanging out in his kennel, sitting in a dog bed. He rises when we enter. They tell me that they took him back from a buyer who had trouble with his prickly personality. They put him in his kennel when I arrived, because he's not a big fan of strangers, and they didn't want him to get aggressive with me. He doesn't launch himself at his kennel door or bark as I would expect an aggressive dog to do. He just watches. When we walk around to the outdoor dog runs, he effortlessly glides through his doggie door into his own private, fenced area to keep an eye on us. When I was on the rescue run with Theresa's organization, I saw kennels of a similar size shared by up to ten or more dogs—and they did not have the flexibility of indoor-outdoor access on demand. Needless to say, there's not a single dog in a cage here. There's not a single paw touching a wire mesh floor. Food and water are plentiful, and the temperature is kept even with the rest of the home. The conditions in the kennels here are better than many doggie day cares I've seen that charge top dollar to entertain and board local pups.

But even if Patrice and Robert are being excellent, responsible breeders, the question that many animal welfare groups and the Adopt Don't Shop movement would ask remains: Why breed at all when there are so many dogs in shelters needing good homes?

When I ask them this question, Patrice and Robert smile knowingly first at each other and then at me, sitting there at seven months pregnant but probably looking even more.

"Why have a child? There are orphans all over the world: underfed, undernourished, undereducated," Robert begins.[3]

"Even in this country," Patrice adds.

"Absolutely. So why would you have a child? It's the same thing. It's something personal, very personal. Obviously, it's your offspring. Our dog's puppies are not our offspring, but nevertheless, we've watched them grow, watched them develop," Robert explains.

"Your baby's going to look like you and your husband," Patrice says before describing the high level of prenatal care that marks the earliest stages of bonding with one's own child, equating it to the type of work she does with her dogs and why it's enriching and valuable to her. "There are a lot of sad cases, and I say definitely go work in a shelter and help them out… So yes, I feel bad that there are dogs in shelters. I feel bad that there are orphans too."

"Right, but do I begrudge you for having your child and having a family?" Robert asks. "No."

It's an argument I've heard before from other breeders, and I can certainly understand their point of view. But hearing Patrice's own perspective on it adds new weight.

"I'm glad you're able to make a choice. I made a choice not to have children," Patrice says. "Because that's who I am. And I'm not insulted by the question. I think it's honest."

As I get into my car to leave Heirloom Wheatens, Patrice waves and closes a gate behind me with a street sign reading WHEATEN COURT on it. In just a few short weeks, I'll be visiting the facility where Izzie was born: Simler's Kennel in the northeast corner of Missouri. While I don't know for sure what I'll find there, I'm quite certain it won't be anything like this, based on the USDA inspection reports my FOIA request turned up.

No. I no longer have any delusions that this sprawling campus is anything like Izzie's birthplace—although this is always what I'd hoped and wished her breeder had been like. I watch as Gladys and Delaney freely chase each other, enjoying their retirement in the tall grass and the setting sun, full bellies and a good night's sleep at the foot of a bed awaiting them both.

CHAPTER SEVENTEEN

Dog Is My Copilot

I'M ABOUT TWO HOURS FROM THE NEAREST MAJOR highway when I arrive at Simler Trail. It's a hot and hazy August afternoon in northeast Missouri, and my windshield is coated in the carcasses of late-summer beetles grown fat on months of plenty. I pass a small cemetery just before the crossroads. A man is mowing the lawn on the side of the road. He waves at me in my rental car as if he's been expecting me. Nothing could be further from the truth.

I've imagined this moment for a very long time. For years, I've stared at the name and address of the breeder listed on Izzie's purchase papers and tried to picture where she came from. Her entire story was contained in just a few short lines.

```
Sire: Simler's Rich
Dam: Simler's Cindee Marla
DOB: 11-13-2010
Breeder: Mrs. Keith Simler
```

The information also included Mrs. Keith Simler's USDA number and her address on Simler Trail. This information was all typed out on an American Pet Registry Inc. (APRI) form with a Jesus fish stamped at the bottom. APRI is an off-brand version of the American Kennel Club. Needless to say, we never filled it out, and we never mailed in our twenty-dollar fee to make Izzie's dubious pedigree official with the registry.

Even though this information is much more than other buyers often get with their purchase, it is sparse to say the least. It was easy to overanalyze the little I had. To me, a lifelong city dweller, there was something distinctly intimidating about the fact that Izzie's breeders share the same name as the road where they live and work. It spoke of a family that had long roots in a place, long enough that their rural road was distinguishable from others in that it was theirs. These were people who were tied to the land in a way I'd never been. It frightened me, thinking that to even set foot on the road was to intrude on their family history.

Now that I'm here, I feel a pang of excitement and fear to see the Simler Trail sign. As much as I've thought about it, some part of me is amazed that the road even has a sign to note its existence. Like so many things that live for years in our imaginations, it can feel as if we, ourselves, made them up. To see that it's real and that I'm actually here is somehow a shock.

I pause at the crossroads, trying to spot the kennel up ahead. After miles of rolling country roads through sun-flooded open fields and hills, Simler Trail is a sudden and dark diversion into the woods. The trail itself is just one narrow, unpaved lane of sharp, gray gravel, and the trees and dense forest crowd in like a tunnel with no light visible on the other side. There are no signs to mark that this is a private road or that I'm turning onto someone's driveway, so with plausible deniability in my back pocket, I proceed.

Within about one hundred meters of turning onto the trail, the day is sunken into damp, green darkness. I go slow, trying to peer through the trees on either side. My GPS tells me now that I've passed Simler's Kennel before giving up entirely and conking out. How can that be? There is truly nothing here, not even a turnoff to access the property. The forest reveals no clues, and the road gives me no choice but to continue straight ahead. I plough forward, as there's no space to make a U-turn here anyway. If a car were to come speeding toward me from the opposite direction, we'd both be stuck unless one of us would concede to reversing until we reached the main road.

After about half a mile, the trees peel away, and the road slopes into open, sun-drenched countryside. It's almost beautiful if not somewhat forlorn for its isolation. On my left, marring the idyllic landscape, is an ancient, rotted-out barn at least two stories tall. It has shed its warped planks around its base like a giant, wilting tulip. You can see straight through the yawning gaps to the field gone to seed behind it. Rusted and twisted farm equipment lies abandoned nearby, seemingly forgotten for decades.

I'm the only car or person in sight as the road now bends downhill, bordered by a handmade barbed-wire fence anchored to tree branches stuck into the ground. An algae-covered pond glows neon green to my left. On my right, two dozen cows wander together in the field, bathing in a clear watering hole. It's not apparent who they belong to—if anyone.

The road dips back uphill, and then, unmistakably, there it is: Simler's Kennel. I recognize it from an undercover video that my animal rights investigator contact Pete shot. As confirmation,

the address marker bears the number I've been looking for. I try
to drive as slowly as possible without attracting any suspicion,
although, this far down the secluded road, there's no plausible
deniability left to hang on to. The Simlers' house sits on the left
side of the road, distressed white clapboard and quaint. As far as I
can tell, I'm the only human being here or for miles around.

But there are dogs.

The kennels straddle the small road, housing around 150 dogs
or perhaps more. Each unit is of a different shape, size, and style,
springing up haphazardly across the landscape like a favela. There
are a few trailers with dogs presumably in stacked cages inside.
Outdoors, there are stacks upon stacks of what appear to be hand-
constructed, thin, metal-and-plywood dog cages. Some appear to
loosely adhere to the Missouri regulations that dogs be allowed
unfettered access to the outdoors. However, that access might be
more of a curse than a blessing on a hot and humid day like today.

In the units housing larger dogs like Labradors and German
shepherds, there appears to be no power or ventilation to protect
them from the elements beyond the shade provided by the tin
roofs above their heads. Instead, the doghouses sit dotting the
field, disconnected from the main property by the road. Red
coolers are zip-tied to the backs of their wire cages, presumably
to provide food or water. But it's hard to tell from the road, as
the rusted No Trespassing signs affixed to the cage areas keep
me from venturing down to the kennels close up. At thirty-four
weeks pregnant, I know I wouldn't be able to beat a hasty retreat
even if I tried. And even in broad daylight, I have that creeping,
horror-film inkling that I'm being watched.

It wasn't supposed to go like this.

As pregnant as I am, I wouldn't have flown to Missouri and

driven three hours from Kansas City on nausea-inducing country roads to get here if I didn't have an interview lined up. For the past two weeks, I'd been in contact with Keith Simler's longtime kennel manager, Jackie Dorris. When I reached out to Simler, it was Jackie who returned my call. She was friendly but cautious in our initial conversations, informing me that Simler is now in his eighties and does not oversee the day-to-day operations of the kennel. Besides, she'd assured me, she's been in charge of the facility for the last thirteen years, so she believed she could handle all my questions herself. I accepted that Simler wasn't willing to talk. After all, it was his late wife, Wanda, who bred Izzie back in 2010. Wanda passed away in 2014, and Keith took up the operation and reapplied for a new USDA license in his own name about a month after her death. Wanda is now buried at that church cemetery I'd passed at the crossroads to Simler Trail itself.

Things had been going smoothly with Jackie in our conversations ahead of my trip to visit her. Usually, she was bright and cordial, although with certain questions, I could sense that her guard was up. To ease her mind and my way to an interview, I sent her a text message with a picture of Izzie's paperwork to show her that yes, in fact, I was telling the truth that my dog had come from her kennel. We chatted about Izzie's papers in a phone call a few days later, and she told me, somewhat apologetically, that there were no more of Izzie's littermates around in her breeding stock and that her dam and sire, Cindee Marla and Rich, were long gone as well. I gently tried to find out where they might have ended up, but she balked. After some prodding, she said simply if not cryptically, "Well, six years is a really long time for what we do."

She expressed some surprise that I'd purchased Izzie in New

York. I asked if that was uncommon, and she said she does not sell to the American Dog Club where I bought her anymore. When I asked her why that might be, she said she likes to keep a rotation of buyers and not sell to one alone too often.

Back in April 2015, my undercover investigator contact, Pete, visited Simler's Kennel on behalf of the Companion Animal Protection Society (CAPS). As he often does, he took hidden camera video and posted it on the CAPS website. It seems like the incident still has Jackie and Simler on edge. For the most part, Jackie is the star of Pete's video after he was handed off to her by Simler much as I was. When I asked Pete how he gained access to Simler's facility, he was unable to give me details, as it could blow his cover for future investigations. But judging from the video alone, it's clear that Pete enters the facility with their blessing as they happily guide him through a tour of the kennels. At one point, the video freezes, and a caption pops on screen to highlight a violation to Missouri state regulations: a wall obstructs the animals' view of what should be unfettered access to the outdoors.

"I was concerned about sensory deprivation with these dogs. Because at Simler's Kennel, they would take a large wall, and they would put it about a foot, if I remember correctly, about a foot in front of the outdoor cages," Pete recalls. "If [the dogs] are inside, all they can see is the dogs across from them, the dogs next to them, and then that's it. And then they go outside, and all they can see are the dogs next to them and a wall in front of them. And they have no understanding of the world, or that there is a world, other than occasionally someone comes in every so often to look at them, turn lights on and off, and maybe fill up their feeder. And that's it."[1]

In the state inspection reports I have from just two months

after Pete's visit, the agent failed to identify this violation or any others.

But Pete's video of Simler's Kennel does not show the same level of horrors that are seen at many other dog-breeding facilities. While it certainly does not paint the operation in a positive light, it is not nearly as bad as it could be. Even Pete admits that Simler's Kennel, by comparison to the hundreds of others he's seen, is not terrible.

"I guess there's got to be two scales for it," Pete says, considering how to best explain his evaluation to me. "So if we're talking about a USDA scale, they're great. They have a few violations, but they're not that bad. And they appear to generally be in compliance. A few violations here and there. If we're talking from an animal welfare perspective, then I would say that they're average, which is to say they are horrible. And most of that would be relevant to the psychological well-being of the animals."

I find this dual scale interesting. Throughout my investigation into the world of USDA-licensed dog breeding, I've been finding that even those who uphold the Animal Welfare Act are still unquestionably abusing their dogs. In 2015, the year that Pete visited Simler's Kennel, the facility had no violations on the record—although it did have many in the past. As a result, I think Simler's Kennel makes a useful case study into how dogs that are well kept by USDA standards are still suffering.

I ask Pete for some examples of what concerned him about the psychological well-being of the dogs he found at Simler's Kennel. He points to one that sticks in his mind and is most apparent above the others in his video there.

"Simler's Kennel is an example of stereotypy for these dogs," Pete says, referring to the group of compulsively repeated behaviors seen in animals that lack mental stimulation. "They seem to be cage crazy. There was a large number of dogs I would see that, when I'd go up to them, they would just start spinning in circles and running in circles absolutely nonstop. Then they wouldn't stop doing that based upon if we moved somewhere, or if we would put our hands up to the cages, or what. They had this running in left-hand circles behavior that was just constant. Dogs don't normally act like that when they're not confined."

But for Simler, Pete's video presents a problem in that it is very easy to find with a quick Google search. Now, a pet shop purchaser can see exactly what the commercial breeding operation his dog came from looks like, providing the transparency that is not afforded by the state or the USDA. Thanks to CAPS and Pete, I don't need a FOIA request to judge the quality of the Simler facility for myself. Either way, with all the challenges the government and the industry put in the way of consumers learning about the reality on the ground at dog-breeding facilities, I find myself believing more than ever in the work Pete does.

Pete says that several other breeders he's investigated have complained to or threatened lawsuits against CAPS for posting his footage online. When I ask CAPS if Simler has done as much, the group's founder tells me she has not heard from Simler or Jackie Dorris to date.

Jackie didn't mention Pete's video by name, but she asked if when I came to visit, I'd be trying to sneak hidden cameras into the kennels. Her tone was cordial, but the anxiety was very real. She said, with only a hint of defensiveness, that she had nothing to hide and has no violations on her USDA record, but still, it was something she wanted to avoid. Of course, she does have violations on her USDA record over the past several years—but that was not the point. I told her the truth: that I don't conduct interviews with hidden cameras. I reminded her yet again that I was not an activist but a journalist, simply trying to learn more about what she does and where my dog came from. Besides, I said, trying to break the ice, "I'll be thirty-four weeks pregnant by the time I get there, and I'm massive. Given that it's August, you'll see very quickly that there's nowhere on my body I could get away with hiding a camera even if I wanted to." She laughed. I don't bother bringing up the fact that just two weeks before we began our conversations, Missouri Governor Jay Nixon vetoed the state's notorious ag-gag bill that would have criminalized this type of undercover access. Technically, if I had wanted, I would have been within my rights to shoot undercover video—although, of course, that isn't what I do.

We'd planned to meet at the kennel at noon on a Saturday in early August 2016. I booked my flight and hotel and then reached out to her once again to confirm that I was coming, full speed ahead. We chatted briefly and ended the conversation by saying that we'd see each other in a few days and that we were both looking forward to it.

So off I went, fingers crossed that the airline would still let me fly, big as I was. They did, begrudgingly, with a small amount of wrangling at the gate. I rented a car and headed off to the hotel to finish preparing my research for the interview and get a good night's sleep ahead of what was sure to be a very long day of driving. Saturday morning, I set off for the northeast corner of the state, ready to finally see where Izzie came from, withholding judgment until I could set eyes on it myself. I fretted along the drive there that I might find Jackie very likeable and yet find her dogs to be in horrific condition. I hoped I'd find the kennel in surprisingly good condition and the dogs healthy and happy so that I wouldn't have to cope with the dissonance of finding her personality at odds with what I knew was right and ethical. Maybe things had changed since April 2015 when Pete's undercover video was shot and posted online?

About thirty minutes away from Simler's Kennel, I gave Jackie a call to check in, letting her know I was close by. Immediately, the excuses began pouring out.

"There's an emergency at the kennel. The dogs are already freaked out enough. I can't be bringing anyone else on the property now. It's, well, it's just we have a situation, and it's very last minute, so I can't bring you out there," she said.

"But I'm already out here," I protested.

I tried and tried, but Jackie was unmovable. It didn't matter. I was not going to be allowed to come to the kennel under any circumstances.

I tried to wiggle in with a new tactic, still driving straight ahead on the road to Simler Trail. I offered to meet off-site for our interview, told her I'd buy her lunch somewhere and we could just chat. I hoped that just meeting in person, I'd maybe be able to talk her into letting me come by.

"Well, I can't because I have a family emergency too, and now we have to leave town right this moment. We're going to be packing into the car and heading to Columbia [Missouri] any minute now."

"Well, I'm only a half hour away," I tried.

"I know," she said with an exaggerated apologetic tone. She was overselling it a bit, in my opinion. "But we'll be long gone by then."

"I've come all this way," I said, the self-pity in my voice as real as can be. "I'm thirty-four weeks pregnant, and you told me to go ahead and book my flight and come out. So I came—and believe me, it wasn't very easy. After this, they're not going to let me fly again for a long while because, as you know, I'm so far along in my pregnancy."

"Gosh, I understand. That's too bad," she said, her words kind, her voice hardening.

"If you have to leave, is there anyone else on the property I can talk to since I've come all this way?"

"They're all too busy, and there's just no way. And Keith [Simler] wants nothing to do with this at all."

We went back and forth for a few minutes until it became clear that I'd be getting precisely nowhere. Her excuses varied between saying that she was cancelling due to a family emergency and that there was an emergency at the kennel. My gut told me that there was no real emergency at all. Instead, I sensed I was dealing with a case of cold feet, or perhaps someone got in her ear and put the kibosh on this interview altogether. As a consolation, she promised we could chat by phone in the following week and said she'd give me a full interview on the record then.

Later when I tell Pete what happened, it takes everything for him not to outright scoff at my naïveté. He alerts me to the fact that I've made, in his opinion, a rookie mistake.

"If you want to do the journalist thing, that's very, very hard. Even just to talk to them," he says.

I tell Pete that I'm not in the business of going undercover like he is. For what I do, it's best to give people a fair shake to present their point of view in the interest of journalistic transparency. He tells me that even still, I shouldn't have let Jackie know ahead of time that I was coming. I should have just shown up.

"It has to always be right this fucking minute. Never set an appointment. Never try and talk to them and say, 'I'll get in tomorrow or next week or in three hours.' It is right now. Because if they have time to think about it, they will change their mind. Just get in there, and fucking work it, and get it done," he instructs.

Maybe Pete's right. And maybe if I hadn't been so pregnant at the time of my trip, I wouldn't have been worried about just marching up to their door, marching past all the NO TRESPASSING signs, and making my case. But I'm no longer making decisions for myself alone.

So here I am on Simler Trail, just a few minutes after my last, fruitless call to Jackie. There's no sign of any emergency at the kennel as she said. At this point, I'm hoping to just show up and find her here or at least someone amid the crisis she vaguely referred to on the phone. But the place is deserted. More importantly, there are no signs that anyone is around to tend to the animals in the oppressive humidity of Missouri's summer. I roll down my window for just a moment to hear the dogs barking. A red tick finds its way inside immediately. I fight it back outside and wonder whether the dogs are also covered in the little pests. Once I see that there's no one around the main house and barn, I decide to keep moving down the road to see if maybe I'll run into someone who will speak to me.

I roll on and on downhill, passing through the rows of stacked kennels up against the side of the road. Another abandoned barn spills hay out into the field, and then, without warning, the dirt road just stops, overtaken by wild weeds. There I am, a sitting duck in the middle of an open field, sprawling out about a half mile in every direction. Even in the sunshine, I feel afraid, scared to be so exposed and, at the same time, so alone in such a vast expanse. There's nowhere to go but directly back where I came from.

I maneuver a U-turn, leaving tracks in the tall, untamed grass. I head back up the hill for my second pass of Simler's Kennel. It's still deserted. I brake suddenly. There's a large black Lab mix of some kind lying motionless just next to the road. It's the only dog in sight that is free from a cage. I stop to take a closer look, concerned that it is only free because it is dead. But my squealing brakes wake him, and thankfully, he lifts his graying chin to see who's stopping before going back to sleep.

I breathe in, trying to slow my racing heart before starting back to the main road. But before even a shred of relief can seep in, I see something that truly shakes me and will stay with me forever.

There, right next to me, in a rough-hewn, stacked, roadside cage, staring straight back into my window, I see Izzie.

The world stops. I force myself to keep looking.

I know it's not her. I know that's impossible. But she looks just like her. A muddle of her wheaten terrier puppies, each no bigger than my fist, circles around her feet. Her nipples sag along her belly. Her expression gives me nothing. She is just a blank face gazing back at me through wire mesh. She has Izzie's same too-thin hair, the same honey-colored eyes, the same squared-off head. But unlike Izzie, when I lock eyes with this listless animal, I see no joy—and maybe no capacity for joy left in her tired, overspent body.

The puppies huddle on the cage floor. Soon, they'll be gone, shipped off to someone as foolish as I was. But it's not the puppies that stun me. It's her who I can't stop staring at: the mother dog who will watch them as they're ripped away from her, who will be forced to breed again on her very next heat, who will suffer this miserable cycle in this miserable cage until her body gives out. Then maybe she'll be killed. Or maybe she'll be rescued to a life in a home. But she'll never be quite like a normal dog. Sure, she'll look like a dog. But some part of what has made this animal so sacred to humanity for millennia will have been robbed from her.

We sit like this for what feels like a long time, taking each other in. To her, maybe I'm just another passerby or a farmhand. Maybe she's not even looking at me but looking off in the distance over my shoulder. In her, I see what Izzie's future would have been if she hadn't been shipped off for sale. This is what her life would have been if she weren't mine. The only difference is that I'm not sure Izzie would have survived this long. It takes everything in me not to get out and grab the dog and her puppies and tear off down the road with them. But I can't save them. Just like I can't save the hundred or more other dogs surrounding me. I know that. So instead, I just stare back helplessly, hoping I can do more in writing than I can in the flesh.

In the weeks that follow, I call Jackie at least a half dozen times. I send her about as many text messages, trying to get that interview she had promised when ditching me in Missouri. My calls are dodged; my voicemails and text messages are ignored. So without a willing participant from Simler's Kennel on the record to recount their side of the story, I'm forced to rely on what undercover investigator Pete, the USDA, and the Missouri Department of Agriculture have found on the property.

Using the USDA's online database that was available to the public at the time of my visit, I searched for Simler. On Keith Simler's current license dating back to April 2014—a year before Pete visited and investigated the facility—there is not a single violation to be found. No mention of dogs compulsively circling, gone cage crazy. Nothing. There is a mention of the late Wanda Simler's license, but no reports are listed under her name. I submit a FOIA request with the federal government, and nine months later, a sixty-four-page file of USDA inspection reports dating back to 2009 under Wanda's license arrives in my inbox. These tell a very different story from what had been available to the public to see.

On March 19, 2013, a USDA inspector cited the kennel for a violation of compatible grouping in which puppies under four months old cannot be housed with any adult dogs other than their mothers. While this may not seem like a very serious rule to break, the inspector's notes under this nondirect violation are unnerving.

"In the inside section of a sheltered enclosure, the inspectors found what appeared to be a deceased newborn puppy. The licensee was unaware that the puppy was in there until the inspectors pointed it out to her," the report reads.[2]

The official documents contain images as well, including a blurry photograph of the dead puppy.

The other images are also hard to stomach: close-up shots of rotten teeth and gums, matted hair pulling the dog's skin at the root, feces caked and ossified on a dog's fur. Teeth problems seem to be a recurring issue in the reports. Also from the March 19 report were reports of multiple female Yorkshire terriers with teeth and fur problems. These were marked as direct violations—the most serious category available to inspectors.

A female Yorkshire Terrier…was observed with severe matting on her head, face, and chest area… The matting on her back legs and abdomen were so tightly matted that the matted hair was pulling on her skin and the skint [sic] was slightly reddened. There were balls of entangled fecal material dangling from her rear end and back legs. Matting of the hair coat can be painful, can lead to the development of skin infections, and reduces the ability of the coat to insulate. Upon closer observation of this dog, it was also noted that there was a heavy accumulation of a light to dark brown and black material covering the surface of many of the teeth. Some of the front and back teeth were completely encased in this material, and the gums above these teeth had receded, exposing the root structures... These signs are consistent with the presence of dental disease, can be painful, lead to the development of other health problems, and can inhibit the ability of the animal to eat normally.[3]

By March 27, 2013, the inspectors returned to note that this violation had been addressed and found no new noncompliant items.

I also FOIA requested any teachable moments issued to the Simlers. The USDA responded that they had none on record.[4]

Additionally, I placed a Sunshine request with the Missouri Department of Agriculture to view the state inspection reports on Simler's Kennel. A month later, a much thinner stack of papers arrived on my doorstep dating back to September 2010, two months before Izzie was born there. For the most part, state inspectors found no violations. The only noncompliance on record with the state at Simler's Kennel dates to June 21, 2016, when the inspector found several dogs with long toenails needing to be trimmed and groomed to prevent discomfort.[5]

In the last year of traveling the country, visiting other breeding facilities, I've somehow been able to distance myself from the truth of Izzie's birth. I've tried to convince myself that I'd someday see where she came from and it would be different. It's true that Simler's Kennel is not the worst out there or even the worst that I've seen for myself. If this collection of state and federal reports are to be believed, things are better today at Simler's Kennel than they were when Izzie was born, and any improvement is a good thing. But it's still not a place where dogs are happily kept, where puppies are born into a loving home, where they're kept safe from the elements and warm at night. I don't fault the Simlers for this. If the abandoned farm equipment surrounding the dog cages is any indicator, breeding dogs is a last resort for them—as it is for so many of these breeders. But they are regulated by a system that asks very little of them. So sure, the Simler facility is mostly operating within the legal constraints provided to it. But from what I know now, legal doesn't mean right.

A long, dazed drive, a bumpy plane ride, and I'm back in Denver. It feels like another planet after where I've been. I'm exhausted as I pull up in front of my house. Dan and Izzie are sitting on our front step waiting for me. They rush to the car when I pull up. Izzie jumps to put her paws on my swollen belly and tries to bring those honey eyes as close to my face as possible. I kneel down in the grass and put her paws on my shoulders.

"Who the hell are you?" I whisper in her ear.

I look for some clue, some sign that she knows where I've been. She gives me nothing but her excitement that I've returned home. I search her face for some way to see the ugliness of her birthplace, as foreign to me as an island on the other side of the world. I find nothing. But she looks different to me now. It's like she's been robbed of some of her magic. She's still my closest ally, my most cherished friend. She's still the same Izzie to everyone else around us—even to Dan. But now that I've seen where she was born, I feel that I know too much. Like a child who dared to ask where babies come from, I sought to find out where puppies come from. And like that curious child, I was disappointed, disgusted, and hurt to learn the truth.

This is Izzie's truth, and now it's mine to bear. And I can love her and give her the best life she could ever hope for, but it will never undo the damage done.

———

Two weeks after my trip to Izzie's birthplace, my water breaks. It's the middle of the night, and I'm not due for about a month. I yelp and squirm out of the soaked sheets, and Dan shoots up in bed.

"What is it? What's wrong?" he asks in a panic.

"My water broke," I chirp and bound out of bed, speed-waddling into the bathroom. I can't stop laughing as my husband swirls around the house, trying to figure out what to pack. I'd been warning him that all the baby books say to have his-and-hers hospital bags packed from week thirty-four onward. But then again, I knew I couldn't really push my argument with a guilt trip, because at thirty-four weeks, I was in rural Missouri trying to get into the breeding facility where Izzie was born. Oddly, the baby books didn't say anything about that.

I ring the on-call doctor and tell her my water broke. She sleepily says to wait for contractions. When I tell her the baby was transverse breech as of my last OB visit, she tells me to head to the hospital right away. I'm calm amid the chaos within me. I shove a bath towel between my legs and go outside to give Izzie a walk. I stand barefoot on the cold concrete pavement as she sniffs around the grass for a place to go. It's a few hours before dawn on the first day of September, and the heat is finally breaking. Every few steps, she pauses and looks back at me in the darkness, checking to see if this is a new nightly routine I'm trying out with her.

"Go ahead. It's okay," I assure her, readjusting my towel under my muumuu. The street is quiet and still, our neighbors' windows all dark and unaware. Back in the house, Dan is frantic. While I at least had my bag packed, we are still woefully unprepared. The whole pregnancy, we'd been puzzling over what we'd do with Izzie if we went into labor in the middle of the night. During the day, it'd be no problem: we'd take her to her usual dog sitter or drop her off at the fancy dog-boarding facility down the block. But the middle of the night was a blind spot that we were still figuring out without any family in Denver or friends that we'd be comfortable waking on a moment's notice.

As Dan runs back and forth upstairs, I take all the cash out of my wallet and lay it out on the front table with Izzie's leash and a big bag of her treats. I text her walker, asking him to start coming every few hours to let Izzie out beginning at 9:00 a.m.—and take whatever cash he needs. In the meantime, I begin working through how long we'll really be in labor or in the hospital before we can get her to her dog sitter who she so loves. I just don't want her to have to spend a night alone in the house.

When Dan finally comes downstairs with our bags in tow, we give Izzie a treat. For the last time, we are a family of three. I kiss her on the fuzzy blank space between her eyes and hope she won't be too afraid.

Dan and I slip out the door and glide across the silent city to the hospital.

"Do you really think we're coming home with a baby?" I ask Dan as he white-knuckles the steering wheel.

"Of course we are. What else would possibly happen?" He runs a deserted red light.

"I don't know," I say, thinking the worst but choosing not to add to his anxiety. I know the baby is lodged inside me sideways like a fallen tree trunk stuck between two riverbanks.

"Maybe they'll patch it up and just send us home," I say.

Dan doesn't answer, too focused on the empty highway.

Four hours and one emergency C-section later, my baby is placed in my arms. He's weightless, tiny, swollen, beautiful, and strange but undeniably alive and irrevocably ours. He wails and wails, his tiny lungs shocked to find the cold and alien air around him instead of the warm water world he had always known.

"Hey," I say and pull his face close to mine. He falls silent, and his eyes jolt open to take me in. This is my child, and nothing will ever be the same.

We made it. We managed to have the baby we were told was impossible. For nine months, I'd been so sure that once he was safely delivered, my fear and anxiety at the possibility of losing him would subside. Instead, I find myself awash in a new terror as the world around me begins to look like a carnival of profound dangers. Blame it on the dissociative experience that is a C-section, but it takes me a full day to realize that he is really my child. Sometimes, I still can't believe it.

Once we're out of the operating room and my phone is returned to me, the first thing I do is check in to make sure Izzie is walked and fed and happy. She is, her walker assures me—and he'll be heading back again to see her in just an hour or two. I'm relieved, but I still can't have her staying home alone overnight. Sure, she could go through the night without an accident, but I can't subject her to the loneliness and the sudden surprise we'll be springing on her when we return.

"Dan, I want you to go and take Izzie to her sitter's house," I say, confined to a hospital bed until the spinal block can wear off.

"I can't leave you here alone," he says, rocking our too-tiny son in his arms.

"I'm fine," I insist. "And there are a million nurses hovering around. You should go and take her to the sitter so that we can relax knowing she's happy."

Dan drags his feet and fights me but eventually relents, leaving his hours-old, premature son to make sure our firstborn is cared for. When he sends me a selfie of the two of them in the car together, I'm so relieved that I burst into tears for about the tenth time of the day. Our little girl is okay.

The next three days are a blur of nurses, suture checks, and pediatrician visits. We learn how to feed and change our baby. We even settle on a name for him after months of deliberations: Race, after the street in Philadelphia where Dan and I met. Very quickly, from within that tiny hospital room, our family unit permanently changes. We all do. But something is missing, and we won't be complete until we're home with Izzie.

When they finally release us, we drive straight from the hospital to pick up Izzie. I sit in the back seat with Race, making sure he's surviving his first trip in his car seat, which suddenly looks so much bigger than it did when we bought it. When we get to her sitter's place, Dan opens the door, and Izzie leaps into the front seat, tongue flopping and eyes bright. She has no idea that everything has changed. She clearly wants to jump into my lap in the back seat, but my anxiety at guarding my incision chills her enthusiasm as she respectfully stays put with Dan up front. We indulge her in the rare treat of an open-window ride. She periscopes her snout into the air, taking in the fresh breeze.

I'll admit it's a challenge at first for Dan and me to integrate Izzie into our dazzlingly terrifying new life with Race. Hours and days seem to melt together as one feeding-burping-changing session bleeds into the next. Then, with half the day gone, Dan and I look at each other and say one of two things: *Have we eaten anything today?* or *When was the last time Izzie walked?* But if our new addition bothers her, she never shows it. In these early days, she seems unaware that Race is a person just like Dan and me and, as a result, someone to be approached and cajoled for food or affection. Instead, she spends his first week or so somewhat frightened of him. We figure that she recognizes our anxiety around him and knows that he is something very precious not yet to be touched, sniffed, or licked.

When Race is just a few days old, Dan and I make use of an unexpected nap to retreat to the kitchen and scavenge our empty refrigerator for scraps. As we sleepwalk past our baby monitor, I freeze and grab Dan to come see too. There's Race in his bassinet, perched on its stand by our bed. And there, in our bed, head low between her paws, eyes trained with tremendous focus on the bassinet and the baby, is Izzie. We stand in silence, watching them together, not sure if what we're witnessing is a fluke or if Izzie is really standing guard over our son. Soon, he begins to squirm and chirp, winding up to awaken. We watch on the monitor as Izzie leaps from the bed and heads for the door. As I rush to mount the stairs to tend to him, Izzie paces the landing, waiting impatiently for me to come help, alerting me before he can even begin to cry.

We watch these two creatures grow together and bond. When summoned close with Race in our arms, Izzie trembles, her nub wagging so fast, it's blurry to my eye. She licks his milk-sticky hands and his sweat-salty feet. She stares at him longingly and lays her head in his lap as his various swings and rockers bring him to her eye level. As the weeks pass and Race's eyes develop, he begins to notice Izzie when she prances into a room, much to her delight. As he learns to open his fists into hands, his smile lights when I guide him to gently stroke her silky ears. When her sharp, phobic barks rattle the house over nothing, he startles and then settles back to sleep, her frantic yelps just another stitch in the sound fabric of our home, something he's known all his life. When he wails and wails as his teeth start to cut in, she paces in shared, helpless agony. And as he lifts his head and starts to crawl, Izzie sniffs his diapered behind and stands cautiously behind him, keeping an attentive eye on his progress. She is, after all, the local expert on navigating the world on all fours. The first time his babysitter notices how bonded she is to him, I have to ask, "Honestly, how does anyone do this parenting thing without a dog?"

But as I strive to enrich my son and make his early weeks and months as beneficial as possible for his lifelong emotional and physical well-being, I think back to what I learned from Overall's test of Izzie—how her earliest days forever capped her lifelong capacity for joy and appreciation of adventure. I think too of what breeder Patrice had told me when I visited Heirloom Wheatens. Just like Patrice does with her puppies, I pour myself into this child. I put him on his tummy during playtime even as he fights me furiously, and I introduce him to new people and environments to teach him to not be anxious and phobic. While none of

us would ever equate a puppy to a human child, I am watching
in real time how any living being can flourish when given all the
best chances to thrive.

As a first-time parent, I'm surprised to find that babies don't
come into the world fully formed. I discover that there's something
about a newborn that isn't quite human yet. All the pieces are
there, but that essential consciousness and awareness takes time
before it can begin shining through. Every day, he becomes more
of a person. And part of this emerging humanity is his growing
interest in our dog: the first time his eyes dart when he hears her
running to the nursery; the first time he sits up and, eye level with
her, babbles directly at her; the first time he watches her peeing in
the grass and bursts into a fit of giggles; the first time he reaches
out to touch her and stops crying.

Watching him grow to know that she is a part of his world
but is somehow different from us is a milestone of its own. In our
own home, I feel as if I am witnessing the millennia of our shared
evolution of man and dog on a tiny scale in rapid playback.

Seeing the innate bond that Race and Izzie have already begun
to develop together without even the words to name it, I feel
stronger than ever that our dogs deserve better.

And I know Race feels it too. His first words say it all.

First comes Mama. Then comes Dada.

Then it's Izzie, Izzie, Izzie.

How Do You Solve a Problem Like Izzie?

IT'S MY JOB TO REPORT THE FACTS AND PRESENT THEM to you as accurately as possible and without bias. Throughout the reporting and the writing of this book, I've done everything I can to ensure accuracy, but I've been somewhat less successful in divorcing myself from my opinions. Or in keeping myself from making new opinions entirely.

I came to this story certain of only one thing: I love my dog. While that truth has not been shaken, I have been changed in the reporting of this story. But my one bias has not. I believe that to have a personal relationship with a dog is a life-altering privilege that humanity should never lose but must always continue to earn through honor and respect. Not every person is entitled to a dog. We take these ubiquitous creatures for granted. I myself have been guilty of this. But for those of us who can appreciate the awesome responsibility and the soul-enriching beauty of this relationship that is older than even the language we have to describe it, it is truly an honor beyond words to be one who has the opportunity to walk beside this creature from its birth to its death.

But where do we go from here?

As I've tried to demonstrate throughout this book, there are two main problems with the commercial breeding of dogs in this country. The first problem is that the laws and regulations at the federal level are not adequate. The second problem is that the USDA's enforcement of these federal regulations is not adequate. With laws that do not protect the dogs and an agency that is not doing its duty to enforce even these minimal standards, we are left with commercially bred dogs that are treated as a factory-farmed commodity and not as a companion animal that has evolved to have a unique bond with us. Worse still, we have an American public that abhors puppy mills and yet does not realize that a USDA stamp of approval is no guarantee that a dog came from a humane operation.

In many cases, breeders are not evil dog-haters. It's easy to paint with broad brushstrokes, and it's true, there are plenty of bad actors out there. But often, they are economically strapped farmers who were left with few options as Big Ag rolled in and pushed them out. They typically live in remote, rural areas and are tied to their land in such a way that it's impossible to simply tell them to get a real job. And because the regulations ask so little of them, it's hard to see why they would move into another line of business. Puppy farming has become an industry of last resort for these farmers, because the barriers to entry are so dangerously low. So it's easy to see why people have fallen into this industry to try and turn a profit, not for the genuine love of dogs. And then it's easy to see how that motivation impacts the care they give these animals.

Changing the rules is challenging but not impossible. To alter many of the provisions in the Animal Welfare Act would not necessarily require an amendment. All it would take is a secretary of agriculture who can be convinced to redefine the rules much as Secretary Vilsack did when he agreed to redefine what constitutes a retail pet store and close the gaping internet-sales loophole. Other provisions that are entirely omitted by the Animal Welfare Act—genetic testing for breed health or a limit on the number of litters a female dog is allowed to breed in her lifetime—would require an amendment.

On the enforcement side, projects like Purdue's efforts with the Canine Care Certified program are a start but may not be sufficient. Experts from across the spectrum of animal care are divided on their thoughts about how to resolve this problem. Some, like John Goodwin at the Humane Society, believe that better regulations are needed but that the USDA already has the infrastructure for enforcement and could be a force for change if they are empowered or pushed to do a much better job. He worries that efforts like the Purdue project are too cozy with the retail pet industry and will, as a result, lead to third-party inspections that are not truly neutral.

"I really think the answer is not to have the industry doing self-inspections but to raise the USDA's rules to the highest standards—to the standards that the American public expects," he says. "At least with the USDA inspectors, they aren't being paid for by the people being inspected. Can you imagine if BP spills oil all over the Gulf by Louisiana, and instead of having government inspectors go over there to oversee the cleanup, we just leave it to BP to inspect? Nobody would trust that, and they shouldn't... The good thing about government agencies is that they are susceptible to voters. We get new governments in. We get a new president who appoints a new secretary of agriculture. We get a new governor who puts in a new head of the state department of agriculture. So there's a system with a mechanism in place to bring about change. It's slow, but at least it's there… I'm agnostic about which agency does [the inspections], but I'm passionate that the current rules need to be dramatically upgraded and need to have better and more consistent enforcement. That's not an endorsement of the USDA, and it's not a criticism either. It's just that there is a system in place, and how do we maximize its impact to shut down puppy mills?"[1]

Others see it differently. Mary LaHay, president of Iowa Friends of Companion Animals, believes that enforcing the regulations is a consumer-protection issue that must come out from being under the oversight of the USDA. After all, she points out, these dogs are not an agricultural product.

"It needs to be under commerce or something like that, where the shoddy business practices can be attended to. Even under the agriculture umbrella, [dog breeding] isn't being given the kind of attention most agricultural products are given," LaHay says. "Any other agricultural product, if there was an issue with it, all the oversight agencies would very quickly be able to trace it back to its original source. And for food and everything, that's important, and I understand that, and I agree with that. But it's not being done that way with puppies. And it needs to be. Agriculture does not give [dog-breeding inspection] the funding it needs, the attention it needs. And [dog breeding] just plain old doesn't belong under agriculture."[2]

Sara Amundson at the Humane Society Legislative Fund also wants to seek reform through consumer-protection efforts, particularly given the interstate-commerce implications of breeding dogs in rural areas and then shipping them to customers hundreds of miles away.

"It's an interstate commerce issue, no ifs, ands, or buts," Amundson says. "That is why none of these states are going to be able to resolve this in isolation. As long as those dogs are being sold across state lines, we've got to have that interplay between the federal government and the state governments."[3]

Animal ethics expert Bernard Rollin also sees the need to get dog breeding out from under the oversight of agriculture, as he is adamant that dogs cannot be considered livestock.

"[Dogs have] assumed a different role in human life," Rollin says. "The role of a member of the family. The role—as one judge put it—of giving and receiving love. With pigs, you generally don't give or receive love, even under good pig-husbandry conditions. But dogs are a different story."[4]

Rollin believes the solution is ultimately in the hands of the consumer. He finds it abhorrent to breed any dogs at all while more than a million perfectly healthy shelter dogs are euthanized every year for the crime of simply not being adopted.[5] To him, it is the consumer who is to blame for not respecting the lifelong— for better or for worse, in sickness and in health—relationship that comes with bringing a dog into the home.

"If you know when you acquire a dog that you're taking on a heavy burden, you're going to be less likely to acquire one than if you think you can dispose of it casually," Rollin says. "I don't want to live in a nanny state. But that means we have to be responsible. It wouldn't be that far out of line for kids to start getting educated in elementary school on pet ownership and what that entails... You're taking responsibility for a life."

Surprisingly, even those who side with the commercial breeding industry agree that change is needed.

"I think we need to have inspectors who are qualified—if, in
fact, we continue to regulate dog breeders at the federal level.
We need to have qualified inspectors who understand dogs and
understand dog breeders, because there's an animal husbandry
aspect in all of it that's not there," Mindy Patterson of animal
ownership–rights organization the Cavalry Group, who often
speaks on behalf of breeders, tells me.[6]

I ask her if her desire to see USDA inspectors with a deeper
understanding of animal husbandry comes from an opinion that
dogs are livestock. I'm surprised when the question throws her.

"You know, I have to think about that," she says. "No one has
ever posed that question to me. I'd have to think about that. But
yeah, I mean, as dogs, I don't know... I'm going to refrain from
giving an answer on that one without giving it some thought, but
I can send you an answer later if you like."

I agree and return to Patterson several times over the weeks
that follow our conversation. She promises that she's working on
an answer to the livestock question and that it will come soon
as she, herself, decides where exactly she stands on the issue.
Ultimately, an answer never comes.

Patterson says that she's well aware that there are bad breeders
out there and that she opposes them as much as anyone else.

"I am all for animal welfare. I am one of the biggest animal
lovers out there. I would never, ever condone wrongdoing or
animal violence of any kind, ever. But you know, [dog breeders]
have been painted with this broad brush of being animal abusers,"
Patterson says. "I'm a mom, and I've got a daughter who's going
to have kids one of these days. I'm broken-hearted that her kids

may not know the privilege of riding a horse or owning a horse or going to the circus. And she'll never see elephants or be able to go see orcas at SeaWorld... All these things are the incremental elimination of animals—the human-animal bond and the human-animal contact and interaction... Because if you don't see them or get to touch them and experience them, then you don't care about them."

Patterson's viewpoint about commercial dog breeding—and circus elephants and SeaWorld, for that matter—is in diametric opposition to anything I've heard from the animal welfare groups. That much, I expected. However, I do find it interesting that she and her opponents on the animal welfare side have one complaint in common: both sides take issue with USDA enforcement.

But of course, Patterson's group and others like it remain wary of animal welfare groups and take aim at the fact that shelters often charge consumers to adopt.

"There are people who believe that breeders shouldn't make money from it, that all dogs should be adopted," she says. "But if you adopt a dog, you're certainly paying for the dog. So it's okay for the rescues to make money, but not a dog breeder? That mentality conflicts with the private ownership and breeding of animals."

In my interview with Brian Klippenstein, just a few months before he became the USDA transition leader for the Trump administration, he echoed many of Patterson's opinions: that money changes hands for rescue dogs and that groups like the Humane Society are trying to eliminate all animal ownership while making millions for themselves by enjoying nonprofit tax exemptions. But his comments about state-by-state regulations will perhaps be more telling as we look at how any presidency that is excessively cozy with Big Ag will treat the USDA's work with commercial dog breeders.

"Each state has the power to regulate. It's such a term of art: where you have enough and you cross over into too much. But we don't think it should be regulated so that a real abuser can operate with impunity," Klippenstein said. "The USDA should have a role, but it shouldn't be exclusionary of the states. And this is just a general sense we have that people nearby probably set up and enforce rules better than folks from a distance. But having the USDA set minimum standards is, you know, that's something we don't oppose."[7]

He went on, however, to speak about the constitutional protections of interstate commerce and the dangers of allowing one state to set standards high enough to effectively legislate away any competitors from other states, something he worked to fight in the egg industry when he ran Protect the Harvest.

"With state regulations, I think you can go too far, where you are just trying to set a standard, or are you trying to shield your state's producers from external competition?" he asked wryly.

As for me, I have trouble buying the argument that state regulators are trying to put anyone out of business. In fact, I worry that relying on states to pass regulations poses a significant challenge to reforming the industry. It creates a patchwork of laws that are more restrictive in some places than others regarding the care of an animal that itself doesn't change when it crosses state lines. But the real problem is that states are being compelled to pass laws because the federal requirements are so weak, as the former assistant attorney general for Missouri told me.

But no matter who enforces it—commerce, agriculture, local police, independent auditing service—it's clear that dogs remain philosophically challenging for us to pin down. And just because we lump them into one government agency doesn't change the truth about what dogs really are.

So I concluded my last interview with the USDA's Gibbens by asking him one more time if dogs are agriculture.

"Not [according to] the Animal Welfare Act, no," he said.[8]

"I guess that's why it's still a bit of a puzzlement why the USDA would be called upon to enforce the Animal Welfare Act, if dogs aren't considered agriculture in it," I said. "And are dogs livestock?"

"Certainly there are people in the industry who would see them that way," Gibbens said. "But we don't view them as livestock. [Are dogs] part of the Department of Agriculture? Absolutely. Is it agriculture in that way? Yes."

So we're still left scratching our heads, staring at these four-legged enigmas at the foot of the bed. At once, we feel so close to them that they are a part of our family. But we allow them to be delivered to our loving arms as a mass-produced agricultural commodity. And at the end of the day, all of us—on all sides of the debate—are confounded by how to classify them and regulate the industry that breeds them. But if our government is going to go to the trouble of regulating dog breeding, shouldn't it at least devise rules that are worthy of enforcing and then, you know, actually enforce them? Because the regulated breeding industry, as it is in place today, is set up to let us love dogs to death.

People will always want dogs in their lives. Among those people, there are those who will always adopt from a shelter or a rescue. You may notice that in these pages, I did not make an attempt to convince you to adopt. Hopefully the facts that I've laid out for you can lead you to make a decision for yourself about what is right. As to whether we should be breeding dogs at all as a society?

That is not a question I feel it's my place to answer. Instead, I've sought to hold the current, inadequate system accountable.

While I believe that convincing everyone to adopt is a tremendously worthy endeavor—and others are currently doing an admirable job of it—I am not quite as optimistic that we can universally change human nature. I hope it happens someday that all dogs are adopted and there are none left without homes and then euthanized. But I don't believe I will see this in my lifetime. To those who have already adopted or who have been convinced to only do so in the future, I offer my support and respect. You have given a home to a dog who truly needs and deserves one.

But as a realist—or as a pessimist—I have to address the fact that people will keep buying dogs for quite some time to come. So in the meantime, it is our duty and our right to improve this taxpayer-funded regulatory system that is charged with protecting the welfare of the dogs that are bred for us. While our lawmakers are vital in this process, the real power lies with you, the consumer. We have to ask the right questions, demand transparency from our government, and refuse to purchase dogs from breeders or retailers who cannot or will not provide us with the information we deserve about where their puppies come from. Purchasing a dog should not be convenient; it should take serious research and soul searching to make this lifetime commitment. But if humanity has already put a few thousand years into transforming the wild canine into a dog, you can invest just a few extra months into finding a responsibly sourced dog of your own.

As I write this, there is a foot of fresh snow accumulating on our front yard. The stone chimney across the street is puffing white smoke into the frozen tree above it. Izzie is staring at me, begging me to put on my boots and open the front door. When I do, she will bolt down the block, diving across piles of snow and dipping her snout into the powder. She will tease me, galloping in close before speeding off out of my grasp. When she quickly gets too cold, she'll run to the door and signal that it's enough. I'll take her in and wrap her in a fluffy beach towel and hold her close to warm her tiny body, her small but immense heart echoing through her frame and into my own. We'll huddle like this, together in the warmth, while the snow keeps falling outside and somewhere out there, maybe not so far away, hundreds of thousands of other dogs tremble in their frozen cages with no concept of hope or redemption.

Will they ever feel joy? I hope we can give them a chance.

Endnotes

CHAPTER ONE

1 "Pet Statistics," American Society for the Prevention of Cruelty to Animals, accessed August 3, 2017, https://www.aspca.org /animal-homelessness/shelter-intake-and-surrender/pet-statistics.

2 Daniel Engber, "Pepper Goes to Washington," *Slate Magazine*, June 3, 2009, http://www.slate.com/articles/health_and_science /pepper/2009/06/pepper_goes_to_washington.html.

3 Associated Press, "Campaign on to End Theft of Family Pets for Science," *Express*, July 10, 1965, https://www.newspapers.com /newspage/254722031.

4 Joyce Tischler, phone interview with author, November 9, 2016.

5 Coles Phinizy, "The Lost Pets that Stray to the Labs," *Sports Illustrated*, November 29, 1965, http://www.si.com /vault/1965/11/29/612645/the-lost-pets-that-stray-to-the-labs.

6 Bernie Rollin, phone interview with author, November 9, 2016.

7 Mary LaHay, phone interview with author November 4, 2016.

8 All Animal Welfare Act regulations and requirements from:

"Animal Welfare Act and Animal Welfare Regulations," United States Department of Agriculture, November 2013, https://www .aphis.usda.gov/animal_welfare/downloads/Animal%20Care%20 Blue%20Book%20-%202013%20-%20FINAL.pdf.

9   All translations of the Animal Welfare Act from: Karen Overall, phone interview with author, August 19, 2016.

10   American Veterinary Medical Association, "AVMA Guidelines for the Euthanasia of Animals: 2013 Edition," February 27, 2013, https://www.avma.org/KB/Policies/Documents/euthanasia.pdf.

11   Ibid.

12   Robert Gibbens, personal interview with author, February 15, 2017.

CHAPTER TWO

1   United States Department of Agriculture, "Introductory Course for Commercial Dog Breeders," accessed November 30, 2017, https ://docs.google.com/spreadsheets/d/18_3vgHixj7EwnQzHvnlgHN 4TDGJVQpQkSxIjqT7xn7g/edit#gid=0.

2   Avenson v. Zegart, 577 F. Supp. 958 (D. Minn. 1984), http://law .justia.com/cases/federal/district-courts/FSupp/577/958/1497077/.

3   Robert Gibbens, personal interview with author, August 2, 2016.

4   John Goodwin, senior director of HSUS Stop Puppy Mills Campaign, email message to author, April 24, 2017.

5   John Goodwin, phone interview with author, July 14, 2016.

6   "About the U.S. Department of Agriculture," USDA, accessed March 31, 2017, https://www.usda.gov/our-agency/about-usda.

7   "About APHIS," USDA-APHIS, accessed March 31, 2017, https ://www.aphis.usda.gov/aphis/banner/aboutaphis.

8   USDA Office of the Inspector General, "Animal and Plant Health Inspection Service Animal Care Program Inspections of Problematic

Dealers," May 2010, https://www.usda.gov/oig/webdocs/33002-4
-SF.pdf.

9   Ed Green, phone interview with author, December 12, 2016.

10 "New Terms Will Appear on USDA Inspection Reports," USDA
    Animal and Plant Health Inspection Service, November 22, 2016,
    September 22, 2016, https://content.govdelivery.com/accounts
    /USDAAPHIS/bulletins/16620a4.

11 Bob Baker, phone interview with author, January 22, 2016.

12 Cathy Liss, phone interview with author, September 22, 2016.

13 Laura J. Fox, "Notice of Violation of Court Order and Intent to
    Enforce and/or Reopen Lawsuit," February 6, 2017, http://blog
    .humanesociety.org/wp-content/uploads/2017/02/2017-02-06
    -Notice-of-Violation_HSUS-v-USDA-No.-15-0197.pdf.

14 "Animal Welfare Enforcement Actions," USDA, February 7, 2017,
    last modified August 18, 2017, https://www.aphis.usda.gov/aphis
    /ourfocus/animalwelfare/enforcementactions.

15 Matt Herrick, Twitter post, February 5, 2017, 11:32 a.m., https
    ://twitter.com/mattmherrick/status/828325492906422272.

16 Brian Klippenstein, phone interview with author, February 8, 2016.

17 American Pet Products Association, "Pet Industry Market Size
    & Ownership Statistics," news release, accessed March 31, 2017,
    http://www.americanpetproducts.org/press_industrytrends.asp.

CHAPTER THREE

1   Pete, phone interview with author, October 13, 2016.

CHAPTER FOUR

1   Joyce Tischler, phone interview with author, February 8, 2016.

2   Treaty of Lisbon, European Union Law, signed December 13, 2007, http
     ://eur-lex.europa.eu/legal-content/EN/TXT/?uri=CELEX:12007L/TXT.

3   Humane Society International (India), "15 Animal Rights in India
     That Every Citizen Should Know," accessed July 13, 2017, http
     ://www.thebetterindia.com/46721/humane-society-india-animal
     -laws-prevention-of-cruelty-act/.

4   United States v. Park, 536 F.3d 1058 (9th Circuit 2008), https
     ://casetext.com/case/us-v-park-33.

5   Associated Press, "Kennel Owners Win Legal Fight with Forest," *Casper
     Star Tribune*, October 12, 2009, accessed March 31, 2017, http://trib
     .com/news/state-and-regional/kennel-owners-win-legal-fight-with
     -forest/article_2ee055fe-8481-53a6-8327-3726184a8bcf.html.

6   "New York Mills Dog Breeder Sentenced for Torturing Animals,"
     EchoPress.com, May 7, 2009, http://www.echopress.com/content
     /new-york-mills-dog-breeder-sentenced-torturing-animals-2.

7   USDA Decision and Order, in re: Pine Lake Enterprises, Inc., AWA
     Docket No. D-10-0014, February 4, 2010, accessed July 13, 2017, https
     ://www.oaljdecisions.dm.usda.gov/sites/default/files/100204AWAD-10
     -0014DO.pdf.

8   Humane Society of the United States, "USDA Applauded for
     Permanently Revoking Licenses of Two Infamous Puppy Mill
     Operators," news release, October 21, 2011, accessed March 31,
     2017, http://www.humanesociety.org/news/press_releases/2011/10
     /usda_applauded_10242011.html.

9   Hal Herzog, phone interview with author, January 27, 2016.

CHAPTER FIVE

1   Alexandra Horowitz, *Inside of a Dog: What Dogs Think and Know*
     (New York: Simon & Schuster, 2009), 91.

2   Pat Shipman, *The Invaders: How Humans and their Dogs Drove Neanderthals to Extinction* (Cambridge, MA: Belknap Press, 2015).

3   Brian Hare, email message with the author, October 7, 2016.

4   E. L. Maclean and B. Hare, "Dogs Hijack the Human Bonding Pathway," *Science* 348, no. 6232 (April 17, 2015): 280–81, http://science.sciencemag.org/content/348/6232/280.

5   Marc Bekoff, interview with author, January 14, 2016.

6   Davis S. Tuber et al., "Behavioral and Glucocorticoid Responses of Adult Domestic Dogs (*Canis familiaris*) to Companionship and Social Separation," *Journal of Comparative Psychology* 110, no. 1 (March 1996): 103–08, doi:10.1037//0735-7036.110.1.103.

7   Peter F. Cook et al., "Awake Canine fMRI Predicts Dogs' Preference for Praise vs Food," *Social Cognitive and Affective Neuroscience*, December 2016, doi:10.1093/scan/nsw102.

8   Franklin D. McMillan et al., "Mental Health of Dogs Formerly Used as 'Breeding Stock' in Commercial Breeding Establishments," *Applied Animal Behaviour Science* 135, no. 1 (November 30, 2011): 86–94, http://www.appliedanimalbehaviour.com/article/S0168-1591(11)00300-5/abstract.

9   Ibid.

10 Ibid.

11 Ibid.

12 "Regulatory Compliance for Commercial Dog Breeders: Introductory Course," USDA, https://www.aphis.usda.gov/aphis/ourfocus/animalwelfare/caw/education+and+training/ct_commercial_dog_breeders.

13 Robert Gibbens, interview with author, February 15, 2017.

14 L. Pierantoni, M. Albertini, and F. Pirrone, "Prevalence of Owner-Reported Behaviours in Dogs Separated from the Litter at Two Different Ages," *Veterinary Record* 169, no. 18 (August 26, 2011): 468, doi:10.1136/vr.d4967.

15 Ibid.

16 Karen Overall, phone interview with author, August 19, 2016.

17 Franklin D. McMillan et al., "Differences in Behavioral Characteristics between Dogs Obtained as Puppies from Pet Stores and Those Obtained from Noncommercial Breeders," *Journal of the American Veterinary Medical Association* 242, no. 10 (May 15, 2013): 1359–363, doi:10.2460/javma.242.10.1359.

CHAPTER SIX

1   Karen Overall, interview with author, November 21, 2016.

CHAPTER SEVEN

1   Leslie Irvine, interview with author, January 14, 2016.

2   Alan Beck, phone interview with author, January 13, 2016.

3   Stanley Brandes, "The Meaning of American Pet Cemetery Gravestones," *Ethnology* 48, no. 2 (Spring 2009): 99–118, http ://anthropology.berkeley.edu/sites/default/files/Brandes%20-%20 AMERICAN%20PET%20CEMETERY%20GRAVESTONES.pdf.

4   Liz Donovan, "The Most Popular Dog Names of 2015," December 7, 2015, http://www.akc.org/content/news/articles/popular-dog-names-2015/.

5   "Popular Names in 2015," Social Security Administration, accessed August 22, 2017, https://www.ssa.gov/cgi-bin/popularnames.cgi.

CHAPTER EIGHT

1   Carolyn Dimitri, Anne Effland, and Neilson Conklin, "The 20th Century Transformation of U.S. Agriculture and Farm Policy," *USDA Economic Research Service, Economic Information Bulletin* 3 (June 2005),

https://www.ers.usda.gov/webdocs/publications/44197/13566_eib3_1_.pdf?v=41055.

2 Bob Baker, phone interview with author, January 22, 2016.

3 Humane Society of the United States, "Puppy Mills and the Animal Welfare Act," 2017, accessed July 13, 2017, http://www.humanesociety.org/assets/pdfs/pets/puppy_mills/usda-licensed-breeders-by-2016.pdf.

4 Jennifer Molidor, "Welcome Jessica Blome," Animal Legal Defense Fund, September 13, 2013, http://aldf.org/blog/welcome-jessica-blome/.

5 Jessica Blome, phone interview with author, February 17, 2016.

6 Virginia Young, "Compromise Dog Breeding Measure Is Rushed into Law," *St. Louis Post-Dispatch*, April 28, 2011, http://www.stltoday.com/news/state-and-regional/missouri/compromise-dog-breeding-measure-is-rushed-into-law/article_200c6417-ffef-58fa-990e-1bbbb0af3807.html.

7 Joel Currier, "State Officials Hail Compromise on Dog Breeding Bill," *St. Louis Post-Dispatch*, June 15, 2011, http://www.stltoday.com/news/local/govt-and-politics/state-officials-hail-compromise-on-dog-breeding-bill/article_5eed7696-3daa-581e-bff3-fbb026b7e793.html.

8 Brian Klippenstein, phone interview with author, February 8, 2016.

9 Robert Gibbens, interview with author, August 2, 2016.

10 Josh Benson, "Commercial dog Breeding in Missouri: Part 1—What a Difference a Law Makes," *Columbia Missourian*, September 2, 2014, accessed March 31, 2017, http://www.columbiamissourian.com/news/commercial-dog-breeding-in-missouri-part---what-a/article_befcce1e-b719-5e60-98f1-748bf7e761df.html.

11 "The Horrible Hundred 2017: Uncovering U.S. Puppy Mills," Humane Society of the United States, May 9, 2017, http://www.humanesociety.org/news/press_releases/2017/05/horrible-hundred-2017-uncovering-puppy-mills.html?referrer=https://www.google.com/.

12 Joe Vansickle, "Chris Chinn," *National Hog Farmer*, May 15, 2010, accessed March 31, 2017, http://www.nationalhogfarmer.com /people/pork-masters-chris-chinn-0515.

13 Mindy Patterson, phone interview with author, October 18, 2016.

14 Sarah Stewart, "4 Oklahoma Breeders on 'Horrible Hundred' List," KFOR, May 4, 2016, accessed July 13, 2017, http://kfor .com/2016/05/04/4-oklahoma-breeders-on-horrible-hundred-list/.

CHAPTER NINE

1 Theresa Strader, interview with author, January 18, 2016.

CHAPTER ELEVEN

1 "Old Song Carries New Tune," Humane Society of the United States, October 30, 2009, http://m.humanesociety.org/news/profile/2009/10 /old_song_new_tune_103009.html.

2 Russell Belk, phone interview with author, July 13, 2016.

3 Bob Baker, phone interview with author, January 22, 2016.

4 T. J. Greaney, "Prop B Supporters Offer Allegations of Dog Dumping," *Columbia Daily Tribune*, October 28, 2010, accessed March 31, 2017, http://www.columbiatribune.com/news/politics/prop-b-supporters -offer-allegations-of-dog-dumping/article_a6727bf3-eec3-5c31 -ba46-2527cf7db898.html.

5 Mike Bober, phone interview with author, July 21, 2016.

6 "Pet Industry Market Size & Ownership Statistics," American Pet Products Association, accessed August 23, 2017, http://www .americanpetproducts.org/press_industrytrends.asp.

7 USDA Office of the Inspector General, "Animal and Plant Health Inspection Service Animal Care Program Inspections

of Problematic Dealers," May 2010, https://www.usda.gov/oig /webdocs/33C02-4-SF.pdf.

8   Sara Amundson, phone interview with author, November 15, 2016.

9   Doris Day Animal League v. Veneman No. 01-5351 (U.S. App. DC Cir. January 14, 2003), http://caselaw.findlaw.com/us-dc -circuit/1362167.html.

10   Ibid.

11   USDA Office of the Inspector General, "Inspections of Problematic Dealers."

12   Robert Gibbens, interview with author, February 15, 2017.

13   Humane Society of the United States, "Today Show Airs HSUS Investigation into Huge Internet Puppy Broker," news release, December 7, 2011, accessed March 31, 2017, http://m .humanesociety.org/news/press_releases/2011/12/purebred _breeders_120711.html?credit=web_id339681617.

14   Purebred Breeders "Statement Regarding Report on Online Puppy Sales," news release, December 6, 2011, accessed March 31, 2017, http://www.today.com/news/statement-regarding-report-online -puppy-sales-wbna45570337.

15   Purebred Breeders LLC, "Purebred Breeders Refutes NBC *Today Show* and Humane Society Story," news release, December 7, 2011, accessed March 31, 2017, http://www.businesswire.com/news/home/20111207006727 /en/Purebred-Breeders-Refutes-NBC-Today-Show-Humane.

16   Trina Robinson and Robbi Peele, "Woman Claims Online Puppy Company Didn't Give Her Right Dog," NBC 6 Miami, January 31, 2014, accessed March 31, 2017, http://www.nbcmiami.com /investigations/Woman-Claims-Online-Puppy-Company-Didnt -Give-Her-Right-Dog-242943441.html.

17   Arielle Schechtman, senior director of communications for PuppySpot, email correspondence with author, January 24, 2017.

18   PuppySpot, "Dog Lovers Can Fetch Their New Best Friend at PuppySpot.com," news release, October 18, 2016, accessed March 31, 2017, http://www.prnewswire.com/news-releases/dog-lovers-can -fetch-their-new-best-friend-at-puppyspotcom-300346391.html.

19   "More about NAIA, National Animal Interest Alliance," Animal Welfare—National Animal Interest Alliance, accessed March 31, 2017, http://www.naiaonline.org/about-us/more-about-naia/.

20   "What You Need to Know About Animal Extremism," NAIA Trust, accessed March 31, 2017, http://www.naiatrust.org/resources /whatyouneedtoknow/.

21   Patti Strand, "NAIA Study Confirms Fewer Dogs, Scarce Purebreds in US Animal Shelters," news release, July 14, 2015, accessed March 31, 2017, http://www.naiaonline.org/articles/article/naia-study -confirms-fewer-dogs-scarce-purebreds-in-us-animal-shelters#sthash .zTsKDY7e.GNW1efvY.dpbs.

22   Greg Liberman, phone interview with author, January 13, 2017.

CHAPTER TWELVE

1   Gabriel Rom, "Former Valhalla Pet Store Owner Hit with More Violations," *USA Today*, April 28, 2016, https://www.usatoday. com/story/news/local/westchester/mount-pleasant/2016/04/28 /pet-store-violations/83661716/.

2   Carly Baldwin, "Dead Dogs Could Have Been in Freezer 'For Months,' Pet Store Owner Says," *Patch.com*, March 2, 2016, accessed March 31, 2017, http://patch.com/new-jersey/eastbrunswick /dead-dogs-could-have-been-freezer-months-pet-store-owner-says.

3   Spencer Kent, "Pet Shop Facing 267 Animal Cruelty Counts Loses License," NJ.com, March 29, 2016, http://www.nj.com/middlesex /index.ssf/2016/03/east_brunswick_revokes_license_of_just_pups.html.

4   Christopher Brennan, "Pet Store Closed after Police Find 67 Dogs—Including Puppies Covered in Feces—in Van," *New York Daily News*, April 5, 2016, http://www.nydailynews.com/news/national/dog-store-closed-police-find-van-full-puppies-article-1.2588680.

5   Noah Cohen, "Just Pups Owner, Brother Charged with 134 Animal Cruelty Counts," NJ.com, April 27, 2016, http://www.nj.com/bergen/index.ssf/2016/04/just_pups_owner_brother_charged_with_134_animal_cr.html.

6   Melanie Anzidei, "Just Pups Hearing in Paramus Court over 403 Health Violations Postponed," NorthJersey.com, May 24, 2016, http://www.northjersey.com/story/news/2016/05/24/just-pups-hearing-in-paramus-court-over-403-health-violations-postponed/94721628/.

7   *State of New Jersey v. Just Pups, LLC. and Vincent LoSacco* C-184-16 (Sup. Ct. Bergen Cty, 2016), http://www.nj.gov/oag/newsreleases16/Just-Pups-Complaint.pdf.

8   Missouri state inspection report, July 27, 2016.

9   Homepage, Southwest Auction Service, LLC, accessed March 31, 2017, http://www.swaauction.com/.

10   Daniel Hubbard, "Just Pups Owner Pleads Guilty, Will Pay $19,000," *Paramus Patch*, last modified November 10, 2016, https://patch.com/new-jersey/paramus/just-pups-owners-pleads-guilty-will-pay-19-000.

11   Paul Milo, "Alpine Couple Suing Just Pups, Pet Store with History of Complaints," *NJ.com*, November 18, 2016, accessed July 13, 2017, http://www.nj.com/bergen/index.ssf/2016/11/alpine_couple_suing_just_pups_pet_store_with_histo.html.

12   William Westhoven, "Industry Rebukes E. Hanover's Just Pups," *Daily Record*, February 13, 2017, accessed March 31, 2017, http://www.dailyrecord.com/story/news/2017/02/13/industry-condemns-east-hanovers-just-pups/97862926/.

13 James Lent, "East Hanover Revokes Pet Store License," *Hanover Eagle*, March 7, 2017, http://www.newjerseyhills.com /hanover_eagle/news/east-hanover-revokes-pet-store-license /article_29bafb95-0753-5760-8fd0-2e82300d6c69.html.

14 Robert Gibbens, interview with author, February 15, 2017.

CHAPTER THIRTEEN

1 Karen Overall, interview with author, November 21, 2016.

2 Nancy Sasso, phone interview with author, July 19, 2016.

3 American Veterinary Medical Association, "Pet Purchase Protection Laws," June 2014, accessed March 31, 2017, https://www.avma .org/Advocacy/StateAndLocal/Pages/pet-lemon-laws.aspx.

4 "The Horrible Hundred 2016," Humane Society of the United States, May 2016, https://drive.google.com/file /d/0B0GqgKr1XwGQSFl3dDJpQ2JPdkk/view.

5 "Inspection Report," United States Department of Agriculture, prepared by Randall E. Coleman, April 19, 2012, https://cbsphilly .files.wordpress.com/2015/09/2012-usda-inspection-report.jpg.

6 Charlotte Huffman, "I-Team Investigates: Where Are Puppy Stores Getting Their Dogs From?" CBS Philly, September 23, 2015, accessed March 31, 2017, http://philadelphia.cbslocal .com/2015/09/23/i-team-investigates-where-are-puppy-stores -getting-their-dogs-from/.

7 "Inspection Report," United States Department of Agriculture, prepared by Randall E. Coleman, April 19, 2012, https://cbsphilly .files.wordpress.com/2015/09/2012-usda-inspection-report.jpg.

8 Tanya Espinoza, email correspondence with author, February 16, 2017.

CHAPTER FOURTEEN

1 City and County of Denver, "Denver Animal Ordinances," accessed March 31, 2017, https://www.denvergov.org/content /denvergov/en/denver-animal-shelter/animal-protection/denver -animal-ordinances.html.

2 John Goodwin, phone interview with author, July 14, 2016.

3 Robert Gibbens, interview with author, August 2, 2016.

4 Cathy Liss, phone interview with author, September 22, 2016.

5 Mike Bober, phone interview with author, July 21, 2016.

6 Brian Winslow, phone interview with author, August 31, 2016.

7 Candace Croney, phone interview with author, August 8, 2016.

8 The Humane Society Veterinary Medical Association, "USDA Urged to Improve Care Standards for Puppy Mill Dogs," Humane Society of the United States, September 21, 2015, http://www.humanesociety.org/news /press_releases/2015/09/usda-care-standards-pm-dogs-092115.html.

9 Michal Addady, "This Is How Much Americans Spend on Their Dogs," Fortune.com, August 26, 2016, http://fortune.com/2016/08/26 /pet-industry/.

10 Brian Winslow, email correspondence with author, October 11, 2016.

11 Wayne Pacelle, "Puppy Mill, Inc.," *A Humane Nation* (blog), November 20, 2008, accessed March 31, 2017, http://blog .humanesociety.org/wayne/2008/11/petland-puppies.html.

12 "Certification Fee Details," Canine Care Certified, accessed November 30, 2017, https://caninecarecertified.org/breeders/certification-fee/.

CHAPTER FIFTEEN

1 Kristin Akin, phone interview with author, August 16, 2016.

2 Cornerstone Farms, accessed August 23, 2017, http://www .cornerstonefarms.net/.

3   "Cornerstone Farms," BBB Accredited Business Profile, accessed March 31, 2017, https://www.bbb.org/stlouis/business-reviews/dog-breeders/cornerstone-farms-in-curryville-mo-310027881.

4   Humane Society of the United States, "The Horrible Hundred 2016: Puppy Mills Exposed," May 2016, http://www.humanesociety.org/horrible-hundred-2016-puppy-mills-exposed.html.

5   Bob Baker, phone interview with author, August 25, 2016.

6   Robert Gibbens, interview with author, August 2, 2016.

7   Inspection report, Missouri Department of Agriculture, Division of Animal Health, October 21, 2014, obtained by Sunshine request.

8   Ibid.

9   Sarah Alsager, public information officer for the Missouri Department of Agriculture, email correspondence with author, January 25, 2017.

10 Inspection report, Missouri Department of Agriculture, Division of Animal Health, August 4, 2016, obtained by Sunshine request.

11 Inspection report, Missouri Department of Agriculture, Division of Animal Health, August 8, 2016, obtained by Sunshine request.

12 United States Department of Agriculture inspection report, August 8, 2016.

13 United States Department of Agriculture, Animal and Plant Health Inspection Service, email correspondence with author, November 9, 2016.

14 Kathleen Summers, phone interview with author, August 26, 2016.

15 "Full Interview with Todd Akin," *Jaco Report*, Fox 2 St. Louis, August 19, 2012, http://fox2now.com/2012/08/19/the-jaco-report-august-19-2012/.

16 David Nakamura, "Obama denounces Rep. Todd Akin's remarks on 'legitimate rape,'" *Washington Post*, August 20, 2012, https://www.washingtonpost.com/politics/obama-denounces-rep-todd-akins

-remarks-on-legitimate-rape/2012/08/20/69b786fa-eaee-11e1-a80b-9f898562d010_story.html?utm_term=.0a806454212b.

17 Naftali Bendavid, "Romney Calls Akin Comments 'Inexcusable,'" *Wall Street Journal*, August 20, 2012, http://blogs.wsj.com/washwire/2012/08/20/romney-calls-akin-comments-inexcusable/.

18 Lori Moore, "Rep. Todd Akin: The Statement and the Reaction," *New York Times*, August 20, 2012, http //www.nytimes.com/2012/08/21/us/politics/rep-todd-akin-legitimate-rape-statement-and-reaction.html.

19 Todd Akin, *Firing Back: Taking on the Party Bosses and Media Elite to Protect Our Faith and Freedom* (Washington, DC: WND Books, 2014).

20 Todd Akin, phone interview with author, August 17, 2016.

21 Debra and Tom Ritter, email correspondence with author, January 10, 2017.

22 Bob Baker, phone interview with author, August 25, 2016.

CHAPTER SIXTEEN

1 Patrice Chevalier and Robert Bergman, interview with author, July 26, 2016.

2 Patrice Chevalier and Robert Bergman, email correspondence with author, August 15, 2016.

3 Patrice Chevalier and Robert Bergman, interview with author, July 26, 2016.

CHAPTER SEVENTEEN

1 Pete, phone interview with author, October 13, 2016.

2 Inspection report, United States Department of Agriculture, March 19, 2013, provided by Freedom of Information Act request.

3   Ibid.

4   United States Department of Agriculture, Animal and Plant Health Inspection Service, email correspondence with author, November 14, 2016.

5   Inspection report, Missouri Department of Agriculture Division of Animal Health, June 21, 2016, obtained by Sunshine request.

EPILOGUE

1   John Goodwin, phone interview with author, July 14, 2016.

2   Mary LaHay, phone interview with author, November 4, 2016.

3   Sara Amundson, phone interview with author, November 15, 2016.

4   Bernard Rollin, phone interview with author, November 9, 2016.

5   "Pet Statistics," ASPCA, accessed March 31, 2017, http://www .aspca.org/animal-homelessness/shelter-intake-and-surrender /pet-statistics.

6   Mindy Patterson, phone interview with author, October 18, 2016.

7   Brian Klippenstein, phone interview with author, February 8, 2016.

8   Robert Gibbens, interview with author, February 15, 2017.

Acknowledgments

My eternal thanks go to my wise and patient agent, Stacy Testa, for her generosity, time, and support—even when I told her I was writing a book about my dog. She is the reason I am lucky enough to see this book come to fruition.

My gratitude to Dominique Raccah and everyone at Sourcebooks, especially my brilliant editor, Anna Michels, whose insight and eloquence shaped this text. I will forever be grateful for her willingness to take a chance on this story.

Also at Sourcebooks, many thanks to production editor Cassie Gutman, art director Adrienne Krogh, and publicist Liz Kelsch. Special thanks to Writer's House digital director Dan Berkowitz and to my fearless transcribers, Rose Ayana and Hannah Peshkin. To my lifelong friends, April Rueb and Justine Cohen, for being such cheerleaders, and to my brother, Reid, for his support. To Amanda Hume at Vert Beauty and Andrea Flanagan Photography for making Izzie and me look presentable in our author photo. And to Katie Calvin-Purkapile, who cared for baby Race so I could continue working on this project—even with a newborn.

Thank you to all of the sources who spoke to me for this book from both sides of the story. Your time, expertise and, in many cases, your bravery shed much-needed light on a complicated topic. And to those of you who have devoted your lives to advocating for these incredible animals, you have my utmost gratitude and admiration.

To my parents: for encouraging me to write and pursue a career in journalism. Thank you for supporting every step of the journey to get here.

And to Dan—the father of my dog. Without you, there are no stories worth telling. You believed in me and fought for this one to be told, even when I had my doubts. Your love makes the impossible possible. Thank you isn't enough: you made this book happen in every single way.

About the Author

RORY KRESS IS A JOURNALIST AND A NATIONAL EMMY
Award–winning television producer. She has reported on
Iraqi refugees in Jordan coping through Rollerblading, surro-
gate mothers giving birth to American babies in India, the
cultural awakening of Jewish youths in Poland, and the conver-
sions of Hispanic Americans to Islam in New Jersey. She was
the news producer for NBC's *Today Show* and is a graduate of
the Columbia University Graduate School of Journalism and
Princeton University. She lives in Denver with her family and
her dog, Izzie.